Unix Shell Programming

Yashavant P. Kanetkar

ISBN 81-7029-753-0

BPB PUBLICATIONS

B-14, CONNAUGHT PLACE, NEW DELHI - 110001

Published by Manish Jain for BPB Publications, B-14 Connaught Place, New Delhi-110001 and Printed by him at Pressworks, Delhi.

Distributors:

BPB BOOK CENTRE
376, Old Lajpat Rai Market, **Delhi-110006** Phone: 2961747

BUSINESS PROMOTION BUREAU
8/1, Ritchie Street, Mount Road, **Madras-600002** Phone: 834796, 8550491

DECCAN AGENCIES
4-3-329, Bank Street, **Hyderabad-500195** Phone: 512280, 593826

COMPUTER BOOK CENTRE
12, Shrungar Complex, M. G. Road, **Bangalore-560001**
Phones: 5587923, 5584641

COMPUTER BOOK CENTRE
SCF No.-65, Sector-6, **Panchkula-134109**, Chandigarh
Phone: 561613, 567538

MICRO BOOKS
Shanti Niketan Building,8, Camac Street, **Calcutta-700017**
Phones: 2426518, 2426519

MICRO BOOK CENTRE
2, City Centre, C G Road, **Ahmedabad-380009** Phone: 421611

MICRO MEDIA
Shop No. 5, Mahendra Chambers, 150 D.N. Road, FORT, 2, City Centre,
Bombay-400001 Phones: 2078296, 2078297

Limits of Liability and Disclaimer of Warranty

The Author and Publishers of this book have tried their best to ensure that the programmes, procedures and functions contained in the book are correct. However, the author and the publishers make no warranty of any kind, expressed or implied, with regard to these programmes or the documentation contained in the book. The author and publishers shall not be liable in any event for any damages, incidental or consequential, in connection with, or arising out of the furnishing, performance or use of these programmes, procedures and functions.

IBM, IBM PC, IBM XT, and IBM AT are registered trademarks of International Business Machines, Inc.
MS-DOS is a registered trademark of Microsoft Corporation.
Unix is a registered trademark of AT & T.

All trademarks referred to in the book are acknowledged as properties of their respective owners.

ISBN 81-7029-753-2

Published by Manish Jain for BPB Publications, B-14, Connaught Place, New Delhi-110001 and Printed by him at Pressworks, Delhi.

Dedicated to
all Unix users

About the Author

Yashavant Prabhakar Kanetkar obtained his B.E. from VJTI Bombay and his M. Tech. from IIT Kanpur. Since 1987 he has been Director of ICIT, a Training and Software Development firm which he set up at Nagpur. Mr. Kanetkar is author of several books including *Let Us C, Exploring C, Working With C, C Projects, Undocumented DOS Through C, Writing TSRs Through C* and *Understanding Pointers In C* published by *BPB Publications* and *Tech Publications, Singapore*. These days he is writing a few more books on C++ and Windows with his team at ICIT. Mr. Kanetkar also writes regular columns titled *The C Column* and *Object: C++* for a leading computer magazine.

Acknowledgments

Unix I was told is difficult to learn. I too found it to be so. However, I have realised that writing about it is more difficult. More so because it's not easy to decide what to include and what to leave out.

Niranjan Bakre and Sangeeta Karandikar helped me to make these choices. In that sense this book is theirs as much as mine, though I retain the responsibility of any inadequacies or mistakes that I have made. I have worked hard to eliminate the mistakes. You would judge it better whether I worked hard enough. Sangeeta also helped in honing the first five chapters, whereas Niranjan executed and improved the shell scripts.

Thanks to Manish Jain of BPB for asking if I might be interested in writing this book. I was and you now hold it, and I hope that it may help to make Unix as pleasant for you as it has been for me.

Most of the figures in this book have been prepared by Shilpa Agarkar. Her remarkable thoroughness has greatly improved this book.

Hemant Kelkar designed the book cover and I hope you too would appreciate his eye for detail and precision.

Thanks to Seema and Aditya for putting up with my bizarre schedules and for listening to my dreams.

Contents

Introduction

Welcome to Unix Shell Programming! There are lots of books about Unix, but most of them assume that you are a computer wizard and would love to learn every single command Unix has to offer. On these scores at least you would find this book refreshingly different.

It doesn't expect that you have worked with Unix earlier. It begins with a description of what you can really do with Unix, how to get started, what commands you should really know, before beginning with the real stuff - the shell programming.

How This Book is Organized

This books has two parts. These parts stand on their own depending on whether you are a novice Unix user or you have already worked with Unix. If you are already familiar with Unix commands you can straightaway begin with Part II. However, if this is your first tryst with Unix you would be better off if you start with Part I. Part I comprises Chapters 1 through 8, whereas Part II consists of Chapters 9 through 16. Contents of each part are mentioned below in brief.

Part I:

Chapter 1 introduces you to fundamental Unix concepts, the major features of Unix OS and the equipment you need to run it. Chapter 2 gives you step-by-step instructions for creating, renaming and removing files and directories. It also describes the file and directory permissions and the philosophy behind it. Chapter 3 discusses the Unix file system, its organization and the commands related to it. Chapter 4 discusses commonly used Unix commands with their important variations. Chapter 5 is devoted to one of the important capabilities of the Unix shell - input/output redirection and piping. Chapter 6 is a self-contained guide to the **vi** editor which helps you create, modify and maintain text files. Chapter 7 talks about the processes launched by the system and by the users and their behaviour. Chapter 8 helps you communicate with other users through the powerful communication facilities offered by Unix.

Part II:

Assuming that you are thorough with the philosophy and the commands introduced in the earlier part, Part II proceeds to teach you the intricacies of shell programming. Chapter 9 introduces the fundamental concepts of shell programming with discussion about shell variables, positional parameters and writing interactive and non-interactive shell scripts. Chapter 10 covers the decision control instruction, the file and string tests and their utility. Chapter 11 discusses the various looping facilities available with the shell and their practical use. Shell metacharacters are VIPs of Unix and you learn about them in detail in Chapter 12. Every programmer keeps a few aces up his sleeves. Some of these are shown in Chapter 13. Features which are away from mainstream shell programming but are quite handy in particular situations are the topic of Chapter 14. This book would lose its charm if it doesn't discuss system administration and the related scripts. Hence a separate chapter has been devoted to it - Chapter 15. To put together all the skills acquired earlier into one big practical program nothing short of a full-fledged project would do. With that intention a Payroll Processing System has been developed in Chapter 16.

Thus, this book takes you from the simple use of single Unix commands through complex commands to shell script programs to an in-depth shell programing project.

Throughout the book there is a strong emphasis on examples, so that you can see how various programming mechanisms work and try your hand at tinkering with them. All chapters also have an exercise at the end so that you can test your understanding of the concepts as you progress. This makes the learning process easier. Don't forget to do the exercises. After all reading about ideas is no substitute for using them.

If you are a relative novice, I hope this book would make a Unix programmer of you. And if you are already a programmer, I hope this book would make you a good Unix programmer. Good luck!

Yashavant Kanetkar

kanetkar@kalptaru.indiagate.com
Aug, 1996

1 *Getting Started*

We are now embarking on a very special journey that of unveiling and exploring the unlimited expanse that is Unix. By the end of this journey, we plan to have you make tentative, if not confident overtures to the Unix Operating system. But first, let us do away with a few civilities. What was the origin of Unix? How did it reach the status it enjoys today? Read on.

A Unix Biography

Unix, as the world knows it today, is the happy outcome of the proverbial rags-to-riches story. What is now heralded as the most powerful and popular multiuser Operating System (OS) had a very humble beginning in the austere premises of AT & T's Bell laboratories, the fertile spawning ground of many a landmark in computer history.

The origin of Unix can be traced back to 1965, when a joint venture was undertaken by Bell Telephone Laboratories, the General Electric Company and Massachusetts Institute of Technology. The aim was to develop an operating system that could serve a large community of users and allow them to share data if need be. This never-to-be enterprise was called Multics, for Multiplex Information and Computing Service. Even after much time, resources and efforts had been devoted to the project, the convenient, interactive computing service as quoted by Ritchie, failed to materialise. This led Dennis Ritchie and Ken Thompson, both of AT & T, to start afresh on what their mind's eye had so illustriously envisioned. Thus, in 1969, the two along with a few others evolved what was to be the first version of the multiuser system Unix. Armed with a museum piece of a computer called PDP-7, a rudimentary file system was developed. Though this was not tapped to the fullest, it had all the trappings of a truly potent multiuser operating system. This system was christened 'Unix' by Brian Kernighan, as a very reminder of the ill-fated Multics. Later, in 1971 Unix was ported to a PDP-11 computer with a 512 KB disk. Unix then was a 16 KB system with 8 KB for user programs and a upper limit of 64 KB per file. All its assembly code being machine dependent, the version was not portable, a key requirement for a successful OS.

To remedy this, Ken Thompson created a new language 'B' and set about the Herculean task of rewriting the whole Unix code in this high level language. 'B' lacked in several aspects necessary for real life programming. Ritchie sifted the inadequacies of B and modified it to a new language which he named as 'C' - the language which finally enabled Unix to stand tall on any machine.

Thus, by 1973, Unix had come a long way from its PDP-7 days, and was soon licensed to quite a number of Universities, Companies and other commercial institutions. With its uncomplicated elegance it was charming a following perhaps more effortlessly than the pied piper of the fables. The essentially accommodating nature of the system encouraged many a developer to polish and enhance its capabilities, which kept it alive and with the times.

By the mid eighties there were more than a hundred thousand Unix installations running on anything from a micro to a mainframe computer and over numerous varying architectures - a remarkable achievement for an OS by any standard. Almost a decade later Unix still holds the record for being the soul of more computer networks than any other OS is.

Hardware Requirements for Unix

From the Lilliputian System on the PDP-11, Unix has emerged to be a rugged stalwart today. There are some prerequisites for a system that can host and take best advantage of it. These are an 80 MB hard disk and at least 4 MB of RAM (Random Access Memory) on a 16-bit microprocessor (80286, or preferably 80386/80486). So you need a PC/AT or higher with the aforementioned configuration to employ Unix to the best of its ability. And how do we connect the terminals to the host machine? Through a 4/8/16 port controller card installed in the expansion slot on the mother board of the host machine. One end of the cable is plugged to the port on the controller card and another end to the serial port (9 pin or 25 pin) of the terminal. Any DOS based machine with a serial port can act as a terminal.

Out of 80 MB disk space almost 40 MB is eaten away by the actual Unix OS files whereas another 10-20 MB is used as swap space. The swap space is used when Unix falls short of memory. At such times it temporarily stores in this swap space the contents of memory which are not immediately required. Whenever these contents are required they are read back from the swap space.

More the number of terminals more should be the memory on the host machine. As a thumb rule we can say that per terminal to be supported 0.75 to 1 MB should be present in the host machine.

Besides the hardware, Unix also requires a considerable amount of human support. This comes in the form of a System Administrator who supervises the working of Unix on any installation.

Salient Features of Unix

The Unix OS offers several salient features, the important of which are discussed below.

Multiuser Capability

Among its salient features, what comes first is its multiuser capability. In a multiuser system, the same computer resources - hard disk, memory etc. - are accessible to many users. Of course, the users don't flock together at the same computer, but are given different terminals to operate from. A terminal, in turn, is a keyboard and a monitor, which are the input and output devices for that user. All terminals are connected to the main computer whose resources are availed by all users. So, a user at any of the terminals can use not only the computer, but also any peripherals that may be attached, say for instance a printer. One can easily appreciate how economical such a setup is than having as many computers as there are users, and also how much more convenient when the same data is to be shared by all. The following figure shows a typical Unix setup.

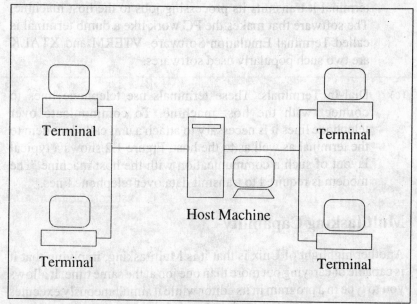

Figure 1.1

At the heart of a Unix installation is the host machine, often known as a server or a console. The number of terminals that can be connected to the host machine depends on the number of ports that are present in its controller card. For example, a 4-port controller card in the host machine can support 4 terminals. There are several types of terminals that can be attached to the host. These are:

(a) Dumb Terminals: These terminals consist of a keyboard and a display unit with no memory or disk of its own. These can never act as independent machines. If they are to be used they have to be connected to the host machine.

(b) Terminal Emulation: A PC has its own microprocessor, memory and disk drives. By attaching this PC to the host through a cable and running a software from this PC we can emulate it to work as if it is a dumb terminal. At such times, however, the memory and the disk are not in use and the PC cannot carry out any processing on its own. Like a dumb terminal it transmits its processing jobs to the host machine. The software that makes the PC work like a dumb terminal is called Terminal Emulation Software. VTERM and XTALK are two such popularly used softwares.

(c) Dial-In Terminals: These terminals use telephone lines to connect with the host machine. To communicate over telephone lines it is necessary to attach a unit called modem to the terminal as well as to the host. Figure 1.2 shows a typical layout of such a communication with the host machine. The modem is required to transmit data over telephone lines.

Multitasking Capability

Another highlight of Unix is that it is Multitasking, implying that it is capable of carrying out more than one job at the same time. It allows you to type in a program in its editor while it simultaneously executes some other command you might have given earlier, say to sort and copy a huge file. The latter job is performed in the 'background', while in the 'foreground' you use the editor, or take a directory listing or whatever else. This is managed by dividing the CPU time intelligently between all processes being carried out. Depending on the priority of the task, the operating system appropriately allots small time slots (of the order of milliseconds or microseconds) to each foreground and background task.

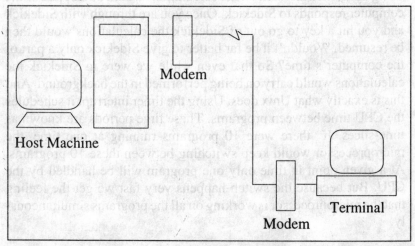

Figure 1.2

The very concept of a multiuser operating system expects the same to be multitasking too. We can say this because even when a user is executing only one command at a time, the CPU is not dedicated to the solitary user. In all probability, there are ten more users who also demand execution of their commands. Unix, therefore, has to be on its toes all the time, obliging all the users connected to it.

Although crude, MS-DOS also provides a multitasking capability. The type of multitasking provided by Ms-DOS is known as Serial Multitasking. In this type of multitasking one program is stopped temporarily while another is allowed to execute. At any given time only one task is run. You can liken this to a situation in which a human working on a computer stops his work to answer a ringing phone and then, having finished with the call, switches back to the computer.

Most of us must have used Sidekick or some other memory resident program. Once we load this into memory, a simple keystroke can take us from Sidekick to another program we may be running or vice versa.

If, for example, we invoke Sidekick in the middle of some calculation being done, then all work on the calculations would be stopped as the computer responds to Sidekick. Once you are through with Sidekick and you hit a key to go out of Sidekick the calculations would then be resumed. Wouldn't it be far better to give Sidekick only a part of the computer's time? So that even while we were in Sidekick the calculations would carry on being performed in the background. And this is exactly what Unix does. Using the timer interrupt it schedules the CPU time between programs. These time periods are known as time-slices. If there were 10 programs running at one time, the microprocessor would keep switching between these 10 programs. At a given point in time only one program will be handled by the CPU. But because the switch happens very fast we get the feeling that the microprocessor is working on all the programs simultaneously.

Thus, multitasking of Unix is different from DOS which does not give time-slices to running programs. And if there are 5 programs running in DOS and even one goes haywire, the entire machine hangs. In any genuine multitasking environment like Unix this does not happen.

Does Unix give equal time-slices to all programs running in memory? No. There may be some programs that are relatively more important. For example, those that wait for user responses are given a higher priority. Programs which have the same priority are scheduled on a round-robin basis.

Communication

Unix has excellent provision for communicating with fellow users. The communication may be within the network of a single main computer, or between two or more such computer networks. The users can easily exchange mail, data, programs through such networks. Distance poses no barrier to passing information or messages to and fro. You may be two feet away or at two thousand miles your mail will hardly take any time to reach its destination.

Security

Unix allows sharing of data, but not indiscriminately. Had it been so, it would be the delight of mischief-mongers and useless for any worthwhile enterprise. Unix has three inherent provisions for protecting data. The first is provided by assigning passwords and login names to individual users ensuring that not anybody can come and have access to your work.

At the file level, there are read, write and execute permissions to each file which decide who can access a particular file, who can modify it and who can execute it. You may reserve read and write permissions for yourself and leave others on the network free to execute it, or any such combination.

Lastly, there is file encryption. This utility encodes your file into an unreadable format, so that even if someone succeeds in opening it, your secrets are safe. Of course should you want to see the contents, you can always decrypt the file.

Portability

One of the main reasons for the universal popularity of Unix is that it can be ported to almost any computer system, with only the bare minimum of adaptations to suit the given computer architecture. As of today, there are innumerable computer manufacturers around the globe, and tens of hundreds of hardware configurations. More often than not, Unix is running strong on each one of them. And lest we forget, due credit for this feat must be given to the Dennis Ritchie's prodigy, C, which granted Unix this hardware transparency. Unix, in fact is almost entirely written in C.

Unix System Organisation

The functioning of Unix is manned in three levels. On the outer crust reside the application programs and other utilities, which speak our language. At the heart of Unix, on the other hand, is the Kernel, which interacts with the actual hardware in machine language. The streamlining of these two modes of communication is done by the middle layer, called the Shell. Figure 1.3 shows the three layers of Unix OS.

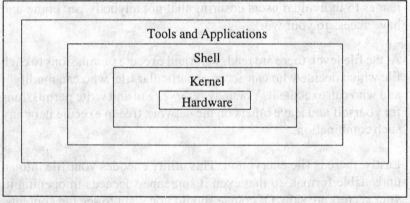

Figure 1.3

The shell, or the command interpreter as it is called, is the mediator, which interprets the commands that we give and then conveys them to the kernel which ultimately executes them. You can imagine kernel as a monarch who is in overall control of everything, whereas the shell as its emissary.

The kernel has various functions. It manages files, carries out all the data transfer between the file system and the hardware, and also manages memory. The onus of scheduling of various programs running in memory or allocation of CPU time to all running programs also lies with the kernel. It also handles any interrupts issued, as it is the entity that has direct dealings with the hardware.

The kernel program is usually stored in a file called 'unix' whereas the shell program is in a file called 'sh'. For each user working with Unix at any time different shell programs are running. Thus, at a particular point in time there may be several shells running in memory but only one kernel. This is because, at any instance Unix is capable of executing only one program as the other programs wait for their turn. And since it's the kernel which executes the program one kernel is sufficient. However, different users at different terminals are trying to seek kernel's attention. And since the user interacts with the kernel through the shell different shells are necessary.

Types of Shells

Different people implemented the interpreter function of the shell in different ways. This gave rise to various types of shells, the most prominent of which are outlined below:

Bourne Shell

Among all, Steve Bourne's creation, known after him as the Bourne Shell, is the most popular. Probably that's why it is bundled with every Unix system. Or perhaps it is the other way round. Because it was bundled with every system it became popular. Whatever the cause and the effect, the fact remains that this is the shell used by many Unix users. This will also be the shell we shall be talking about extensively through the course of this book.

C Shell

This shell is a hit with those who are seriously into Unix programming. It was created by Bill Joy, then pursuing his graduation at the University of California at Berkeley. It has two advantages over the Bourne Shell.

Firstly, it allows aliasing of commands. That is, you can decide what name you want to call a command by. This proves very useful when lengthy commands which are used time and again are renamed by you. Instead of typing the entire command you can simply use the short alias at the command line.

If you want to save even more on the typing work, C shell has a command history feature. This is the second benefit that comes with C Shell. Previously typed commands can be recalled, since the C shell keeps track of all commands issued at the command line. This feature is similar to the one provided by the program DOSKEY in MS-DOS environment.

Korn Shell

If there was any doubt about the cause-effect relationship of the popularity of Bourne Shell and it's inclusion in every package, this adds fuel to it. The not-so-widely-used Korn Shell is very powerful, and is a superset of Bourne Shell. It offers a lot more capabilities and is decidedly more efficient than the other. It was designed to be so by David Korn of AT & T's Bell Labs.

The First Faltering Steps

We have done enough homework on Unix now to venture for our first practical contact with it. Given that your terminal is secured to the host computer and is powered on, your display prompts you for your login name. Each user is given a unique login name and a password, which are like an entry pass to connect to the host machine as a user.

If you haven't been given a login name and a password, you won't be able to gain access to Unix. After you enter your login name, you are prompted to enter the password which when keyed in does not appear on the display. Obviously this is to ensure that no chance or may be premeditated passer-by is able to sneak in on it.

When you try to access your system, Unix will display a prompt that looks something like this:

    login:aa1
    Password: heman1

After receiving the login prompt, you enter your login name (**aa1** in the above example), after which you receive the Password prompt. At this stage you must type in your password (**heman1** in this example). The password of course would not appear on the screen. The password you use should be kept private. It is the method used by Unix to prevent unauthorized entry into the system. The password should be changed frequently. On many systems, after a specified period of time, your password expires (ages) and the next time you login the system requires you to change your password. In addition, you can change your password whenever you like on most systems by using a command to alter the password. We would discuss how to change your password in a later chapter.

Sometimes you may not type the login name or password properly. When you do this, the system will respond with the following message:

    login: aa1
    Password: heman1
    Login incorrect

    Wait for login retry:
    login:

Note that the system does not tell you which one is incorrect, the login name or the password. Again, this is a security measure. Even if you type your login name improperly, you will still get the password prompt. You usually get three to five attempts to get it right before your terminal is disconnected. Many times a message is displayed to the system administrator telling him or her that several unsuccessful attempts were made on your login name.

Once the correct login name and password have been supplied, you find some welcome messages from the suppliers of the Unix version installed on the host machine, followed by a command prompt. The command prompt is a $ (dollar) if you are operating in Bourne shell, or a % if in C shell. What powers await you here will be unwound as we progress. For now, take it from me that they do.

You are prompted for the login and the password every time you put on your terminal. Its purpose is to identify the user and allow access to the system only after verifying the identity of the user. You will not be prompted for the login if there is some problem in cables through which your terminal is connected to the host machine.

Once at the $ prompt you can issue commands. There are several hundred commands available in Unix. Let us begin with the most elementary one.

```
$ who am i
aa1    tty3a    Jun 10 09:15
```

A word of caution before we proceed. All Unix commands are to be typed in small-case letters. Once you enter the above command and press the Enter key the shell interprets your command and then dispatches a message to kernel to identify the user. The kernel retrieves the information about you and displays it on the screen. This information consists of "aa1" which is our login name, "tty3a" signifies the terminal number or the serial port line by which your terminal is connected to the host machine. The date and time at which you logged in are also displayed.

In fact the **who am i** command is a special case of the **who** command. The **who** command is more powerful and displays data about all the users who have logged into the system currently. This is shown below:

```
$ who
aa1     tty3a    Jun 10  09:15
aa2     tty3c    Jun 10  09:25
ajay    tty3d    Jun 10  08:22
shilpa  tty3b    Jun 10  07:10
```

The format of the output is same as that of **who am i**. The first entity is again the user's login name followed by the terminal line he is using and login dates and times.

The end of a Unix session is marked by a logout. This is done by either typing exit at the $ prompt or hitting **Ctrl d**. Terminating your session this way indicates that you have logged out of the system. Simply turning the power at your terminal off does not result in an actual exit. Anyone switching on the terminal would then automatically find himself logged in, bypassing the login procedure. Needless to say, that would mean goodbye to your file security.

Unix Commands

Having covered this much ground let us now get into the thick of the things. Most of us would be entering the Unix arena after traversing that of DOS. So just so as to feel at home, we will first have a look at some commands in Unix that are parallel to those available in DOS. That's the point from where we would begin the next chapter. But before you turn over to the next chapter where you are going to meet a plethora of commands, remember a few things that apply to all Unix commands.

(a)   All Unix commands must always be entered in small case letters.

(b)   Between the command name and the options that may be available with the command there must always be a space or a tab. For example, **ls -l**. Here **ls** is the command whereas **-l** is the option and the two have been separated by a space. The option is usually preceded by a minus (-) sign. The options available with a command are often known as switches.

(c)   Two or more options available with a command can usually be combined. For example, the command **ls -l -a** is same as **ls -la**.

(d)   If you make a typing mistake, press Backspace to erase characters. Don't try to back using arrow keys and then attempt deleting using the Del key.

(e)   To cancel the entire command before you press Enter, press the Del key.

(f)   Don't turn off the computer if you have made a mistake and all is not going well. DOS users are used to just turning off the computer if a command behaves strangely possibly by falling into an infinite loop or some such thing. Unix doesn't respond well to such an approach. Instead we need to suggest politely to Unix to stop execution of the command which is creating a problem. One way do so is by hitting the Del key. If still the command is not abandoned try **Ctrl d** and you would be returned to the login prompt. And if it is really a bad day for you even **Ctrl d** may not be able to do the job. At such times you got to contact the system administrator who would then kill your process from memory. How exactly he achieves this we would explore in a later chapter.

What's in The Name?

A lot if the name happens to be the name of a Unix command. Unix commands have strange names. Unlike DOS environment where you have jazzy names for each utility there appears to be a lack of imagination as far as naming of the utilities under Unix is concerned. Under DOS you have C compilers bearing names like Turbo C, Quick C, Zortech C, Lattice C, Vitamin C etc., whereas under Unix the C compiler is simply named as **cc**. If a DOS developer writes a utility for searching expression in a file he is likely to call it as 'search' or 'explore' or 'peek' or some such name. A similar utility under Unix bears a name 'grep' standing for '**g**lobally search a **r**egular **e**xpression and **p**rint it'! When a Unix developer developed a utility which could convert a file (let's say from lowercase to uppercase) while copying it, he decided to name it as **cc**. However, **cc** was already there standing for C Compiler. Hence he chose the next best option - **dd**. What a lack of imagination! What we must understand is how come Unix commands have such strange names. This is because when Ken Thompson gave Unix as a case study to his students, the student groups started building utilities around Unix. Nobody outside these groups believed that Unix would ever become popular and successful. The names given to utilities were to serve as reminders to persons who were developing or using it. You would agree that the names would have been different and better had people gone about the development of Unix more systematically.

Exercise

[A] Pick up the correct alternative for each of the following questions:

(a) Unix OS was first developed by
   (1) Dennis Ritchie
   (2) Bjarne Stroustrup
   (3) Ken Thompson
   (4) Brian Kernighan

(b) Unix OS was first developed at
   (1) Microsoft Corp., USA
   (2) AT & T Bell Labs, USA
   (3) IBM, USA
   (4) Borland International, USA

(c) Unix OS cannot run on which of the following Microprocessor
   (1) 8086

(2) 80286

(3) 80386

(4) Pentium

(d) Unix is written in
   (1) C language
   (2) Ada language
   (3) Perl language
   (4) Pascal language

(e) In a typical Unix setup the host machine is attached to the terminals through
   (1) I/O card
   (2) Sound blaster card
   (3) Disk controller card
   (4) 4/8-port controller card

(f) Unix is
   (1) Single user, single tasking OS
   (2) Single user, multitasking OS
   (3) Multiuser, multitasking OS
   (4) None of the above

(g) If every user working on a Unix setup is to use the printer, then the printer should be attached to
   (1) The host machine
   (2) Any of the terminal
   (3) The terminal from where the first login was made
   (4) None of the above

(h) For dial-in terminal facility which of the following is a must
   (1) Multimedia kit
   (2) Modem
   (3) Printer
   (4) Terminal emulator

(i)   Which of the following is a popular terminal emulation software
    (1) VTERM
    (2) VT100
    (3) COMIT
    (4) Perl

(j)   Which of the following is a command for searching a pattern in a file.
    (1) find
    (2) grep
    (3) lookup
    (4) None of the above

[B]   State whether the following statements are True or False:

(a)   Unix uses serial multitasking to support various programs running in memory.

(b)   Unix supports multitasking by giving time slices to various programs running in memory.

(c)   In Unix we can communicate only between users connected to one host and not with users connected to another host.

(d)   Every legal user has to have a login id and a password.

(e)   Any user having access to Unix automatically gets an access to all the files present in it.

(f)   Unix can be ported to a new hardware platform with minimum changes in the Unix code.

(g)   The Unix kernel acts as an agent between the shell and the hardware.

(h)   In a typical Unix environment there are several kernels and one shell.

(i)   Bourne shell offers a command history feature.

(j)   **who** is a special case of **who am i** command.

(k)   A command switch for any Unix command always begins with a / sign.

[C]   Answer the following:

(a)   What do you mean by password ageing?

(b)   What do you mean by multiuser, multitasking OS?

(c)   What are the minimum hardware requirements for installing Unix?

(d)   Can Unix be installed on a PC/XT with 80mb hard disk and 16mb RAM? If not why not?

(e)   Name any 5 salient features of Unix OS.

(f)   Which are the different ways of establishing a logical connection with the host machine?

(g)   What is the basic difference between DOS, Windows 95 and Unix?

(h)   Which different types of shells are available in Unix?

(i)   What are the long forms of the following Unix commands?
cc   dd   grep   unix

(j)   Which different security mechanisms are available in Unix?

2

Gaining Confidence

In the last chapter we saw how to execute the **who** command which gives information about the user who has invoked this command after logging in. Remember that in a multiuser system like Unix knowing who you are and where do you stand is crucial. That is why we tackled the **who am i** command first. We also know that **who** lists all the users that might have logged in. Let us now find out how are you related with these users. We know that the System Administrator is in overall control of the Unix installation. In fact he is the one who has to first create your account with Unix so that you can login. For that matter unless he creates an account for a particular user the user is unable to login since Unix won't recognise such a user. Creation of an account involves the following activities:

(a)   Providing login name to the user
(b)   Providing initial password to the user
(c)   Putting the user in one of the groups
(d)   Providing a default working shell to the user
(e)   Providing a default working directory to the user

A typical Unix installation might have 25 to 50 users. If this installation is in a University then the users may be categorised as second year students, third year students and so on. Accordingly, while creating such users the system administrator would put all third year students in one group, all second year students in another group etc. Similarly, in an industrial setup all users from Accounts department may be kept in one group, all users from Purchase department in another group and so on. By dividing all users into groups it becomes easier for the system administrator to manage them. At the same time it is more convenient for the users themselves to share their work, their files and their data. The way the system administrator gives different login names to different users he also provides names to the groups to which the users belong. The following figure shows the organisation of the users and groups which would give you an idea about where do you stand among the user community.

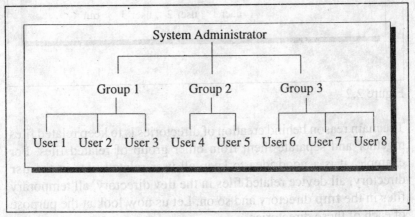

Figure 2.1

The Unix File System

Before we learn any more Unix commands it is essential to understand the Unix File System since Unix treats everything it knows and understands, as a file. All utilities, applications, data in Unix is stored as files. Even a directory is treated as a file which contains several other files. The Unix file system resembles an upside down tree. Thus, the file system begins with a directory called **root**. The root directory is denoted as slash (/). Branching from the root there are several other directories called **bin, lib, usr, etc, tmp** and **dev**. The root directory also contains a file called **unix** which is Unix kernel itself. These directories are called sub-directories, their parent being the root directory. Each of these sub-directories contain several files and directories called sub-sub-directories. Figure 2.2 shows the basic structure of the Unix file system.

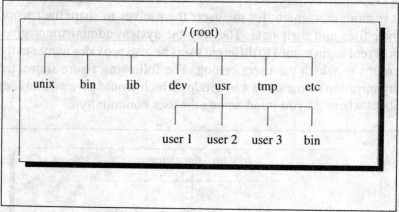

Figure 2.2

The main reason behind creation of directories is to keep related files together and separate them from other group of related files. For example, it is a good idea to keep all user related files in the **usr** directory, all device related files in the **dev** directory, all temporary files in the **tmp** directory and so on. Let us now look at the purpose of each of these directories.

The **bin** directory contains executable files for most of the Unix commands. Unix commands can be either C programs or shell programs. Shell programs are nothing but a collection of several Unix commands.

The **lib** directory contains all the library functions provided by Unix for programmers. The programs written under Unix make use of these library functions in the **lib** directory.

The **dev** directory contains files that control various input/output devices like terminals, printer, disk drives etc. For each device there is a separate file. In Unix each device is implemented as a file. For example, everything that is displayed on your terminal is first written to a file associated with your terminal, and this file is present in the **dev** directory.

In the **usr** directory there are several directories, each associated with a particular user. These directories are created by the system administrator when he creates accounts for different users. Each user is allowed to work with his directory (often called home directory) and can organise his directory by creating other sub-directories in it, to contain functionally related files.

Within the **usr** directory there is another **bin** directory which contains additional Unix command files.

The **tmp** directory contains the temporary files created by Unix or by the users. Since the files present in it are created for a temporary purpose Unix can afford to dispense with them. These files get automatically deleted when the system is shutdown and restarted.

All the aforementioned directories are present on almost all Unix installations. The following figure captures the essence of these directories and their purpose.

Directory	Contains
bin	Binary executable files
lib	Library functions
dev	Device related files
etc	Binary executable files usually required for system administration
tmp	Temporary files created by Unix or users
usr	Home directories of all users
/usr/bin	Additional binary excutable files

Figure 2.3

Following are the salient features of the Unix File System:

(a)   It has a hierarchical file structure.
(b)   Files can grow dynamically.
(c)   Files have access permissions.
(d)   All devices are implemented as files.

These features would be discussed in detail in the following pages.

Creating Files

Now that we understand how the file system is organised in Unix let us learn a few elementary file related commands. We would first learn how to create files. There are two commands to do so: **touch** and **cat**. And this is how they are to be used.

```
$ touch sample
```

This creates a file called 'sample'. However, the size of the file would be zero bytes since **touch** doesn't allow you to store anything in a file. Then does **touch** serve any purpose? Yes, when we want to create several empty files quickly. This can be done by saying,

```
$ touch sample1 sample2 sample3 sample4 sample5
```

You would agree that this is a refreshingly simple way of creating empty files. But what if we want to store a few lines in a file? Just type the command,

```
$ cat > test
```

Now press the Enter key and you would find the cursor positioned in the next line, waiting for you to type the matter that you want to store in the file 'test'. Type in two lines of text:

```
Valderama, Valderama pass the ball to Asprilla
Asprilla, Asprilla shoot the ball into the net
```

Once you are through with this press the keys **Ctrl d**. In Unix the keys **Ctrl d** indicate the EOF or end of file character. Therefore, when we press these keys the **cat** command recognises the EOF character and promptly saves the matter you typed on the disk in the file 'test'. Naturally, you would once again get back the $ prompt on the screen.

To display the contents of a file under DOS, we use the **type** command. In Unix, its counterpart is **cat**, derived from concatenate. Saying **cat recipe** at the command prompt displays the contents of file **recipe** on the screen. Thus, to see the contents of the file **test** that we created above we should say,

```
$ cat test
```

Now we know two uses of the **cat** command. One is to create new files and another to display the contents of an existing file. **cat** has a few more aces up its sleeve. It can concatenate the contents of two files and store them in the third file.

```
$ cat sample1 sample2 > newsample
```

This would create **newsample** which contains contents of **sample1** followed by that of **sample2**. A word of caution. If **newsample** already contains something it would be overwritten. If you want that it should remain intact and contents of **sample1** and **sample2** should get appended to it then you should use the 'append output redirection operator', >>, as shown below:

```
$ cat sample1 sample2 >> newsample
```

Indulging in File Play

Now that we know how to create files and display them let us indulge ourselves in more file related commands. Like those for copying files, renaming them, deleting them, listing them etc. Here we go...

In DOS, we **copy** a file, while in Unix we **cp** it. For example,

    $ cp letter.a letter.b

This will copy the contents of **letter.a** into a file **letter.b**. If **letter.b** does not exist, it will be created. However, if it does exist, Unix takes the liberty to overwrite it without warning you.

Look at the following **cp** command:

    $ cp letter.a letter.b letters

In such a use of **cp**, all files mentioned are copied to the indicated directory. Provided that the directory **letters** exists, both files **letter.a** and **letter.b** would be copied to it.

Just as in DOS, in Unix too you can copy files from or to different directories by specifying their name along with the path. For example,

    $ cp /usr/aa16/chapter1 /usr/aa16/newbook/chap1

Here the file **chapter1** is copied from the directory **/usr/aa16** to the directory **/usr/aa16/newbook**. When copied to this directory it would have the name **chap1** instead of **chapter1**.

While on filenames, we might as well point out that unlike DOS, Unix files do not have to follow a stringent 3-character extension rule. What's more, the dot in the filenames is treated as any other character constituting the filename, having no significance whatsoever as a separator of filename and extension.

Also note that in the above example we have used absolute pathname to refer to the file **chapter1**. The absolute pathname started at the root directory /.

Sometimes instead of absolute pathname we may use a relative pathname. This refers to the pathname starting from the directory in which you are now. When you type a full pathname starting at the root directory, the pathname starts with a /. When you type a relative pathname starting at the current working directory, the pathname doesn't start with /. That's how Unix (and you) can figure out which kind of path it is.

The counterpart of the **del** command in DOS is the **rm** command in Unix. **rm** removes the given file or files supplied to it. It works differently for different options supplied with it. This leads us to a slight digression wherein we need the most populous entity in Unix - options or switches. Unix commands have an abundance of options to manipulate their executions. For instance, saying

```
$ rm -i file
```

where **-i** is a switch, removes **file** interactively; i.e. you are asked for confirmation before deleting the file.

In DOS, to remove a directory, you are first required to empty the directory, and then delete it. Unix offers a single command for the same.

```
$ rm -r dir1
```

This command recursively (**-r**) removes all contents of **dir1** and also **dir1** itself. That gives us a trailer of the powers of Unix, doesn't it?

rm used with the **-f** option removes files forcibly, irrespective of whether you have write permission to them or not. This would be more clear in the next section where we deal with file permissions. For the time being just remember that such an option exists with Unix.

Renaming of files in DOS is interpreted in Unix as moving them. However, **mv** is more capable than **ren** of DOS as we would see. Suppose we want to rename the file **test** to **sample** we should say,

```
$ mv test sample
```

The **mv** command also has the power to rename directories.

```
$ mv olddir newdir
```

olddir will be renamed to **newdir**, provided **newdir** is not already existing.

But why call the operation 'moving' of files rather than 'renaming' of files. Because moving a file implies removing it from its current location and copying it at a new location. However, moving is different than copying in that the source file is erased from its original location and copied at the specified destination. This sense of **mv** command is exemplified by the following command:

```
$ mv file1 file2 newdir
```

On execution of this command **file1** and **file2** are no longer present at their original location, but are moved to the directory **newdir**.

Let us now 'move' on to other file related commands.

Listing Files and Directories

ls is to Unix as **DIR** is to DOS. It gives the directory listing, or lists the contents of the current or specified directory. As you might have fallen in the habit of expecting, **ls** too does more than what plain simple DIR can do. No wonder, considering the whole gang of options (switches) it has on its side. Literally. There are around two dozen options to go with **ls** (what were they thinking of?) that list the contents in ways to suit every fancy of yours. Let us begin with the plain and simple **ls** without any options.

```
$ ls
carribeans
kangaroos
kiwis
```

        pakde
        pommies
        springboks
        zulus

No, don't fall for the filenames that are present in the current directory. What you should note unlike DIR of DOS **ls** is intelligent enough to display the filenames in alphabetical order.

> $ cat > .cricket
> Surat is different than Sharjah
> So sixes don't come so easily at Sharjah
> Ctrl d

Did you expect an error because our filename began with a '.'? Well, filenames can begin with a dot. Since no error has occurred while creating this file we should be confident that **ls** is bound to list it. Let us try it out.

> $ ls
> carribeans
> kangaroos
> kiwis
> pakde
> pommies
> springboks
> zulus

Where has the file **.cricket** gone? Well, well. It is there in the directory but it is treated as a hidden file. For that matter any filename which begins with a '.' is treated as a hidden file. And if we want to list even the hidden files we need to use the **-a** option of **ls**.

> $ ls -a

```
        ..
        .cricket
        carribeans
        kangaroos
        kiwis
        pakde
        pommies
        .springboks
        zulus
```

Now there is another problem? What are the two entries . and .. signifying? . stands for the current directory whereas .. stands for the parent of the current directory. These two entries automatically get created in the directory whenever the directory is created.

Try the following command:

```
    $ ls p*
    pakde
    pommies
```

Let us tackle here a new entity called 'metacharacters'. No, this is no digression. If you talk of **ls**, you generally talk of metacharacters, and vice versa. Metacharacters are characters that the shell never takes at face value. They are representative of one or a group of characters, and constitute Unix's way of indulging us users. These allow us to formulate all sorts of criteria to be satisfied by a string. To understand them better, we deal with them one by one.

Take the most pertinent one, the question mark. When the shell comes across a '?'. it understands that the symbol signifies any single character. Consider the following example:

```
    $ ls ?ain
    gain
    main
    pain
```

rain

Thus, assuming the four listed files to be present in the current directory, the shell substituted 'g', 'm', 'p' and 'r' in turn to display those files ending in 'ain'.

The * is interpreted by the shell as presence (or absence) of any number of characters. Thus saying **ls *** is same as saying **ls**, wherein all the files in the current directory are listed . In fact when we said **ls p***, the shell interpreted it as 'list all files whose names begin with p'. Hence 'pommies' and 'pakde' were listed.

To list all files in directory **mydir** which end in, say, **x**, we would say,

    $ ls /mydir/*x
    cc_fax
    i_tax
    myUnix

Whatever be the length of the name, if the last letter is an **x**, it qualifies for listing.

Another very powerful means for specifying criteria for file selection is by supplying ranges. If you want to list all files whose name start with a vowel, you can say

    $ ls [aeiou]*

This indicates that the first character of the filename to be listed must be any one of the letters given vithin the square brackets, and the remaining can be anything.

If your requirement is to list those files whose names do not begin with a vowel, what do you do? List out all the other 21 alphabets? No way. Again Unix indulges your whim. You simply tell it to list those files whose names do not begin with a vowel.

```
$ ls [!aeiou]*
```

The ! symbol complements the condition that follows it. Hence the above command would list all those files whose first character is anything other than a vowel.

Remember that the [ ] is always substituted by a single character. We can specify a group of characters within [ ], as in,

```
ls [a-m][c-z][4-9]??
```

This will list all 5 character filenames in the current directory whose first character is in the range a to m, the second character is in the range c to z, the third character is in the range 4 to 9, whereas the fourth and fifth are any valid characters.

Take a deep breath before reading any further. Because what is going to follow is a longggg listing... the one obtained by the -l option used with ls.

```
$ ls  -l
total 22
-rwxr-x--x   1   user1   group   24 Jun 06 10:12   carribeans
-rwxr-x-wx   1   user1   group   23 Jun 06 00:05   kangaroos
-rwxr-xr-x   1   user1   group   12 Jun 06 12:54   kiwis
drwxr-xr-x   1   user1   group   10 Jun 06 11:09   mydir
-rwxr-xrwx   2   user1   group   22 Jun 06 14:04   pakde
-rwxrwxr-x   2   user1   group   16 Jun 06 22:25   pommies
-rwxr-xr-x   1   user1   group   04 Jun 06 23:16   springboks
-rwxr-xr-x   1   user1   group   04 Jun 06 10:17   zulus
```

Intimidated? Relax as we go along all would flow smoothly. Let us begin with the first line of the output. 'total 22' indicates that the total number of disk blocks that the files in the current directory have occupied is 22. Generally each block in Unix is of 1024 bytes. But this is something which can be changed to some other multiple of 512.

Unix treats all entities - files, directories, devices - as files. Thus to distinguish between all of them it uses file types. In fact in all the lines listed in the output of the command **ls -l** the leftmost character indicates this type. A '-' indicates that the file is an ordinary file, whereas a 'd' indicates that it is a directory. Other possible file types are given in the following figure.

File Type	Meaning
-	Ordinary file
d	Directory file
c	Character special file
b	Block special file
l	Symbolic link
s	Semaphore
p	Named pipe
m	Shared memory file

Figure 2.4

The character special files and the block special files are normally present in the **/dev** directory. These files are used to handle character oriented devices like terminals or block oriented devices like disks. When these files are listed the file size entry for these files is replaced by major and minor device numbers. Usually these files are never found in user's directory.

The next nine characters following the file type character are the file permissions. Each column in succession gives the number of links, owner name, group name, size of file in bytes, date and time when the file was last modified, and finally the file name.

The concept of an 'owner' comes with the multiuser OS. By default, the person who creates the file is the owner of that file. A 'group' may be formed of a given number of users, who may be working on similar data.

How many links the file has essentially determines by how many different names the file is accessible. When a file has two links, it is not physically present at two places, but can be referred to by either of the names. This is a very useful feature. If you accidentally delete a file with a single link or a single name, there is no bringing it back, as Unix has no file undelete facility. But if a file has 2 links (thereby two names) your file is safe even if one of the links gets severed. A link is severed when the file is deleted.

So if a file is very important for you and you want to avoid its accidental deletion you should establish more than one link for such a file. The command to do so is fairly straight-forward.

$ ln poem mypoem

This establishes one more link for the file **poem** in the form of the name **newpoem**. If you now take a long listing you would find that both these files are listed each showing the presence of 2 links.

The concept of having several links to a file offers another advantage. If one file is to be shared between several users, instead of giving each user a separate copy of the same file we can create links of this file in each user's directory. This avoids unnecessary duplication of the same file contents in different directories.

By default any new file that we create has one link whereas any new directory we create has two links. Why 2 links for a directory? Because that directory name appears in two directory files. For example, if we create a directory **dir1** in a directory **aa1**, the directory file **aa1** would have an entry **dir1**, whereas the directory file **dir1** itself would also have an entry **dir1** (in the form of . which stands for current directory). Can you figure out the situation where a directory has 4 links? If you are able to do that can you determine the maximum number of links that a directory can have.

Let us get back to possibly the most important field in the output of **ls -l**: the permission field. The permissions signify who all can access the file, and for what purpose. This is decided by the files permissions. A set of nine characters denote these permissions. Let us now take a closer look at these permissions. There are three types of permissions to a file.

  r   read
  w   write
  x   execute

There are three entities to which any combination of these permissions are assigned. These entities are the owner, the group, and the rest (those outside the group). Of the nine characters, the first three characters decide the permissions held by the owner of the file. The next set of three characters specify the permissions for the other users in the group to which the file owner belongs, while the last set decides the permissions for the users outside the group. Out of the three characters belonging to each set the first character is for indicating the 'read' permission, the second character is for 'write' permission and the last is for 'execute' permission.

The permissions for the file **carribeans** from the long listing are **rwxr-x--x**. Thus, they signify that

(a)   the owner can read, write as well as execute the file **car-ribeans**.

(b)   the members of the group can read and execute the file, but cannot write to it. A - indicates that the permission is denied.

(c)   all others can only execute **carribeans** (not literally).

These permissions can be encoded numerically. The weights assigned to the three permissions are:

Permission	Weight
read (r)	4
write (w)	2
execute (e)	1

Thus, when all three permissions are available, the total weightage or value is $4 + 2 + 1$, i.e. 7, as is the case with the owner of **carribeans**.

The group permissions of **carribeans** are **r-x**, hence the value is $4 + 0 + 1$. i.e. 6. The permissions for the rest are **--x**, thus the value assigned is $0 + 0 + 1 = 1$.

In a nutshell, therefore, we can say that **carribeans** has the permission 761. When everybody has all the permissions, **rwxrwxrwx**, they would amount to 777.

The existing file permissions can be changed by the owner of the file or by the superuser. The way to change these permissions is by using the **chmod** command. It 'changes the mode' of the file it is executed on. If we want the owner of **carribeans** to have all the permissions and the group and others none, we say,

```
$ chmod 700 myfile
```

If you now take a long listing you would find that the permissions of the file **carribeans** have become **rwx------**.

This way of changing file permissions is referred to as the absolute mode. There is another syntax for **chmod** that changes permissions, which constitutes the symbolic mode. Its general form is,

```
$ chmod [who] [+/-/=] [permissions] file
```

The **who** here refers to whom the permissions are to be assigned. It may be the user or owner (u), the group (g) or others (o). If none is specified, all are assumed. The + refers to add permission, - refers to remove permission and = instructs **chmod** to add the specified permission and take away all others, if present.

The specified permission, of course, can be **r**, **w** or **x**. The command to give write permission to all would be

```
$ chmod +w carribeans
```

In order to take away execute permission from others as well as group we would say

```
$ chmod go-x myfile
```

What if we are to give a read permission to group and others and take away their write permission for a file called **yankees**? In such a case we should use **chmod** as shown below:

```
$ chmod go+r,go-w yankees
```

What would happen if execute the following command:

```
$ chmod go=r,u=rw file1
```

This removes all existing permissions and replaces them with read permission for group and others and read & write permission for owner of the file **file1**. Instead of using u/g/o and +/-/= we can straightaway use the weight (read = 4, write = 2, execute = 1) associated with each permission as shown below:

```
$ chmod 744 file1
```

This would assign the permission **rwxr--r--** to **file1**.

Can you interpret the following commands? Try your hand at them.

```
$ chmod 777 file1
$ chmod 654 file1
```

```
$ chmod 457 file1
```

Masking File Permissions

Let us first create an empty file called **sample** using the **touch** command and then try to list it.

```
$ touch sample
$ ls -l sample
-rw-r--r-- 1  user1  group  24 Jun 06 10:12 carribeans
```

How come that the file permissions for this file have been set to 644? Ideally speaking, whenever you create a file Unix should ask you what permissions you would like to set for the file. But then Unix never spoon-feeds you. It assumes that you are an intelligent user who understands the importance of file security and then sets up certain default permissions for the files that you create. What Unix does is it uses the value stored in a variable called **umask** to decide the default permissions. **umask** stands for user file creation mask, the term mask implying which permissions to mask or hide. The **umask** value tells Unix which of the three permissions are to be denied rather than granted. The current value of **umask** can be easily determined by just typing **umask**.

```
$ umask
0022
```

Here, the first 0 indicates that what follows is an octal number. The three digits that follow the first zero refer to the permissions to be denied to the owner, group and others. This means that for the owner no permission is denied, whereas for both, the group and others, a write permission (2) is denied. Whenever a file is created Unix assumes that the permissions for this file should be 666. But since our umask value is 022, Unix subtracts this value from the default system wide permissions (666) resulting in a value 644. This value is then used as the permissions for the file that you create. That is the reason why the permissions turned out to be 644 or **rw-r--r--** for the file **sample** that we created.

Similarly system-wide default permissions for a directory are 777. This means that when we create a directory its permissions would be 777 - 022, i.e. 755. You must be wondering of what significance would execute permission be for a directory, since we are never going to execute a directory. But remember execute permission for a directory has a special significance. If a directory doesn't have an execute permission we can never enter into it.

Can we not change the current **umask** value? Very easily. All that we have to say is something like,

$ umask 242

This would see to it that here onwards any new file that you create would have the permissions 424 (666 - 242) and any directory that you create would have the permissions 535 (777 - 242).

Directory permissions

Read, write and execute permissions for files are alright, but these permissions for directories have more to them than meets the eye. We know that directories too are treated by Unix as files. A directory, as Unix perceives, is a file which contains the names of the files present in the directory. Hence a read permission on a directory allows the listing of the directory contents and nothing else. No changing over to that directory or removing or modifying files.

If one has only a write permission to a directory, it is as good as having no permissions at all. You can't read it, so listing of its contents is not allowed. Neither can you enter it, as no execute permission exists. Rather like blindfolding somebody, tying up his limbs and then 'generously' telling him to eat whatever he can see!

A variation of the same syndrome is in assigning only an execute permission. With an execute permission, you can do a **cd** (**cd** stands for change directory) and enter the directory, but that's it. You can neither read nor modify or create files in the directory.

Since we don't favour any Nazi or sadistic tendencies, we would want to allow others just so much freedom as ensures our safety. As owners, we would certainly like to have all three permissions. For users of the same group, a read as well as execute permission can pose no threat. The read permission will allow them to see the contents and the execute permission to enter into the directory. Anything further may prove detrimental to our health.

For all others, a read permission is all we need to grant. All and sundry are not expected to wander into our domains.

Thus, the best combination of permissions to be granted to directories may be **rwxr-xr--**, which numerically amounts to 754. Security at the directory level plays a significant role. For instance, a trespasser may easily delete files to which he has no permissions, provided he has access to the directory in which it is present.

If we have a read permission to somebody's directory we can do a **ls** on it. If we have an execute permission to this directory we can go into it using the **cd** command. Finally, if we have a write permission to it we can copy a file into this directory using the **cp** command. And then we may have a combination of these permissions. Figure 2.5 shows what we can achieve through such permissions.

Still Better Directory Permissions

We saw above that 754 permissions for a directory are powerful enough to guard your directories from intruders with malicious intentions. To make it virtually impregnable we may add a 'sticky' bit to it. Contrary to its name there is a lot more to it. When this bit 'sticks' onto the directory, no matter what a hacker does he can never delete any files in this directory. With the sticky bit attached to the

Directory Permissions for group and others	cd	ls	cp Into	cp From
r--	error	works	error	error
-w-	error	error	error	error
--x	works	error	error	error
rw-	error	works	error	error
r-x	works	works	error	works
-wx	works	error	works	error
rwx	works	works	works	works

Figure 2.5

directory only the owner of the directory or the superuser can delete files from this directory. Let us understand this with an example.

Suppose we have assigned the most liberal directory permissions (777) to a directory called **mydir**. The following command confirms this.

```
$ ls -ld mydir
drwxrwxrwx   2   user1    group    50   Jun 11 10:50 mydir
```

Note that we have used the option **-d** since we want to see the long listing of a directory. We (**user1**) being the owners of this directory we can set the sticky bit for this directory by saying,

```
$ chmod u+t mydir
```

Let us now see if any change has taken place in the permissions of the directory.

```
$ ls -l mydir
drwxrwxrwt  2  user1  group  50  Jun 11 10:50  mydir
```

Notice the 't' at the end of the permissions. The sticky bit has been set up. Here onwards it would guard all the files in this directory against an intruder trying to remove or modify them. The intruder may read your existing files or create a few himself, since your generous permissions permit it, but delete, he cannot, come what may. Let's confirm this.

Assume that there is a file called **chap1.bpb** in the **mydir** directory. Let us attempt to delete it.

```
$ rm /mydir/chap1.bpb
chap1.bpb: mode 644 ?y
rm: chap1.bpb not removed.
Permission denied.
```

I hope that sets to rest any doubt that you may have about the power of the sticky bit. So to ensure that your files in an important directory remain fail-safe first assign the permission 754 to this directory and then add the sticky bit to it. If we are to carry out both the jobs simultaneously we can use the weight 1 associated with a sticky bit as shown below:

```
$ chmod 1754 mydir
```

Can an intruder modify files that are present in the directory whose sticky bit is set? That depends upon permissions of the individual files present in this directory.

Can we not set the sticky bit for a file, and thereby ensure that nobody can delete it? No, because significance of a sticky bit with reference to a file is different. When a sticky bit is applied to a file, the file sticks around in memory even when its execution is over. This ensures that next time we have to execute it, it is not necessary to read it back from disk, thereby saving the read time. Great. So we should set the sticky bit for every file that we create. Not really. Because only superuser can set the sticky bit for a file. Moreover, sticky bit can be set only for a binary executable file. When set for any other file it carries no meaning. So if we can't set the sticky bit ourselves at least let us see which file has a sticky bit set. One good example is a file called **vi**.

```
$ ls -l /usr/bin/vi
-rwx--x--t  5  bin bin 132424   Dec 15 1991 /usr/bin/vi
```

Note the 't' in the permissions field. **vi** stands for 'visual editor' and since on any installation many users work with **vi** the superuser usually sets up a sticky bit for this file. This ensures that once executed there is no need to reload **vi** from disk during subsequent executions. Quite an economy of time, you would agree.

Removing A File Forcibly

Now that we understand file permissions let us see how can we remove a file to which we do not have a write permission. This can be achieved by using **rm** with **-f** option as mentioned earlier. For example, if we have permission **r--** to a file **letter**, we can delete the file by using

```
.  $ rm -f letter
```

Ordinarily we cannot delete a file unless we have a write permission to it. Had **rm** not provided the **-f** option we would have been first required to add the write permission to the file using the **chmod** command and then delete it using **rm**.

As you must have guessed, the **-f** option is applicable only to files of which you are the owner. You of course cannot forcibly delete somebody else's files using the **-f** option of **rm**.

Other Useful *ls* Variations

We already know the **-a** and **-l** option of ls. Let us wander a little further. Try the **-r** option. It lists all the files in the present directory including the files present in any sub-directories that may be present in the current directory. When it encounters any sub-directory firstly all files in this sub-directory are listed before listing the next file in the current directory.

Two more options are useful. **-s** and **-i**. The **-s** option lists the files along with their sizes (in blocks, not bytes), whereas, the **-i** option lists the files along with their inode numbers. At this stage we don't know what are inode numbers. As we progress we would see that they are crucial in understanding how files are created on the disk.

lc and **lf** are look-alikes of **ls**. The first one displays the files in columnar fashion, whereas the second puts a * after all executable files and a / after all sub-directories present in the current directory.

```
$ lc

carribeans    chap3.bpb    chap6.bpb    kiwis      pommies
chap1.bpb     chap4.bpb    cricket      mainfile   springboks
chap2.bpb     chap5.bpb    kangaroos    pakde      zulus

$ lf
carribeans*   chap3.bpb    chap6.bpb    kiwis      pommies
chap1.bpb     chap4.bpb    cricket*     mainfile*  springboks
chap2.bpb     chap5.bpb    kangaroos/   pakde/     zulus/
```

Thus, **lf** provides a handy way to determine which is an ordinary file, which is a directory and which is an executable file.

So much about the variations of **ls**. I hope you got the idea by now? If you're really interested in the whole bunch (are you sure?) of options available with **ls** you are referred to the Unix manual.

Directory Related Commands

When the user logs in he is always brought to his default working directory (often called home directory). A convenient way of finding in which directory you are a **pwd** command is provided. **pwd** stands for 'present working directory'.

```
$ pwd
/usr/user1
```

The current working directory is displayed as **/usr/user1**. Note how the detailed path is listed so as to leave no doubt in the mind of the user. The **/** denotes the root directory of the Unix file system. Within this root directory there is a sub-directory called **usr** within which there is another directory called **user1**. That's where we are working right now. Hence the path from the root directory is listed as **/usr/user1**. Note that unlike DOS where \ (backslash) is used to specify a path, in Unix a / (slash) is used.

mkdir

Another commonly used directory command is **mkdir**. It is a counterpart of MD or MKDIR of DOS. Case is one issue Unix is vehemently touchy about. So while **mkdir** is fine, MKDIR simply won't touch the right chords.

```
$ mkdir  book
```

The above command creates a directory named **book**.

Among the options available with **mkdir** is **-p**, which allows you to create multiple generations of directories, at one go. That means, it creates all the parent directories specified in the given path too. Here's an example.

```
$ mkdir -p works/bpb/unix/book
```

The **-p** option tells Unix to first create **works**, then within it **bpb**, next its child directory **unix**, and lastly **book**, nested within all these. Neat, isn't it? And then they say Unix wasn't meant to be user friendly.

Suppose you want to create a directory which should have permissions 754 irrespective of the **umask** value you can use the command,

```
$ mkdir -m 754 newdir
```

Confirm the permissions set for this directory using **ls -l**. You would find the permissions to be **rwxr-xr--**.

Also note in this long listing that the number of links for this directory are 2. By default any new file created has 1 link, whereas any new directory created has 2 links. Why this disparity? Because whenever a directory is created two entries for this directory are made. For example, assume that **newdir** was created in the parent directory, say **chapters**. As we know a directory file contains a list of all files and sub-directories present in the directory. Thus, one entry of **newdir** would be in the **chapters** directory file. The second entry of **newdir** would be present in the directory file **newdir** itself, in the form of a '.'. The '.' as we know signifies the current directory.

rmdir

Dedicated to removing directories is the command **rmdir**, though **rm** is also capable of the job. With the **-p** option, **rmdir** wields enough power to remove not only the specified directory, but also its parent directories. However **rmdir** only removes the empty directories.

Thus, to remove the directory **book** created earlier, we say

```
$ rmdir  works/bpb/unix/book
```

In order to remove the parent directories of **book**, we say

```
$ rmdir -p works/bpb/unix/book
```

Here on removing the **book** directory if the **unix** directory falls empty
then it is removed. On removing the **unix** directory if the **bpb**
directory falls empty then that too gets removed and so on. This
process stops when **rmdir** bumps into a non-empty parent directory.

cd

In Unix parlance too, **cd** is for changing over to a new directory.

```
$ mkdir  newdir
$ cd  newdir
```

This would take you in **newdir**. To confirm that you really do reside
in **newdir** now, we can use **pwd**.

```
$ pwd
/usr/user1/newdir
```

cd when given without any argument is interpreted by the shell as a
request to change over to the current user's home directory. Stray
where you please, a **cd** will bring you back where you belong - to
your home directory.

```
$ cd
$ pwd
/usr/user1
```

While using **cd** you can tell Unix in two ways exactly which directory
you want to go to:

- Using full pathname or absolute pathname
- Using a relative pathname (the pathname starting from where you are now)

If you try to move to a directory that doesn't exist or if you incorrectly type the directory name or pathname, Unix reports an error.

A Bit of Mathematics

Unix keeps a very useful feature handy. The calculator called **bc**, possibly short for base conversion, which is one of its functions, or the 'best calculator' - your guess is as good as mine. It is invoked by typing **bc** at the shell prompt. Once you type **bc** at the prompt, you are in the calculator mode, and the $ the prompt disappears. That is the only way the reserved and laconic Unix indicates to you that it has braced itself to carry out even the most mind-boggling calculations. The input to the calculator is taken line by line. Enter an expression and Unix supplies the result as shown here:

```
$ bc
10 / 2 * 2
10
2.5 * 2.5 + 2
8.25
quit
```

The input and results are self-explanatory. Typing **quit** ends your tryst with **bc**. While working with floats if you want precise answers all that you need to do is set the variable **scale** to a value equal to the number of digits after the decimal point till which you want the answer to be printed.

```
$ bc
scale = 1
2.25 + 1
3.35
```

Foxed? How come even after setting the **scale** we are getting answer upto second place after the decimal point? That's the point. After setting the **scale** variable if the answer of an expression turns out more than what **scale** can provide then the value in **scale** is ignored and the correct answer is displayed.

Another of **bc**'s useful features is that of base conversion. You no longer have to sweat it out what 11010011 amounts to in decimal, or what 89275 is in hexadecimal or octal. Two commands, **ibase** and **obase** rescue you.

```
$ bc
ibase = 2
obase = 16
11010011
89275
1010
A
quit
```

By setting the variable **ibase** to 2 and **obase** to 16 all input that we supply is taken as a binary number whereas all output is displayed in hexadecimal.

bc also supports functions like sqrt, cosine, sine, tangent etc.

```
$ bc
sqrt (196)
14
s ( 3.14 )
unimplemented
```

sqrt( ) is an in-built function whereas **s( )** and **c( )** which stand for sine and cosine respectively would work only when **bc** is invoked with the **-l** option.

```
$ bc -l
```

```
scale = 2
s ( 3.14 )
0
```

Note that the trigonometric functions expect their arguments in radians and not in degrees.

bc also allows setting up of variables. The life of these variables is until you exit **bc** (by typing quit). These variables can be used in programs. Yes, **bc** is a programmable calculator in its truest sense.

```
$ bc
for ( i = 1 ; i <= 5 ; i = i + 1 ) i
1
2
3
4
5
quit
```

This C like program prints numbers from 1 to 5 using a **for** loop which gives values 1 to 5 to the variable **i**. Giving values is alright but how do you print the variable's value? Simply by mentioning it's name, as justified by the **i** following the closing parentheses in the above program.

The scope of **bc**'s programming ability is vast. What we have done here is only the tip of the iceberg. It can support loops, decisions, function definitions, several operators etc. Just say **man bc** and explore on your own what more **bc** has to offer.

Another utility that aids computation in Unix is **expr**. The almighty **bc** need not be beseeched for analysing a simple expression here or a formula there. **expr** can handle that easily. It gives the result of the expression it acts on

```
$ expr  100 + 50
```

```
150
$ expr 3 \* 2
6
```

Why the \ preceding the '*' in the second expression? Remember while working with shell a * always expands to all files in the current directory. The \ just takes away this special meaning of *.

Though useful **expr** can't handle floating point arithmetic. In such cases we have no recourse but to invoke **bc**.

There is another math related command available in Unix: **factor**. When **factor** is invoked without an argument, it waits for a number to be typed in. If you type in a positive number less than 2^46 (about 7.2e13) it will factorise the number and print its prime factors; each one is printed the proper number of times. Then it waits for another number. It exits if it encounters a zero or any non-numeric character. For example,

```
$ factor
15
       3
       5
28
       2
       2
       7
q
$
```

If **factor** is invoked with an argument, it factors the number as above and then exits.

Unix provides another handy utility called **units**. It converts quantities expressed in various standard scales to their equivalents in other scales. It works interactively in this fashion:

```
$ units
You have: inch
You want: cm
* 2.540000e+00
/ 3.937008e-01
```

What the above output means is if we are to convert inches to centimeter we got to multiply the inches with 2.54 or divide inches by 0.3937008. The way **units** understands various units possibly no human being can. For example, it understands distance through units like cm, meter, km, inches, feet, mile, nautical mile, yard etc. It knows that quantity of liquid can be measured in liters, quarts, pints, gallons etc. And of course it understands units like weber, henry, faraday, coulomb, newton, joule, kelvin, rankine etc. It understands all the currencies in the world and knows their conversion rates. We couldn't have expected more. As on date **units** understands 484 different units a list of which can be seen by displaying the file **/usr/lib/unittab** using the **cat** command.

Miscellaneous Commands

Before getting down to business, let us first go through a few commands that help us get a stronger feel of the ambience. These are commands that in general give us information about the network and we, its users.

```
$ logname
user1
```

The command **logname** prints the login name of the user.

Unix knows each user not only by the login name, but also by two numbers called the user and group identity numbers. Those, obviously are distinct for each user and are used by Unix for operations regarding that user. To print these, say at the shell prompt

```
$ id
uid=202(user1) gid=50(group)
```

If we are to find the name of the Unix system we are using we can use the command **uname** as shown below.

```
$ uname
scosysv
```

In addition to above information if we want to know the details like the release number, version number, OEM number, type of the microprocessor (80386, 80486 etc.) on which Unix is being run, type of bus the microprocessor has, number of CPUs present in the host machine etc. we can use the **uname** command with the **-X** option.

For each terminal on the network, Unix uses a file. The output displayed on its monitor is picked from the file associated with the terminal. Thus, there is a different file for each terminal. All these files are present in the **/dev** directory. To Unix, all devices are nothing but files. It sees each terminal as a special file. To find out the name of your terminal file, say

```
$ tty
/dev/tty1a
```

So all your transactions with the Unix system are via the file **/dev/tty1a**.

To see who all are currently sharing the network with you, there is the command **who** which gives a list of all the users on the system, their terminal names and the date and time at which they logged in. If you are not interested in everybody, just want to get some information on yourself, there is the rather philosophical sounding command **who am i**. It is a special case of **who**, listing only one user, yourself.

```
$ who am i
```

      user1   tty1a   Apr 20   01:02

To display the current date and time, there is the **date** command.

     $ date
     Sat Apr 20 04:40:10 IST 1996

So that was the instant we entered the **date** command, IST signifying Indian Standard Time. The output of the date command can be modified by a variety of switches. For example,

     $ date '+DATE : %d-%m-%y %n TIME : %H:%M:%S'
     DATE : 17-06-96
     TIME : 10:55:25

Note that the format in which you want to print the date must be enclosed within a pair of single quotes and the format should begin with a + sign. As can be guessed **%d**, **%m** and **%y** signify day, month and year, whereas **%H**, **%M** and **%S** signify hour, minute and second. The **%n** ensures that what follows is displayed on a new line.

Under Unix a lot of significance is attached with time. Hence a real time clock keeps time, and according to it times of creation or modification of files and directories, login and logout times etc. are recorded. The real time clock also sees to it that Unix performs certain actions it is instructed to at the specified time. With quite a lot depending on the system time, the privilege of changing the set time is reserved for the superuser alone.

Exercise

[A]   Fill in the blanks

(a)   Binary executables required for system administration are usually placed in _____ directory.

(b)   All user directories are usually placed in _____ directory.

(c)   Hidden files in Unix always begin with a character __.

(d)   To list hidden as well as the normal files in the current directory the command you would use is ____.

(e)   Usually the size of each block in Unix file system is of ___ bytes.

(f)   If there are three links for a file then the number of copies of the file would be ____.

(g)   The default system-wide permissions for a file are ___ and that for a directory are ___.

(h)   The default value of **umask** is ___.

[B]   State whether the following statements are True or False:

(a)   All devices in Unix are implemented as files.

(b)   All device related files are usually present in **/tmp** directory.

(c)   A terminal file is always a block special file.

(d)   Directories do not have execute permission.

(e)   The wildcard characters '*' and '?' have the same meaning in Unix as they have in DOS.

(f)   The minimum number of links for any directory file are 2.

(g)   A directory can have more than 2 links.

(h)   A common user cannot set sticky bit for his file.

(i)   Setting a sticky bit for a non-executable file is meaningless.

(j)   A user can change his password using **pwd** command.

(k)   The way we use **cd** to change directory we can use **md** to make a new directory.

[C]   Log into a Unix system and try to perform the following operations:

(a)   Create 5 empty files **empty1**, **empty2**, **empty3**, **empty4** and **empty5**.

(b)   Create a file called **text** and store your name, age, sex and address in it.

(c)   Display the contents of the file **text** on the screen.

(d)   Make a copy of the file **text** into another file **newtext**.

(e)   Create a file **matter** and type any two sentences in it.

(f)   Combine the contents of the file **text** and **matter** into another file **txtmat**.

(g)   Delete the file **text**.

(h)   Create one more link called **tmpfile** for the file **matter**.

(i)   Change the permissions for the file **newtext** to 666.

(j)   Rename the file **newtext** to **oldtext**.

(k)   Create a directory **mydir** in the current directory.

(l)   Move the files **oldtext** and **matter** to the directory **mydir**.

(m)   Create another directory **newdir** within the directory **mydir**.

(n)   Copy the contents of **mydir** directory to the **newdir** directory.

(o)   Delete interactively all empty files created earlier.

(p)   Setup sticky bit for the directory **newdir**.

(q)   Delete the directories **mydir** and **newdir** at one shot.

[C]   Suppose there are following files in present working directory:

art
part
part1
part2
part3
mozart
tart
quartz

Which of the above files would qualify for the following searches:

(a)   ls a?

(b)   ls a*

(c)   ls *.*

(d)   ls [!abc]art

(e)   ls [a!bc]art

(f)   ls [b-dku-z]*

[D]   Answer the following:

(a) What does a sticky bit for a directory and a executable file signify?

(b) State two different ways in which you would identify whether a given file is an ordinary file or a directory.

(c) How would you identify whether a given file is an executable file or not without executing it?

(d) Suppose the path **dir1/dir2/dir3/dir4** exists in your directory. All these directories are empty. How would you remove all of them at one shot?

(e) Write a program using **bc** to find factorial value of a number.

(f) Write a program using **bc** to print squares, cubes and square roots of all numbers from 1 to 50.

(g) Write a program using **bc** to print sine and cosine values of all angles from 0 to 360 degrees in steps of 5 degrees.

(h) How will you find the current Rupee to Dollar and Dollar to Yen conversion rate?

(i) What does uid and gid signify?

(j) How would you find with which version of Unix you are working and the processor on which this version is running?

(k) If the path **dir1/dir2/dir3** exists then how many links would the directory **dir2** have?

(l) Write the Unix equivalent of the following DOS commands:
DIR   DEL   COPY   TYPE
CD   MD   RD   REN

(m) What is the meaning of **.** and **..**?

(n) How will you change over to the parent of parent of current directory without using any directory names?

(o) How will you print the listing of the parent directory from the current directory?

(p) If you have gone to some other directory, how will you come back to your default directory without using the default directory name?

(q) How will you copy a file "aaa.c" present in current directory to a directory "ddd" present in the parent directory?

(r) How will you forcibly remove a file to which you don't have write permission?

(s)   How will you print the contents of files "aaa" "bbb" "ccc" using a single command?

(t)   How will you list the current directory in columnar format?

(u)   How will you list all files in current directory whose second character is a digit?

(v)   How will you list all filenames starting with 'a' or 'b' or 'k'?

(w)   What are the typical characteristics of a Unix file system?

(x)   What will be the effect of following Unix commands?

umask

chmod 777 aaa.c

chmod u+w g-w abcd.out

chmod ug+rw a=x ffff.out

chmod u+t mydir

Which is the ideal directory permission? What operations can be performed by user, users in the group and others in a directory with ideal permissions?

(y)   What is the usual permission settings for a file and a directory?

(z)   How will you find out prime factors of a number 218?

3 The Unix File System

As an average user one may be satisfied by just tinkering around with the utilities Unix offers on a silver platter. No doubt, it's no mean offering. But it's worth going back-stage and getting the feel of how Unix actually runs the show. Knowing about what goes on inside a Unix file system is, in fact, a must for anyone who cares for serious programming.

A 'file system' is a group of files and relevant information regarding them. Your whole hard disk may comprise a single file system or it may be partitioned to house several file systems. However, the reverse is not true. No file system can be split over two different disks. Creation of file systems is dealt with in a later chapter. For the present, let us concentrate on understanding an already installed file system. The disk space allotted to a Unix file system is made up of 'blocks', each of which are typically of 512 bytes. Some file systems may have blocks of 1024 or 2048 bytes as well. The block size depends upon how the file system has been implemented on a particular installation. It may also change from one Unix version to another. Should you want to find out the block size on your file system, use the **cmchk** command which reports the block size.

```
$ cmchk
BSIZE = 1024
```

The block size rarely exceeds 2048 bytes. Whenever a file is created one block is made available for storing this file's contents. Thus, on a file system whose block size is 2048 bytes if we create a small file of 1000 bytes still one block (2048 bytes) would be assigned for this file's storage, thereby wasting precious 1048 bytes. Then won't it be worthwhile having as small a block size as possible? No, because if the block size is 512 bytes and we create a file of 2000 bytes then to store it on the disk four disk accesses would be necessary. Remember disk accesses are time consuming. More the disk accesses required more would be the time required for reading/writing this file.

All the blocks belonging to the file system are logically divided into four parts. The first block of a file system is called the 'Boot block' which is followed by 'Super block', 'Inode Table' and 'Data Blocks'. Let us understand these blocks one by one.

The Boot Block

This represents the beginning of the file system. It contains a program called 'bootstrap loader'. This program is executed when we 'boot' the host machine. Although only one boot block is needed to start up the system, all file systems contain one (possibly empty) boot block.

The Super Block

The super block describes the state of the file system - how large it is, how many maximum files can it accommodate, how many more files can be created etc.

The Inode Table

We know that all entities in Unix are treated as files. The information related to all these files (not the contents) is stored in an Inode Table on the disk. For each file, there is an inode entry in the table. Each entry is made up of 64 bytes and contains the relevant details for that file. These details are:

(a)   Owner of the file
(b)   Group to which the owner belongs
(c)   Type of file

(d)   File access permissions
(e)   Date and time of last access
(f)   Date and time of last modification
(g)   Number of links to the file
(h)   Size of the file
(i)   Addresses of blocks where the file is physically present

Data Blocks

These contain the actual file contents. An allocated block can belong to only one file in the file system. This block cannot be used for storing any other file's contents unless the file to which it originally belonged is deleted.

Surrogate Super Block and Inode Table

Judging by the information stored in the Inode Table, we can see that this must change whenever we use any file, or change its permissions, etc. Making these changes on the disk would gobble up a lot of precious CPU time. To remedy this, a copy of the Super Block and Inode Table gets loaded into memory (RAM) at start-up time. Since memory access is faster than disk access, a lot less time is consumed in recording the changes in the RAM copies of Super Block and Inode Table every time some modification occurs. The original Super Block and Inode Table on the disk are updated after a fixed interval of time, say every 30 seconds, by a command called **sync. sync** synchronises the inode table in memory with the one on disk by simply overwriting the memory copy on to the disk. Thus, the changes that may have been recorded in the copy in memory during the last interval of 30 seconds get duly registered on the disk.

How Does Unix Access Files

Internally a file is identified by Unix by a unique 'Inode number' associated with it. We can obtain the inode number associated with a file by using the command **ls -i**.

```
$ ls -i reports
reports 12324
```

Here 12324 is the inode number. We know that a directory in Unix is nothing but a file. A directory file contains the names of the files/sub-directories present in that directory along with an inode number for each. The inode number is nothing but an index into the inode table where the information about the file is stored. For example, amongst several slots present in the inode table slot number 12342 contains information about the file **reports**.

Suppose the file **reports** is present in a directory called **mydir**. If we attempt to **cat** the **reports** file let us see how Unix would handle this situation. Firstly, it would check whether we have a read permission to the **mydir** directory file. If so, it would find out whether this directory file has an entry **reports** in it. If such an entry is found then it would pick up the inode number for this file from **mydir**. This inode number as we know is an index into the in-core (memory) inode table. Using this inode number the information about **reports** is accessed from the inode table. From this information it is ascertained whether we have a read permission for the **reports** file. If so then the contents of the **reports** file are read from the disk addresses mentioned in the inode entry of **reports** and displayed on the screen.

Storage of Files

Amongst other information, each inode entry in the inode table consists of 13 addresses each, which specify completely where the contents of the file are stored on the disk. These addresses may be numbered 0 through 12. Of these, the first ten addresses, 0 through 9 point to 1 KB blocks on disk. For example, a file of size 3 KB may have its entries as shown in Figure 3.1. The address 4970 signifies where the first 1 kilobytes of the file are stored. The next 1 KB chunk is at 5231, and the next at 3401.

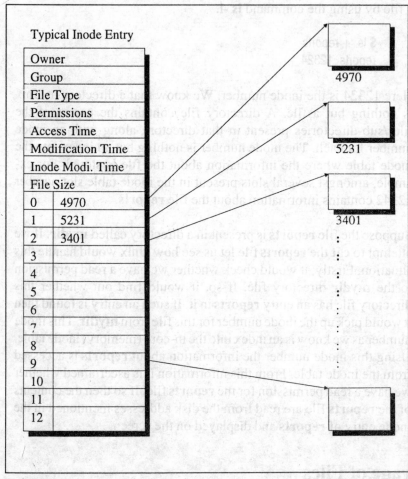

Figure 3.1

These addresses may be scattered throughout the disk, as files are stored in chunks wherever empty blocks of disk are available. This is specially the case with large files, for which a very big chunk may be impossible to find. Thus, the addresses 0 to 9 can handle a file of a maximum size of 10 KB. For files larger than this, Unix has a very interesting way of indicating their location. Have a look at Figure 3.2.

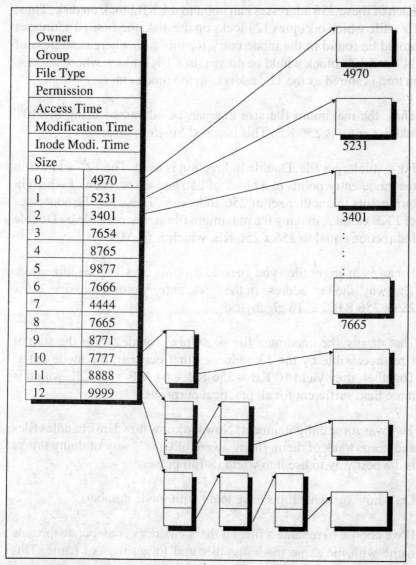

Owner	
Group	
File Type	
Permission	
Access Time	
Modification Time	
Inode Modi. Time	
Size	
0	4970
1	5231
2	3401
3	7654
4	8765
5	9877
6	7666
7	4444
8	7665
9	8771
10	7777
11	8888
12	9999

Figure 3.2

As can be seen from the figure the 10th entry also contains an address of a 1 KB block. This block doesn't contain the file contents. Instead, it consists of 256 four-byte slots which can store 256 more addresses. Each of these 256 addresses can point to a 1 KB block on disk. Thus, for a file which occupies 12 blocks on the disk, the first 10 addresses would be found in the inode entry for this file, whereas address of 11th and 12th block would be present in a 1 KB block whose address in turn is stored as the 11th address in the inode entry.

Thus, the maximum file size that can be addressed using the 10th address entry is 256 KB. This is called Single Indirection.

For a still larger file, Double Indirection is used. The 12th address in the inode entry points to a block of 256 addresses, each of which in turn points to another set of 256 addresses. These are the addresses of 1 KB chunks, making the maximum file size accessible by Double Indirection equal to 256 x 256 KB, which is 64 MB.

For an even larger file - you guessed it - Unix uses Triple Indirection. This way, the last address in the inode entry yields a massive 256 x 256 x 256 KB, i.e. 16 gigabytes!

That means, the maximum file size Unix provides for is the sum of sizes accessible by the 13 addresses that occur in the inode entry. Together, they yield 10 KB + 256 KB + 64 MB + 16 GB, which is more than sufficient for all practical purposes.

That was some enlightenment! Now we know how Unix handles files and keeps track of them. Being aware of Unix's way of doing things is the best way to use it to wield its full power.

Let's now see what links have to do with inode numbers.

If we choose to rename a file, all that Unix does is associate the new name with the same inode number and forget the old name. This association may be thought of as a link with the inode number, or in essence with the file. Unix provides for its files to have more than

one such links. For instance, a file called **reports** in the root directory
may have a link called **results** in a sub-directory. The way to create
a link is by saying,

$ ln reports impdir/results

Assuming that **impdir** is a directory present in root, it now contains
the entry for **results**, whose inode number is, say, 12324. We can
check what the inode number of **reports** was, in the first place, by
using **ls** with **-i** option.

$ ls -i reports
12324 reports

This is no coincidence - the inode numbers of **reports** and **results**
have to be the same, as they are referring to the same file. The file is
physically present in only one location, but can be accessed by either
of its two names. What if you were to delete **reports**?

$ rm reports

This would tell Unix to discard the name **reports** as a link to the file
with same inode number 12324. However, the file is still very much
present on the disk. The root directory no longer holds an entry for
reports, but the other link, **results** in **impdir**, is intact. Hence the file
is also intact, and will remain so until all links to it are deleted. If we
use **rm** to delete **results**, only then will the file be physically deleted.

Disk Related Commands

One of the major concerns of the System Administrator of a Unix
installation is efficient hard disk management. Since the Unix file
system is installed usually on a hard disk its upkeep is of primary
importance. The System Administrator has to regularly monitor the
integrity of the file system and the amount of disk space available.

Neglecting this may eventually lead to a system crash. Let's see what are the commands usually used for the upkeep of hard disk.

Checking Disk Free Space

If we want to see how much of the disk is being used and what part of it lies free, Unix has for us a command called **df** (for disk free). This command reports the free as well as the used disk space for all the file systems installed on your machine.

```
$ df
/   (/dev/root   ):     12970 blocks      27857 i-nodes
```

We have on our machine only one file system installed, the root file system or simply **/dev/root**. **df** reports the number of free disk blocks and free inodes for this file system. If we want a more detailed information about disk usage we should say,

```
$ df -ivt
Mount Dir Filesystem  blocks   used   free  %used iused ifree %iused
/          /dev/root  282098  269146 12952  95%   7410  27854  21%
```

Now, the available blocks and inodes are reported numerically as well as percentages of total available blocks and inodes. This possibly gives a better idea of how much disk space is free.

One thing that you must note is that **df** counts blocks in sizes of 512 bytes irrespective of the actual block size as reported by the **cmchk** command. Hence the actual amount of free disk space in bytes will be the free space reported by **df** multiplied by 512. For our file system this comes out to be,

$$12952 * 512 = 6631424 \text{ bytes (approximately 6.32 MB)}$$

Phew! That's close to exhaustion. If steps are not taken immediately soon the entire disk space is going to be consumed. That's the time the System Administrator goes into action and cleans the file system of any unused files, empty files, empty directories, unreasonably big files etc. In fact a program can be written to identify and delete such files. This program is discussed in a Chapter 15.

dfspace Makes More Sense

How much space do you think you have on your hard disk if it has 27857 free inodes or 12970 blocks? Finding it difficult to comprehend? Naturally so, because we understand the disk space better in terms of bytes and megabytes than in terms of inodes and blocks. And **dfspace** does exactly that. It reports the free disk space in terms of megabytes and percentage of total disk space.

```
$ dfspace
dfspace: not found
```

Don't get offputted by that message. It came because the **dfspace** command is present in **/etc** directory. This directory doesn't get searched when we execute any command. So to execute it we need to say,

```
$ /etc/dfspace
/      :   Disk space:  6.32 MB of 137.74 MB available ( 4.59%).

Total Disk Space:   6.32 MB of 137.74 MB available ( 4.59%).
```

Now **dfspace** does all the mathematics internally and reports free disk space for the root file system. Had there been other file systems installed their free space would also have been reported. Additionally it also reports the total disk space available. Note that the disk space available (6.32 MB) tallies with what we calculated earlier while discussing the **df** command. Only difference being this time the calculations were done by **dfspace**.

Disk Usage - The *du* Command

du sounds similar to **df** but is different in its working. **df** and **dfspace** report the disk space available in the file system as a whole whereas **du** reports the disk space used by specified files and directories. For example:

```
$ du
226    ./backup
418    ./fa/backup
1182   ./fa
4      ./check
16     ./dbf
1662
```

Here **du** is reporting the number of blocks used by the current directory (denoted by '.') and those used by sub-directories within the current directory. Thus, when invoked without any arguments it assumes that blocks occupied by current directory and the directories lying within it are to be reported.

If we specify a directory then **du** descends down this directory locating any sub-directories lying in it and reports the blocks used by the directory and the sub-directories. For example,

```
$ du /dev
2     /dev/string
4     /dev/rdsk
4     /dev/dsk
2     /dev/mouse
20    /dev
```

Thus, the number of blocks occupied by each sub-directory within **/dev**, as well as those occupied by **/dev** are displayed. If we want only the blocks occupied by the directory and not those occupied by the sub-directories within it we can say,

```
$ du -s /dev
20  /dev
```

du is often used to single out directories that occupy large amounts of disk space. Unused and redundant files and directories can then be eliminated from them, thereby freeing the valuable disk space.

The *ulimit* Command

Though most files in Unix occupy few tens of blocks, in some odd case a program may go awry and create files which occupy huge amounts of disk space. Sometimes things might take such a bad turn that the file might occupy several megabytes of disk space and ultimately harm the file system. To avoid creation of such files Unix uses a variable called **ulimit**. It stands for 'user limit' and contains a value which signifies the largest file that can be created by the user in the file system. Let's see the current value of the **ulimit** variable.

```
$ ulimit
2097152
```

This implies that the user cannot create a file whose size is bigger than 2097152 bytes, or 2048 KB. If you happen to create a file which exceeds this size, its size would be curtailed to 2048 KB and the program creating this file would be aborted.

A user can reduce this value by saying,

```
$ ulimit 1
```

Here onwards no file can be created whose size is bigger than 512 bytes. Once reduced this value remains effective till the user doesn't log out. Thus this change will be effective only for the current session and the system will return to its default value when you log out.

An ordinary user can only reduce the **ulimit** value and is never permitted to increase it. A super-user is an exception to the rule and can increase or decrease this value.

Exercise

[A]   Answer the following:

(a)   Why can't the following call to **dfspace** work?
       $ dfspace
(b)   What does the block size signify?
(c)   Which command is used to write in-core super block and inode table information to the disk?
(d)   What information does a super block contain?
(e)   What does the 'i' in inode connote?
(f)   Why there is a in-core copy and a disk copy of inode table and super block?
(g)   Outline the steps performed by Unix whenever we attempt to access a file.
(h)   What is the maximum file size permitted by a Unix file system?
(i)   When a file is deleted what happens to its entry in the inode table?
(j)   Can a file have more than two links?
(k)   Can a file have links across file systems?
(l)   Does the **df** command report the free disk space in bytes?
(m)   How would you find out how much space is used by the directory **/usr/aa1/mydir**?
(n)   What is the size of each entry in the inode table?
(o)   If a file occupies 10 blocks on the disk is it guaranteed that these blocks would be in adjacent locations on the disk?
(p)   What are the 4 components of a Unix file system?
(q)   What are the contents of an Inode block?

[B]   What will be the effect of following Unix commands?

       (a) umask 022

(b) umask
(c) ulimit 512
(d) ln dir1 dir2 (dir2 is existing on the disk)
(e) du ../..
(f) du .

4 Essential Unix Commands

T he journey on which we embarked three chapters ago continues, meeting more commands as we travel. Some quite handy, some not quite so. But nevertheless we must know them. So here we go...

Password

Though all users have access to the same resources under Unix, it is no public library where anyone may pick any information as he pleases. It is more like an account in a Swiss Bank, where even money and power prove useless. If you are the only one who knows the password to your account, rest assured that you will be the only one who can access it. Too good to be true? Well yes, there is one person who can encroach on your data - the superuser. He can override any obstacles and get through to any of your files. That is why by universal consent the system administrator is made to be a person who is totally above board, unbiased, scrupulous and impervious to kickbacks of any nature. After all, the life's work of many is at the mercy of this being's integrity.

We have seen that Unix asks for the user's password at login time. If you have some data that's for your eyes only and you happen to notice that some shady looking characters are making it a habit of looking in the background every time you log in, with all due faith in mankind, take it as a warning bell. You would do well to change your password.

You can change your password whenever you're logged in, by using the **passwd** command as shown below:

```
$ passwd
```

It asks you to enter your old password to prove that you're still who you were when you logged in (computers are notoriously skeptical). Then the **passwd** program asks you to enter your new password twice, to make sure that you type it, if not correctly, at least consistently. None of the three passwords you type appears on screen, of course.

The new password may be framed by you, or it may be a Unix creation. You are asked what you would prefer. Suppose you decide to create your own password. The choice of your password deserves some thought. You want something easy for you to remember but difficult for other people to guess. Here are some bad choices for passwords: single letters or digits, your name, the name of your spouse or significant other, your kid's name, your cat's name, or anything less than six letters long. (Bad guys can try every possible five letter password in just a few hours.)

Good choices include something like your college roommate's name misspelled and backward. Throw in a digit or two or some punctuation, and capitalize a few letters to add confusion so that you end up with something like Ame101paJ. Another good idea is to use a pair of words, like Egg;Head. Password names have no limit on length but often only the first eight matter.

Some system administrators do something called password aging, this strategy makes you change your password at least once a month. Some administrators put rules in the **passwd** program that try to enforce which passwords are permissible and some even assign passwords chosen randomly. This idea is terrible because the only way you can remember a password you didn't choose is to write it on a piece of paper and stick it on your terminal, which defeats the purpose of having passwords.

In any event, be sure that no one but you know your password. Change your password whenever you think that someone else might know it. Unix stores passwords in a scrambled form so that even the system administrator can't find out what yours is. If you forget your password, the administrator can give you a new one, but he can't tell you what your old one was.

If you really want to be paranoid about passwords, don't use a password that appears in any dictionary. Some truly fiendish system breaker may decide to use Unix's password encryption program to encrypt every word in a dictionary and then compare every encrypted word to your password - another thing to keep you awake at night.

Whichever password we create Unix stores it in a file **/etc/passwd**. We can even **cat** this file on the screen as shown below:

```
$ cat /etc/passwd
root:x:0:1:Superuser:/:
daemon:x:1:1:System daemons:/etc:
bin:x:2:2:Owner of system commands:/bin:
sys:x:3:3:Owner of system files:/usr/sys:
adm:x:4:4:System accounting:/usr/adm:
uucp:x:5:5:UUCP administrator:/usr/lib/uucp:
auth:x:7:21:Authentication administrator:/tcb/files/auth:
asg:x:8:8:Assignable devices:/usr/tmp:
cron:x:9:16:Cron daemon:/usr/spool/cron:
sysinfo:x:11:11:System information:/usr/bin:
dos:x:16:11:DOS device:/tmp:
mmdf:x:17:22:MMDF administrator:/usr/mmdf:
network:x:18:10:MICNET administrator:/usr/network:
nouser:x:28:28:Network user with no access privileges:/:/bin/false
listen:x:37:4:Network daemons:/usr/net/nls:
lp:x:71:18:Printer administrator:/usr/spool/lp:
ingres:x:777:50:Database administrator:/usr/ingres:
oracle:x:200:100:oracle ver. 6.0:/usr/oracle:/bin/sh
audit:x:79:17:Audit administrator:/tcb/files/audit:
aa1:x:202:50:user number 1:/usr/aa1:/bin/sh
aa2:x:203:50:user number 2:/usr/aa2:/bin/sh
aa3:x:204:50:user number 3:/usr/aa3:/bin/sh
aa4:x:205:50:user number 4:/usr/aa4:/bin/sh
```

aa5:x:206:50:user number 5:/usr/aa5:/bin/sh
aa6:x:207:50:user number 6:/usr/aa6:/bin/sh

The above output shows that **/etc/passwd** holds lot of useful information about the users. Each field of information is separated from the next using a ':'. The following figure shows the meaning of each field in the last line of the above output.

Typical value	Meaning
aa1	Login name
x	Encrypted password
202	User ID
50	Group ID
This is account of aa1	Comment, given while creating an account
/usr/aa1	Default working directory
/bin/sh	Default working shell

Figure 4.1

Note that there is another **passwd** file present in **/bin** directory. In fact this is the one that gets executed when we change the password. Thus, **/bin/passwd** is an executable file which permits changing of the password, whereas **/etc/passwd** contains the data about each user.

cal is for Calendar

Unix's understanding of time is superb. We saw earlier how the **date** command works. It displays the current date and time. But what if we want to refer to a calendar? That's the time when we use the **cal** command. It is capable of printing calendar for any year in the range 1 to 9999. To invoke it all that we have to do is type **cal**.

    $ cal

```
Fri Apr 26 18:21:10 1996
        Mar                       Apr                       May
 S  M Tu  W Th  F  S      S  M Tu  W Th  F  S      S  M Tu  W Th  F  S
                1  2      1  2  3  4  5  6                   1  2  3  4
 3  4  5  6  7  8  9      7  8  9 10 11 12 13      5  6  7  8  9 10 11
10 11 12 13 14 15 16     14 15 16 17 18 19 20     12 13 14 15 16 17 18
17 18 19 20 21 22 23     21 22 23 24 25 26 27     19 20 21 22 23 24 25
24 25 26 27 28 29 30     28 29 30                 26 27 28 29 30 31
31
```

The output shows the current date as well as the calendar of preceding, current and succeeding month. Obviously, Unix must not be storing all these calendars in memory but must be generating them through calculations when we invoke the **cal** command.

Should you want to see calendar of only a specific month, say, February 1997, you will have to be more explicit while using the **cal** command.

```
$ cal 2 1997
     February 1997
  S  M Tu  W Th  F  S
                    1
  2  3  4  5  6  7  8
  9 10 11 12 13 14 15
 16 17 18 19 20 21 22
 23 24 25 26 27 28
```

The 2 here indicates February. In place of 2 we could have used feb, or just a 'f'. However, you can't use **cal j 1997** to obtain january 1997's calendar. This is because 'j' might as well stand for June or July. If we become more specific and say **cal ja 1997**, it works.

This utility displays the calendar for the month and year specified by the user. Due consideration has been given to the leap years and the calendar is framed accordingly. Try out this utility for September 1752 and I am sure you would be taken aback. No, there is nothing wrong with the program. It just so happened that the King of England decreed that 11 days (3rd to 13th) be knocked off from this month. This he did to adjust the number of days while switching over from Julian to Gregorian calendar. As a result, many people missed their Birthday celebrations.

The *banner* Command

This command prints a message in large letters which looks like a banner. All that you have to say is

$ banner Strange Ways

And here is the output that it produces...

```
    #####
    #   #  ##### #####    ##     #   #  ####   ######
    #       #   #    #   #  #    ##  # #   #   # #
    #####   #   #    #  #    #   # # #      #     #####
        #   #   ##### ######  # # # # ### #
    #   #   #   #   # #    #  #   ##  #    # #
    #####   #   #   # #    #  #    # #  ####   ######

    #     #
    #  #  #  ##    #     #  ####
    #  #  #  # #   #  #   # #
    #  #  #  # #   #    #   # ####
    #  #  #  ######   #         #
    #  #  #  #     #  #     #    #
    ## ##   #     #  #      ####
```

That's really no fancy effect. But then fancy and finesse have never been Unix's forte.

If you want that instead of splitting the words in two different lines they should be displayed in the same line then they should be enclosed in inverted commas as shown below:

$ banner "Strange Ways"

Remember that a banner can accommodate only 10 characters in one line. So the 'ys' in the above message are just not displayed.

The *touch* Command

We had our first tryst with the **touch** command in Chapter 2. Let's explore it a little further. Not only does it create empty files, but it also allows you to change the modification and access times of a file. When you run a **cat** command on a file you are accessing it, when you are making changes in a file you are modifying it, whereas when you are preparing a new file afresh you are creating it. Unix keeps track of times at which each of these activities are performed for every single file on the file system.

touch comes into picture when you want to change these times without really accessing or modifying the file. For example,

$ touch -a myfile

would change the access time of **myfile** to whatever is the current time.

The time displayed by **ls -l** is the last modification time for each file. If you want to see the last access time you may use **ls -lu**.

As you must have guessed the **-m** option is used with the **touch** command for changing modification time to current time. If you just say,

$ touch myfile

then modification as well as the access time is set to current time.

What if you want to set the access time for a file to a particular time instead of current time? Well, no problem.

```
$ touch -a 0425120596 story
```

This would set the access time of **story** to the specified time. The unintelligible looking series of digits is the supplied time. Read it as two digits each for month, day, hour, minutes and year.

The *file* Command

Suppose you have created a bunch of files and have lost track of what does each file contain. You can find out the contents of each by running a **cat** command on each file. You would agree this would be too tedious. Saying **cat** * too would not serve the purpose since there would be too much of output to look at. Unix being a fatherly old chap helps you out in such a situation. It provides us the **file** command. Let's try this one out.

```
$ file *
a.out:       iAPX 386 executable not stripped
ban:         empty
bin:         directory
cal.out:     ascii text
catfile:     commands text
clean:       c program text
cmd:         commands text
etc:         directory
etran.dbf:   empty
mdata.c:     c program text
story:       english text
ss:          commands text
totdir:      ascii text
trash:       ascii text
```

file command recognizes several types of files as shown in the output. Before determining the contents it of course reads each file. We typed an English paragraph in the file **story**, a few Unix commands in the file **cmd** and some garbage in the file **trash**. And, **file** being what it is reported **story** to be an 'English text file', **cmd** to be a 'command text file' and **trash** to be an 'ascii text file'. **file** also recognizes empty files and directories and reports them accordingly. Note how the contents of the file **a.out** are being reported. Can you make out much from that message? Frankly, I cannot.

Links with DOS

Many users move to the multiuser OS like Unix after having spent a lot of time with a single user OS like MS-DOS. At least during the initial phases of this switch they want to (or are required to) shift files from a DOS machine to their directory in the Unix file system. Unix obliges such users. To accommodate and win them over, it incorporates the capability to recognise DOS disks. Thus, a user can easily view, list, copy or delete files from a DOS formatted disk. The commands for carrying out these operations are fairly straight-forward. Some of these commands are exemplified below.

If you want to read some DOS formatted floppy, you simply have to say:

    $ dosdir a:

This will give you the list of all files on the floppy similar to the way DIR lists them. If we want to see the contents of a directory 'project' we will have to say:

    $ dosdir a:/proj

Note that the drive specification in this command is followed by a '/' and not the customary '\' that we employ in DOS.

In order to see the contents of a DOS file, we can use

$ doscat a:filename

Similarly, **dosmkdir**, **dosrmdir**, **dosrm** and **dosls** also function on DOS formatted disks as their counterparts, **mkdir**, **rmdir**, **rm** and **ls** work in Unix environment. Not only this, we can also format a floppy so that DOS understands it using the command **dosformat**.

Though all these utilities are useful, the most important utility in this area is **doscp**, since it is the one which would help you move files from DOS to Unix and vice versa. The trailing **cp** in **doscp** suggests that it is a function for copying files. But that's only half the picture. **doscp** copies a Unix file onto a disk which is in DOS format, with all necessary conversions to make it readable by DOS. For example,

$ doscp trial a:

will copy the file **trial** from current Unix directory to the DOS formatted floppy in A drive.

Likewise, we can copy several files at a time:

$ doscp $HOME/proj/*.prg a:/progs

This copies all '.prg' files from the **proj** directory in the home directory to the **progs** directory in drive A.

File Related Commands

Unix envisages a host of possible ways in which we might want to operate on files, and hence provides a sizeable number of commands that help us manipulate files. Many of these file related commands are called filters. We would explore why they are called filters in Chapter 5. For now let us take a look at some of the more commonly used commands with their numerous options.

wc

A simple and useful command, it counts the number of lines, words and characters in the specified file or files. It comes with the options **-l, -w** and **-c** which allow the user to obtain the number of lines, words or characters individually or in any desired combination.

```
$ wc -lc file1 file2
file1  20  571
file2  30  804
```

Thus, the file **file1** constitutes 20 lines and 571 characters. Similarly for the file **file2**.

The **wc** command is capable of accepting input directly form the keyboard. By entering **wc** without any arguments, it waits for the user to type in the input. On terminating input (using Ctrl d), the appropriate counts are displayed for the input that you supplied.

sort

As the name suggests the **sort** command can be used for sorting the contents of a file. Apart from sorting files, **sort** has another trick up its sleeve. It can merge multiple sorted files and store the result in the specified output file. While sorting the **sort** command bases its comparisons on the first character in each line in the file. If the first character of two lines is same then the second character in each line is compared and so on. That's quite logical. To put it in more technical terms, the sorting is done according to the ASCII collating sequence. That is, it sorts the spaces and the tabs first, then the punctuation marks followed by numbers, uppercase letters and lowercase letters in that order.

The simplest form of **sort** command would be:

```
$ sort myfile
```

This would sort the contents of **myfile** and display the sorted output on the screen.

If we want we can sort the contents of several files at one shot as in:

> $ sort file1 file2 file3

Instead of displaying the sorted output on the screen we can store it in a file by saying,

> $ sort -oresult file1 file2 file3

The above command sorts the three files **file1**, **file2** & **file3** and saves the result in a file called **result**.

And if there are repeated lines in each of these files and we want that such lines should occur only once in the output we can ensure that too using the **-u** option which outputs only unique lines.

> $ sort -u -o result file1 file2 file3

If the files have already been sorted and we just want to merge them we can use:

> $ sort -m file1 file2

Sometimes we may want to combine the contents of a file with the input from the keyboard and then carry out the sorting. This can be achieved by saying:

> $ sort - file1

where '-' stands for the standard input i.e. the keyboard.

We can even sort only the input from standard input by just saying,

> $ sort

Since no file has been specified here it is assumed that the input is to come from the standard input device.

That is only part of the capability of **sort**. **sort** is used most fruitfully for files which are essentially databases, or which have its information organised in fields. Fields are a group of characters separated by a predetermined delimiter, or a newline. In most cases, the delimiter is a space or a tab, separating different chunks of information.

Now that we know what fields are, we can specify the fields to be used for sorting. Such fields are often known as sort keys. The syntax of the **sort** command includes optional **+pos1** and **-pos2**, signifying the starting and ending position of the **sort** key. If **-pos2** is not included, then the key is assumed to extend till the end of the line.

Assume that a file **students** has four fields, for roll number, names of the students, their marks, and their grades. These fields would be numbered 0, 1, 2 and 3.

    $ sort -r +1 -2 students

Saying thus would **sort** the file **students** on the field containing the names of the students. The +1 indicates that the sort key begins at the second field and the -2 indicates that it ends before the third field. This yields names of the students as the sort key. We can even have multiple sort keys using this feature of the **sort** command.

The **-r** switch indicates a reverse **sort**. So, the records arranged in reverse alphabetical order of names would be displayed on the screen.

If we want to sort the same file according to marks we must use the **-n** option which specifies that the sorting is to be done on a numeric field. If not specified then the marks 100, 40, 50, 10 would be incorrectly sorted in the order 10, 100, 40, 50.

The following figure summarises all the options that we have used with **sort** along with a few more useful ones that you may try on your own.

Option	Meaning
-b	Ignores leading spaces and tabs.
-c	Checks if files are already sorted. If they are, sort does nothing.
-d	Sorts in dictionary order (ignores punctuation).
-f	Ignores case.
-m	Merges files that have already been sorted.
-n	Sorts in numeric order.
-ofile	Stores output in **file**. The default is to send output to standard output.
-r	Reverses sort.
-tc	Separates fields with character (default is tab).
-u	Unique output: if merge creates identical lines, uses only the first.
+n[-m]	Skips **n** fields before sorting and then sorts through field **m**.

Figure 4.2

cut

Like sort, **cut** is also a filter. True to its name, it cuts or picks up a given number of character or fields from the specified file. Say you have a large database of employee information. If from this you want to view only a few selected fields, for instance name and division, **cut** is the answer. If the name happens to be the second field and the division the seventh you would say

```
$ cut -f 2,7 empinfo
```

If we are to view fields 2 through 7 we can say,

```
$ cut -f 2-7 empinfo
```

The **cut** command assumes that the fields are separated by tab character. If the fields are delimited by some character other than the default tab character, **cut** supports an option **-d** which allows us to set the delimiter. The file **empinfo** may have the information for each employee stored in the following format

```
name:age:address:city:pin:division
```

Each piece of information is separated by a colon, hence we require the field delimiter to be recognised as ':'. The command for listing the name and division fields would now be

```
$ cut -f 2,7 -d":" empinfo
```

The **cut** command can also **cut** specified columns from a file and display them on the standard output. The switch used for this purpose is **-c**. For example,

```
$ cut -c1-15 empinfo
```

As a result, the first 15 columns from each line in the file **empinfo** would be displayed.

grep

grep is an acronym for 'globally search a regular expression and print it'. The command searches the specified input fully (globally) for a match with the supplied pattern and displays it. While forming the patterns to be searched we can use shell metacharacters, or regular expressions, as professional Unix users call them. Some metacharacters like '', '?', '[ ]' and '!' we learnt in Chapter 2. Knowing the versatility of the metacharacters, what powers they yield to **grep** can easily be imagined. Added to that is its capability to search in more than one file, enhanced by the use of various options or switches.

Let us begin with the simplest example of usage of **grep**.

    $ grep picture newsfile

This would search the word 'picture' in the file **newsfile** and if found, the lines containing it would be displayed on the screen.

We can use **grep** to search a pattern in several files. For example,

    $ grep picture newsfile storyfile

Here, the word 'picture' would be searched in both the files, **newsfile** and **storyfile** and if found, the lines containing it would be displayed along with the name of the file where it occurred. This way we would be able to make out the file from which the line is being listed.

For a search pattern comprising more than a single word, single quotes can be used to enclose the same, as in,

    $ grep 'the picture taken' -i -n newsfile storyfile

The above command searches for the pattern enclosed within ' ', without heeding the case (**-i** makes it case insensitive). The **-n** option also causes the numbers of the lines in which the pattern was found to be printed by the side of each line.

To tailor even the weirdest criteria for searching, **grep** has at its disposal the metacharacters.

    $ grep [Rr]ebecca myfile

Here **grep** would search for all occurrences of 'Rebecca' as well as 'rebecca' in **myfile** and display the lines which contain one of these words.

```
$ grep b??k myfile
```

This command would display all four letter words whose first letter is a 'b' and last letter, a 'k'. The two '?' symbols represent one character each. Thus, lines containing words like book, back, beak etc. would be listed.

grep realises that you may not always want to see what you search. Sometimes you may wish the output to be the other way round, wherein you may wish to see only those lines which do not contain the search patterns. The option **-v** makes this possible.

```
$ grep -v a* myfile
```

With that, all those lines that do not contain words starting with 'a' are displayed. Just in case you failed to appreciate it, note the point that unlike a '?', a '*' also denotes zero characters. Hence all occurrences of an isolated letter 'a' would also qualify for the search.

We can be more explicit in building the patterns to be searched. For example, a pattern '^[abc]' would help search only those lines which begin with 'a', 'b' or 'c'. Likewise, we can build search pattern which helps only those lines to qualify which end in that pattern. For example, the search pattern '[s-z]$' would help search those lines which end with any character between 's' to 'z'

Figure 4.3 lists out the various options available with **grep** along with the meaning of each to serve as a quick reference for you.

Option	Meaning
-c	Returns only the number of matches, without quoting the text.
-i	Ignores case while searching.
-l	Returns only filenames containing a match, without quoting the text.
-n	Returns line number of matched text, as well as the text itself.
-s	Suppresses error messages.
-v	Returns lines that do not match the text.

Figure 4.3

dd

The unintuitive **dd** is a disguise for an extremely versatile command for file manipulation. **dd** converts and copies a file, allowing plenty of choices. For example,

```
$ dd if=report of=document conv=ebcdic, ucase
```

Unix sure is one of few words. The information packed in that one line is: Convert the input file **report** from ascii to ebcdic, and while doing this conversion map alphabetic characters in uppercase and copy them to the output file called **document**. If the input and output files are not mentioned, then by default, the standard input and output are assumed.

Following is the list of other options available with **dd**:

Option	Meaning
count=n	Copy only n input records
conv=ascii	Convert ebcdic to ascii
conv=lcase	Convert alphabets to lower case

conv=noerror	Continue processing if error encountered
conv=...,...	Several comma separated conversions
skip=n	Skip **n** input records before starting copy

Viewing Files

So far we have used the **cat** command to view the contents of a file. However, if the file is bigger than 24 lines then the matter would naturally scroll off the screen. If we want to stop the scrolling we can do so by hitting the pause key and resume it by hitting any other key. This of course needs a bit of a practice otherwise the matter scrolls off the screen before you can reach for the pause key. To exercise a tighter control over the way we can view files Unix provides several utilities. Out of these the **head** and **tail** commands help in viewing lines at the beginning or at the end of the file respectively.

Unless otherwise specified the **head** command assumes that you want to display first 10 lines in the file. Should you decide to view first fifteen lines you simply have to say,

```
$ head -15 myfile
```

The **tail** command is the counterpart of **head** and by default it displays the last 10 lines in the file. As with **head** here too we can specify the number of lines if we decide to override this default value.

The disadvantage of **head** and **tail** is that they cannot display a range of lines. Moreover, what is displayed is final. That is, if we have displayed the first 50 lines in a file we cannot move back and view say the 10th line. Unix provides two commands which offer more flexibility in viewing files. These are **pg** and **more**. They more or less work in the same manner, except for a few minor differences. Each of them helps you view a file page by page with lot of useful options like:

(a) Set the number of lines to be displayed per page.

(b) Ability to move either forwards or backwards in a file just at the touch of a key.

(c) Skip pages while viewing the file page by page.

(d) Search the file for a pattern in forward or backward direction.

On executing each of these commands one pageful of file contents are displayed on the screen after which a prompt is displayed at which the user can give various commands that are understood by **pg** or **more**.

Here we will look at only one example of usage of each command. For more variations the reader is referred to the Unix manual or the on-line help provided by both the commands on pressing the 'h' key at the prompt displayed at the end of page.

  $ pg +10 -15 -p "Page no. %d" -s myfile

This command starts displaying the contents of **myfile**, 15 lines at a time from 10th line onwards. At the end of each displayed page a prompt comes which displays the page number on view. This prompt overrides the default ':' prompt of the **pg** command. The -s option ensures that the prompt is displayed in reverse video.

Let us now look at an example of the **more** command.

  $ more +10 -15 -s -d myfile yourfile

This command too would bring about more or less the same effect as the one that we used with **pg** above. The difference being it would display contents of two files **myfile** and **yourfile**. Also, the -s option would squeeze multiple blank lines in a file to a single blank line. This helps in maximizing the useful information displayed on the screen especially when you know that a file contains several successive blank lines. The -d option changes the normal --**more**-- prompt displayed at the end of each page to a more explanatory '[Hit space to continue, Delete to abort]'.

The most obvious difference between **pg** and **more** is **pg** permits you to set the prompt whereas **more** doesn't. Also, while using **more** at the end of each page a number appears which indicates how much percentage of file have we viewed so far.

Taking Printouts

Unix permits sharing of one printer amongst all users or several printers amongst several users. When several users makes a request to print, their requests are put on a queue and then printed according to the precedence. A print scheduler runs in the background which manages the print jobs of different users.

The **lp** command is used to send the user's print job to the print queue. When we submit the job for printing using the **lp** command it returns a 'request id'. This id can be used to keep track of our job or to cancel it if required. When we cancel the print request our job gets removed from the print queue.

When we print a file using **lp** it adds a banner page at the beginning of our printout. This helps the user in identifying his printout from the heap of printouts that are printed by different users. The simplest form in which **lp** can be used is:

```
$ lp file1  file2
request id is lp-32 (2 files)
```

We can submit the print job and then continue to work with something else. We would like to be informed that our print job has been processed so that we can go to the printer and collect our printout. We can do so by invoking **lp** using the **-w** option:

```
$ lp  -w  file1  file2
request id is lp-44 (2 files)
```

Now as soon as the printing is over we would be so informed by a message on our screen. If we have logged off by the time the printing is over then the message would be mailed to us.

lp comes with several such useful options. Figure 4.4 shows the commonly used options with the **lp** command.

Option	Meaning
-w	Sends a message to the user when the file is printed.
-n num	Prints **num** number of copies (the default is 1).
-o nobanner	Does not print the banner page.
-P list	Prints the page numbers specified by **list**.
-d printer	Specifies a printer other than the default printer.
-q level	Sets a priority level for the print job (lowest is 39).

Figure 4.4

Once the print request has been made using the **lp** command we can watch its progress using the **lpstat** command which shows the status of our print job. There are various options that can be used with the **lpsat** command. Out of these the most comprehensive information is obtained using the **-t** option. This information includes status of all print jobs on the queue, the type of printer, whether it is accepting any fresh print requests etc. When we tried it this is what we got:

```
$ lpstat -t
scheduler is running
system default destination: lp
device for lp: /dev/lp0
lp is accepting requests since Sat Apr 20 14:25:34 1996
available.

lp-13    aa1    190    Apr 23 13:10
```

```
lp-12    root    208    Apr 23 13:21
lp-14    root    311    Apr 23 13:25
lp-15    aa2     126    Apr 23 13:18
```

If for some reason having submitted the job for printing we decide to cancel it, we can do so using the **cancel** command. For doing this we must know the request id that is displayed on our terminal when we submit the print job using **lp**. Even if we forget this id we can always find it using the **lpstat** command. To cancel the print job all that we have to say is:

```
$ cancel  lp-13
```

where **lp-13** is the request id of our print job. The **cancel** command responds with,

```
request "lp-13,190 canceled
```

We can once again verify this cancellation by using the **lpstat** command and you are sure to find your print job request id missing. Quite naturally, you can cancel only your print jobs, whereas the superuser can cancel anybody's print jobs.

As we said earlier, the print jobs submitted to the print queue are managed by the print scheduler called **lpsched**. This scheduler is usually executed at the time of booting. If not, then the system administrator can run it by saying

```
# /usr/lib/lpsched
```

Also, it is only the system administrator who can terminate the printing services if the printer goes bad by using the command

```
# /usr/lib/lpshut
```

File Compression

You would always have more files than what you can accommodate on your disk! This is a very common fact, you would agree. Unix takes care of this to a certain extent by providing you utilities which can pack the same information in lesser bytes thereby saving you precious disk space. These utilities are known as **compress** and **pack**.

Although you can't do anything with the file which has been compressed or packed unless you expand it back to the original format, for files you don't need to refer to very often, they can save a lot of disk space.

The usage of both the commands is more or less same. To compress a file called **trial.txt**, we can say,

    compress -v trial.txt

The optional **-v** (for verbose) option tells **compress** to report how much space it saved. For example, in the above case it reported the following:

    trial.txt: Compression: 43.21% - replaced with trial.txt.Z

How much would be the compression is solely dependent on the contents of the file. On compression the original file is replaced by another which has the same name with **.Z** extension added to it.

Sometimes it may so happen that the contents of the file are such that on compression no saving in disk space is likely to occur. In such a case the **compress** utility informs you so and doesn't create a **.Z** file in such an event.

To get the compressed file back to its original state, we can use the **uncompress** utility as shown below:

    $ uncompress trial.txt.Z

On doing this **trial.txt.Z** is deleted and the original **trial.txt** is recreated back in its original form and shape.

Remember that once a file has been compressed we cannot view it using the normal **cat** command. Unix provides a utility called **zcat** for this purpose. It displays an uncompressed version of a compressed file to the terminal, without changing the compressed file or storing the uncompressed version in a file.

Like **compress, pack** is also able to compact a file, but is uses a different compression scheme. Let us try it on our **trial.txt** file.
@PROGRAM = $ pack trial.txt

>   /usr/bin/pack: trial.txt: 37.1% compression

As you can note, this time the degree of compression is smaller. The packed contents are stored in the file **trial.txt.z** and the original file **trial.txt** is deleted. To view the contents of a packed file we can use the **pcat** command. To get back the original file from the packed file there is a utility called **unpack**.

> $ unpack trial.txt
>   unpack: trial.txt: unpacked

Like **compress, pack** leaves the file untouched if packing doesn't save any space. Quite often it is found that **compress** offers a higher degree of compression as compared to **pack**, though occasionally the reverse may be true.

The On-line Unix Manual

The Unix manual is possibly the best thing that has happened to the Unix world. It provides on-line help about every single Unix command, with all the options that the command can support. To invoke the manual just type the command **man** along with the command you wish to seek help on. For example,

$ man cd

And here is the output it produces on the screen...

cd(C)   cd(C)

Name

cd - change working directory

Syntax

cd [directory]

Description

If specified, **directory** becomes the new working directory; otherwise
the value of the shell parameter $HOME is used. The process must
have search (execute) permission in all directories (components)
specified in the full pathname of directory.

Because a new process is created to execute each command, cd
would be ineffective if it were written as a normal command; therefore,
it is recognized and executed by the shell.

If the shell is reading its commands from a terminal, and the specified
directory does not exist (or some component cannot be searched),
spelling correction is applied to each component of directory, in a
search for the name. The shell then asks whether or not to try and
change directory to the corrected directory name; an answer of n
means 'no', and anything else is taken as "yes".

The Korn Shell command, **ksh**, has extensions to the syntax for **cd**.
Please refer to ksh(C) for more information.

Note

Wildcard designators will work with the **cd** command.

See also

pwd(C), sh(C), chdir(S)

The manual page that is displayed on the screen is identical to the manual supplied with the operating system itself. The on line manual comes with lots of information like the use, syntax, switches available with the command, examples etc. The following guidelines would help you in understanding the manual page:

(a)   'Name' is the first titled section and it describes the name of the command followed by a brief description of the command.

(b)   The 'Syntax' section shows exactly how the command is used.

(c)   Square brackets indicate optional arguments.

(d)   Ellipses (...) indicate that the previous argument can be repeated.

(e)   In the description section the purpose of the command, its working and its options are outlined. After reading the description try out the command with its various options yourself. That's the real way of learning.

(f)   Some commands have a 'Files' section. It lists the system files used by the command.

(g)   The 'See also' section points out the related commands and information.

The **man** files are not merely text files, hence they cannot be **cat** on the screen. Instead, **man** is a complex program that searches and then displays manual text from special files which contain text processing codes.

Though the on-line manual is a great idea, it is written in a style that at times can be difficult to decipher. At many places it appears that the authors of the manual assumed that you have read all the other parts of the manual and know what all the commands are called. Still it is of immense help when you just can't remember the options for a command or what to type where on the command line after the command name.

Even though the on-line manual is the final word on how a command works it is ill-suited for browsing through the various available commands since one has to know the name of the command you want to see. For browsing, one can use the printed manual.

Exercise

[A]   State whether the following statements are True or False:

(a)   The command **$ man man** would give help about the **man** command.

(b)   If the fields in a file are separated using **/** we can separate them out using the **cut** command.

(c)   AABBCC is a valid password.

(d)   To change our existing password we execute the file **/etc/passwd**.

(e)   There are two **passwd** files in the system, one to store password and another to change password.

(f)   September of every year always had and will have 30 days.

(g)   banner "aaa\nbbb" will display 'aaa' and 'bbb' as large characters split over two lines.

(h)   A DOS formatted floppy can be used in Unix and a Unix formatted floppy can be used in DOS.

(i)   The **wc** command works only on text files.

(j)   Once a job is submitted for printing using the **lp** command we have to take the printout even on second thoughts we realise that we should not have printed the file.

(k)   Once a job is submitted for printing using the **lp** command we have to remain logged in till our file gets printed.

(l)   We cannot submit a new job for printing unless our earlier job has been printed.

(m)   If the printer goes out of order the system administrator can ensure that the system refuses to accept new printing jobs.

(n)   Only system administrator can cancel your printing job.

[B]   How would you perform the following operations:

(a)   Change the modification time of a file to midnight of 01/01/1996.

(b)   Convert all capital letters in a file to smallcase letters.

(c)   Change the prompt to 'What next' while using the **more** command.

(d)   Merge and sort the contents of files **a**, **b** and **c** and display the sorted output on the screen.

(e)   Extract the address field from a file which contains records having fields name:age:address:phone.

(f)   Merge the contents of file **f1** with the input supplied from the keyboard and store the sorted output in a file **f2**.

(g)   Copy all files from **/usr/aa1/cobol** directory to a DOS formatted floppy in drive B.

(h)   Display all lines in a file which contain the word 'Poem' from a file **english.txt**. You should be able to report all occurrences like POem, PoEm, POEm etc. You are not allowed to use a command line option to ignore the case while searching.

(i)   Search all lines in a file which end with a semicolon.

(j)   Search all lines in a file which do not end with a semicolon.

(k)   Report number of lines which contain a number for each file in the current directory

[C]   Answer the following:

(a)   How would you display the strings 'aaa' and 'bbb' in two different lines using the **banner** command?

(b)   You are given a file **myfile**. Without opening this file how would you make a fair estimate about its contents?

(c)   What is the difference between the commands **compress** and **pack**?

(d)   A file contains records with each record containing name of city, name of state and name of country. How would you sort this file with state as the sort key.

(e)   A file contains records with each record containing name of city, name of state and name of country. How would you sort this file with country as the primary sort key and state as the secondary sort key.

5 I/O Redirection and Piping

N ow that we have discussed the essential Unix commands that would help us get started with Unix, let us shift gears and look at something different: Input/Output Redirection.

In all operating systems, there is a standard input device and a standard output device. In Unix, as also in most other operating systems, the standard input device is the keyboard and the standard output is the display screen. Trailing behind in popularity is the standard error device, which is the display screen.

Unless otherwise instructed Unix commands/programs get their input from the standard input device and send their output to the standard output device. Any error messages if they occur are sent to the standard error device.

Thus if a command is described as reading from the standard input and writing to the standard output, that means it takes input from your keyboard and sends output or error messages to your screen.

Special files that instruct all the programs to accept standard input from the keyboard and direct the standard output to the display, are provided by Unix. The three streams, i.e the standard input, standard output and standard error are denoted by the numbers 0, 1 and 2 respectively.

Stream	Device	Value
Standard Input	Keyboard	0
Standard Output	Terminal Screen	1
Standard Error	Terminal Screen	2

Figure 5.1

Why not just use the terms keyboard and screen for the standard input, output, and error? Because Unix allows you to change the standard input and output temporarily by using what is known as redirection and piping.

Sometimes it is useful to redirect the input or output to a file or a printer. For example, you might want to redirect a directory listing from the screen to a file. Unix provides redirection symbols for the purpose.

The symbol > implies redirection of output and the symbol < implies redirection of input. The symbol > sends the output of a command to a file or a device, such as a printer. The symbol < takes the input needed for a command from a file rather than from the keyboard.The symbol >> adds output from a command to the end of a file without deleting the information already in the file.

The > operator tells Unix, "Don't display this output on screen instead, put it somewhere else". Likewise the < operators says, "The input for this command is not coming from the keyboard this time look for it somewhere else."

The "somewhere else" can be a file or a printer for output redirection and a file or a keyboard for input redirection. You would agree that attempting to receive input from the printer or sending the output to the keyboard would be a losing battle.

Let us put these operators to a practical stint. Consider this command:

```
$ cat file1 > file2
```

On executing this you will promptly be returned to the $ prompt. The redirection operator declares **file2** to be the standard output, ousting the terminal screen from that role. Thus the output of **cat** which is normally sent to the screen is now sent to **file2** and not to the screen. If the file **file2** does not exist, it is created. If it does exist, it is wiped clear and refilled with the new data.Thus, the output going to the screen has been redirected to a file.

Note that this change in standard output is temporary. When the command ends, your terminal once again becomes the standard output.

Now let's look at input redirection. The Unix manual says that **cat** reads from the standard input if no input file is given. This allows us to do the following:

```
$ cat
Did you hear the story about the optimist and the pessimist? The op-
timist goes to the window every morning and says, "Good morning,
God". The pessimist goes to the window and says, "Good God, morn-
ing".
Ctrl d
Did you hear the story about the optimist and the pessimist? The op-
timist goes to the window every morning and says, "Good morning,
God". The pessimist goes to the window and says, "Good God, morn-
ing".
```

First we typed **cat** and then hit the enter key. Thus we provided no input filename. Then, what we typed next was gathered as standard input, and **cat** passed it on to the standard output, the terminal screen. You may recall that a Ctrl d at the beginning of the line acts to mark the end of keyboard input; it simulates reaching the end of an ordinary file.

Any command that accepts standard input also accepts input redirection. So let's try that out with **cat**:

```
$ cat < newfile
One of the best things about getting older is that all those things you
wanted and couldn't afford when you were younger, you no longer
want.
```

Here the file **newfile** became the standard input, and **cat** read its contents and displayed them on the screen. The same thing could as well have been achieved by saying,

```
$ cat newfile
One of the best things about getting older is that all those things you
wanted and couldn't afford when you were younger, you no longer
want.
```

Though both the commands produce the same output there is a subtle difference between the two. In the latter example **newfile** was not the standard input. Instead, the standard input remained the terminal, and the internal programming of **cat** caused the **newfile** file to be opened in addition to the standard input.

Indeed, **cat**, like many file-reading programs, can read the standard input and a file input during the execution of the command. The standard method (and the one used by **cat**) is to use a hyphen instead of a filename to stand for standard input. Here is an example that uses the file **newfile** as the first input and the standard input (here the keyboard) as a second input:

```
$ cat newfile -
We all shall plant some trees we will never sit under.
Ctrl d
One of the best things about getting older is that all those things you
wanted and couldn't afford when you were younger, you no longer
want.
We all shall plant some trees we will never sit under.
```

As you can see, **cat** concatenated the two inputs. Since the filename came first, it was printed first. Then the keyboard input, represented by the hyphen, was printed.

Sometimes we may use both the redirection operators at once as shown below.

$ cat < currentfile > newfile

The first part of redirection, **< currentfile**, indicates that input is to be taken from the file **currentfile**, and the second part of redirection, **> newfile** establishes that output is to be routed to the file **newfile**. The order in which the two indirection operators are used doesn't matter. We could have obtained exactly the same effect even by saying,

$ cat > newfile < currentfile

Another redirection operator which is popularly used is the append operator, **>>**. It is similar to **>**, except if the target file already exists, the new output is appended to its end. For example,

$ who >> logfile

This command appends the current list of users who have logged in to the end of the file **logfile**.

Redirection is a very useful tool and is frequently used to redirect the output of a process running in the background as we would see in a later chapter. Can you make out what the following commands would achieve?

(a) $ ls > filelist
(b) $ banner Hi-Fi > message
(c) $ cat par.3 par.4 par.5 >> report
(d) $ cat file1 > file1

(e)	$ cat < file1 > file1
(f)	$ cat > file < file1
(g)	$ date ; who
(h)	$ date ; who > logfile
(i)	$ (date ; who) > logfile

Don't jump to conclusions. Try your hand at the above commands. You are in for a few surprises.

There are a few more redirection operators, but they are used mainly while writing shell scripts rather than at command prompt. So we will postpone their discussion to a later chapter. For the moment we will just make a list of these operators along with the purpose of each. Refer Figure 5.2 for this list.

Operator	Action
> file	Make file the standard outpt.
< file	Make file the standard input.
>> file	Make file the standard output, appending to it if it already exists.
<< word	Take shell input up to the first line containing word or upto end of file.
n> file	Make file the output for file descriptor n.
1>&2	Redirect standard output to standard error.
cmd1 | cmd2	make standard output of cmd1 the standard input of cmd2.

Figure 5.2

Piping

The philosophy of Unix commands is that each does a small job but does it quite comprehensively. Quite often a single Unix command does not suffice to solve a problem or do a task. That's the time we can try joining commands together. The chief tools for this are redirection and the pipe. If you have migrated to Unix from some other operating system you probably know about these facilities. However, their true power is tapped best (arguably) by the Unix commands.

Redirection facility of Unix lets us connect commands to files. The Unix piping facility lets us connect commands to other commands. This facility is of utmost importance in combining Unix commands and operations. It can be really useful to redirect the output of one program so that it becomes the input of another program, thereby joining the two programs. To send the output of one command as input for another, the two commands must be joined using a pipe (|) character.

It is possible to join commands using a pipe since many Unix commands accept input from the standard input and send output to the standard output. Incidentally, such commands are known as filters.

Thus a filter is a program which can receive a flow of data from standard input, process (or filter) it, and send the results to the standard output.

How can one tell if a command is a filter? Simple. Read its description using the **man** command. If it can take input from the standard input and if it sends its output to the standard output, then it is a filter. Figure 5.3 shows a list of commonly used filters in Unix.

Filter	Purpose
cat	Concatenates and displays files
pg	Paginates display for terminals
more	Displays a file one screenful at a time
head	Prints the first few lines of a file
tail	Displays the last few lines of a file
grep	Searches files for a pattern
sort	Sorts and merges files
nl	Adds line numbers to a file
pr	Prints files to the standard output
wc	Counts lines, words and characters
tee	Creates a tee in a pipe
uniq	Reports repeated lines in a file
tr	Translates characters in a file
cut	Cuts out selected fields of each line of a file
paste	Merges lines of files
lpr	Sends requests to line printer

Figure 5.3

Let us now see a few examples of piping.

    $ ls | wc -l

Here the output of **ls** becomes the input to **wc** which promptly counts the number of lines it receives as input and displays this count on the screen. Instead of displaying this count, what if want to store the count value in a file? Simple, use the output redirection as shown below:

    $ ls | wc -l > countfile

This example shows that piping and redirection can go together.

Let's consider another example,

```
$ who | sort
```

Here, instead of displaying the output of **who** on the screen it is piped to **sort**. **sort** sorts whatever it receives as input (output of **who**, in this case) and displays the sorted output (sorted according to first charac-ter in each line) on the screen. Why on the screen? Because **sort** being a filter unless otherwise mentioned it sends the output to the screen. Once again, if we want we can redirect this sorted output to a file by saying,

```
$ who | sort > sortedlist
```

There are several situations where we can use the pipe operator. Some of these are given below.

```
$ who | grep shailesh
$ ls | grep file1
$ who | wc -l
$ ls | sort -r
$ ls -r | more
$ cat file1 file2 file3 | pg
$ cal 1996 | head -10
$ cal 1996 | tail -5
$ cat poetry | grep love
```

In all the above examples we can visualize the data flowing through the pipe from one program to the next with each program doing something to the information being passed through it. This process is equivalent to piping in real life, only difference being you do not hear the gurgles as the matter flows through the pipe.

In many cases, input from a pipe can be combined with input from files. The trick, as in combining redirection with files, is to use the special symbol - (a hyphen) for those commands that recognise the hyphen as standard input. For instance, consider this command:

```
$ who | sort - logfile > newfile
```

The output from **who** becomes the standard input to **sort**. Meanwhile, **sort** opens the file **logfile**. The contents of this file are sorted together with the output of **who** (represented by the hyphen), and the sorted output is redirected to the file **newfile**.

By now we know that redirection routes the output to files while pipes route the output to other programs. What if you want to do both? Unix offers the **tee** command to achieve this purpose. It reads the standard input and sends it on to the standard output. It also redirects a copy of what it has read into the file (if any) of your choice. For example:

```
who | tee logfile | sort
```

Here, the output of **who** becomes the standard input of **tee**. **tee** now sends one copy of the input to **sort** through one pipeline, whereas the other copy is stored in a file called **logfile**.

What if we want to store the output of **who** in two files and still manage to send one copy to **sort**. Simple just mention the two filenames after the **tee** command as shown below:

```
$ who | tee logfile newlogfile | sort
```

Let us stretch this a little further. We want to store the output of **who** in **file1** and **file2**, display the same output on the screen and store the sorted output in **file3**. Observe carefully how this can be done:

```
$ who | tee file1 file2 /dev/tty3a | sort > file3
```

Here, in addition to **file1** and **file2** we have used the file associated with our terminal (**/dev/tty3a**). Hence **tee** sends the output of **who** to all the three files. What is sent to **/dev/tty3a** is promptly displayed on the screen. The copy which is sent to **sort** is first sorted and the sorted output is then stored in the file **file3**.

Before using the pipeline shown above use the **tty** command to confirm the file associated with your terminal and use that filename in place of **/dev/tty3a**.

If you wish to append the output of **tee** to a file, just use its **-a** option as shown below:

```
$ cat file1 file2 | tee -a completefile | more
```

In this pipeline the output of **cat** (contents of the files **file1** and **file2**) are appended to the existing contents of the file **completefile**. Another copy of output of **cat** is sent to **more** for displaying on the screen.

So far we have redirected only the standard input and the standard output. We can however also redirect the standard error. The following example shows this can be done.

```
$ cat myfile > newfile 2> errorfile
```

If the file **myfile** exists, then the contents of that file would be copied into **newfile**. However, if it does not exist, then an error message would be produced. However instead of displaying the error message on the screen it would be redirected to a file **errorfile**. Note that the **>** symbol redirects the standard output whereas **2>** redirects the standard error. While redirecting the standard output instead of **>** we may as well use **1>**.

Assuming that the file **myfile** did not exist let's check out the contents of **errorfile**.

```
$ cat errorfile
cat: cannot open myfile
```

This is the error message produced by the **cat** command when it failed to locate the file **myfile**. Obviously, had **myfile** existed its contents would have been copied into the file **newfile**.

Thus the facility of piping and redirection in Unix provides a lot of flexibility. It owes its success largely to two factors. The first is the Unix's treatment of devices as files. This allows the same commands to work equally well with files and with terminals, hard disk drives, and other input/output devices. The second factor is that a lot of Unix commands are designed as filters which take the input from the keyboard and send to the output to the screen. This makes connecting Unix commands a very natural process. The fact that **more, cat, sort, pg** etc. are filters is what lets us link them together with pipes.

Whenever we write programs to work under Unix environment we should give a careful thought to whether it should be developed as a filter to exploit the capabilities of redirection and piping.

We are certainly not through with redirection in all its garbs. However, for the time being that is all that we have to say about the topic. We are going to do a lot more I/O redirection when we write shell programs in later chapters. Till that time get used to the concept by trying your hand at the following.

Construct pipelines to execute the following jobs:

(a)   Output of **who** should be displayed on the screen with value of total number of users who have logged in displayed at the bottom of the list.

(b)   Output of **ls** should be displayed on the screen and from this output the lines containing the word 'poem' should be counted and the count should be stored in a file **file1**.

(c)   Contents of **file1** and **file2** should be displayed on the screen and this output should be appended to the file **file3**.

(d)   From output of **ls** the lines containing 'poem' should be displayed on the screen along with the count.

(e)   Names of cities should be accepted from the keyboard. This list of cities should be combined with the list of cities present in the file **cityfile**. This combined list should be sorted and the sorted output should be stored in a file **newcity**.

(f)   All files present in a directory **dir1** should be deleted. Any error, if it occurs while carrying out this operation should be stored in a file **errorlog**.

Exercise

[A]   Answer the following:

(a)   What would be the effect of the following commands?
```
cat < file1 > file2
wc -l < aaa
who | sort
who | wc -l > aaa
sort
date > aaa
banner > aaa
(date;banner Cheerio) > aaa
ls | grep poem
grep poem file | sort | wc -l | banner
ls | tee /dev/tty | grep poem | wc -l
sort a.txt b.txt c.txt | dd conv=ucase | more
cal 1994 | head -15
date > aaa
cat aaa > bbb 2> ccc
```

(b)   What do you mean by a filter? Give examples of filers.

(c)   Which of the following are filters?
```
date    head    grep    tail    ls
more    who     pg      ps      tee
```

(d)   Can we redirect the output to keyboard and redirect input to screen?

(e)   What is the internal value associated with the standard error device?

(f)   Can you write the following command in a more compact form?
cat < file1 | grep John > result

(g)   What is the difference between the commands:
wc -l < file1
wc -l file1

(h)   What is the difference between the commands:
cat < file1 > file2
cat > file2 < file1

[B]   Construct pipelines to carry out the following jobs:

(a)   List all files beginning with the character 'P' on the screen and also store them in a file called **file1**.

(b)   List all files beginning with the character 'P' on the screen twice in succession.

(c)   Output of **who** should be sorted and displayed on the screen along with the total number of users. The same output except the number of users should also be stored in a file **file1**.

(d)   Merge the contents of the files **a.txt**, **b.txt** and **c.txt**, sort them and display the sorted output on the screen page by page.

(e)   Display the list of last 20 files present in the current directory. Also store this list in a file **profile**.

6 *vi, The King of All Editors*

V **i** (short for visual editor) divides Unix users in two camps: those who hate it and those who love it, nothing in between. People who hate it say that **vi** is the worst thing to have happened in the Unix world, whereas those who love it are totally biased towards it and would go any length supporting its cause. I too have strong opinion about **vi** (and other editors available under the Unix platform) which will be abundantly clear in the later sections of this chapter.

Why *vi*

There are three editors available in almost all versions of Unix: **ed**, **ex** and **vi**. The **ed** program is the original editor that has been a part of Unix since the very beginning. If you use it, you begin to appreciate how far software design has progressed since 1975. The **ed** program is basically a line editor, which means that **ed** assigns line numbers to the lines in the file; every time you do something, you must tell **ed** which line or lines to do it to. If you have used the EDLIN program in DOS, **ed** should look familiar.

An improved version of **ed**, called **ex**, understands all the commands of **ed**. Compared to **ed** it is a shade better in user-friendliness with more informative error messages. If **ed** is an ugly toad than **ex** is a less ugly toad. If there is any way you can get another text editor to use other than **ed** and **ex** do it without a second thought. If you don't think that **ed** and **ex** can't really be that bad, just invoke them once and you will never use them again.

Compared to **ed** or **ex** the **vi** text editor is head and shoulders above them in almost every way. It is a screen editor rather than a line editor; it shows you as much of the file as it can fit on the screen. You don't have to beg it to display bits and pieces of your file. Definitely a step forward, you would agree.

In fact **vi** created a sensation when it first appeared on the Unix scene since it was the first full screen editor. It allowed the user to view and edit the entire document at the same time. Creating and editing files became a lot easier and that's the reason it became an instant hit with the programmers.

The bad news is that deep down **vi** is just a souped-up version of **ed**. There are several disadvantages in using **vi**. These are:

(a)   The user is always kept guessing. There are no self- explanatory error messages. If anything goes wrong no error messages appear, only the speaker beeps to inform you that something went wrong.

(b)   The guy who wrote **vi** didn't believe in help, so there isn't any online help available in **vi**. Incidentally, **vi** was written by Bill Joy when he was a student at University of California.

(c)   There are three modes in which the editor works. Under each mode the same keypress creates different effects. Hence meaning of several keys and their effects in each mode have to be memorised.

(d)   **vi** is fanatically case-sensitive. A 'h' moves the cursor one position to the left whereas a 'H' positions it at the top left corner. Moreover, you are required to remember both.

That's **vi** for you in brief. I don't intend to depress you, but all the same, let's eliminate any rosy ideas that you might have imagined about **vi**. Then how come **vi** is so popular even today. One of the major reasons is that **vi** is available on almost all Unix systems. Yes even if it is installed in Siberia.

vi can handle files that contain text. No fancy formatting, no fonts, no embedded graphics or junk like that, just plain simple text. You can create files, edit files, and print them. It cannot do boldface, running headers or footers, italics, or all that other fancy stuff you need in order to produce really modern, over-formatted, professional-quality memos!

Like all Unix programs, **vi** is a power-packed editor but lacks the finesse that modern-day editors possess. It's possibly the last word in how a program can be non-user-friendly. While using **vi**, you time and again realise that it possibly wants to make users aware that Unix demands a certain level of maturity and knowledge when it comes to using even its elementary editors. In many ways,**vi** sets standard in Unix and presents the true no-nonsense picture that Unix is built over.

Even the most experienced computer user may take a while to get accustomed to **vi**. In fact one needs to develop a taste for **vi**. And once you do that you would realise it is the best editor in the world. Learning **vi** will be a gaint step towards mastering the intricacies of Unix. So let's meet it head on.

Modes of Operation

The **vi** program has three modes of operation:

(a) **Command Mode:** In this mode all the keys pressed by the user are interpreted to be editor commands. For example, if you hit a **h** the cursor is moved one position to the left. In command mode the keys that are hit are not displayed on the screen.

(b) **Insert Mode:** This mode permits insertion of new text, editing of existing text or replacement of existing text. Each of these operations can be performed only after changing over from the command mode to insertion mode using appropriate commands. The insertion mode is also known as input-text mode.

(c)   **The ex Command Mode:** This mode permits us to give commands at the command line. The bottom line of the **vi** screen is called the command line. **vi** uses the command line to display messages and commands. All commands entered in the **ex** command mode are displayed in the command line. This mode is so called because commands given in this mode are compatible with the commands of the **ex** editor.

The First Editing Session

Let us now create a file, add text to it, save this file on the disk and then quit out of **vi**. To invoke **vi** type **vi** and the name of file you want to create as shown below:

    $ vi letter

When you type the **vi** command and the file name, **vi** clears the screen and displays a window in which you can enter and edit text. The _ (underscore) on the top line shows the cursor waiting for you to enter a command here. Every other line is marked with a ~ (tilde), the symbol for an empty line. The screen as it looks like is shown below:

```
_
~
~
~
~
~
~
~
~
"letter" [New file]
```

If you have successfully entered **vi**, you are in command mode and **vi** is waiting for your command. How do you create text? Let us now add text to the file **letter**.

- Press the **i** key to enter the insert mode of **vi**. (Do not press the Enter key). You can now add text to the file. (the **i** is not printed on the screen)
- Type in some text. May be the piece shown below. Take care to press the Enter key to begin on a fresh line.

> Dear sonny,
> A weaver bird is building a nest in the dogwood tree next to our kitchen window. It builds it with such completeness, such perfection, and with such confidence. Where does that kind of knowledge come from?
>
> Bye,
> Mom.

The text that we type goes into a place in memory known as buffer.When you have finished creating text, press the Esc key to leave the insert mode and return to command mode. Now you can edit the text you have created or write the text in the buffer to a file and return to the $ prompt. We would try to save the file to the disk rather than editing it.

To do this, hold down the shift key and press **z** twice (**ZZ**). The editor remembers the file name you specified with the **vi** command at the beginning of the editing session, and moves the buffer text to the file of that name. A notice at the bottom of the screen gives the file name and the number of lines and characters in the file. Then the shell gives you a $ prompt.

Instead of using **ZZ** to save and quit you can also use **:w** and **:q** commands for writing and quitting a file. Note that any command which begins with a **:** is a command to be given in **ex** command mode.

The **:w** command writes the buffer to a file. The **:q** command leaves the editor and returns to the shell. You can type these commands separately or combine them into the single command **:wq**. It is easier to combine them.

Don't bother about any typing mistakes that you may commit. We would soon see how to edit the text present in the file.

If you press Esc key and a bell sounds, you are already in command mode. The text in the file is not affected by this, even if you press the Esc key several times.

Learning The Ropes

Having had our first tryst with **vi** let us now move further on. Let us see how we can edit a file. To edit an existing file you must be able to add, change, and delete text. However, before you can perform those tasks you must be able to load the file from disk into buffer and then move to the part of the file you want to edit. To load the file, type this line:

    $ vi tidbits

Remember to substitute the name of the file you want to edit for **tidbits**. The **vi** program shows you a full-screen view of your file. If the file isn't long enough to fill the screen, **vi** shows tildes (~) on the blank lines beyond the end of the file. The cursor (the point at which you are working) appears at the beginning of the first line of the file. Figure 6.1, for example, shows the file **tidbits** (created using **cat > tidbits**) as it would appear in **vi**.

A clock in an office can never get stolen.
Too many employees watch it all the time.
Two stone-cutters were asked what they were doing. The first said, "I am cutting this stone into blocks." The second replied, "I am on a team that is building a temple." It's the attitude that matters!

~

~

~

~

~

~

"tidbits" [New file]

Figure 6.1

To edit your text, you need to move the cursor to the point on the screen where you will begin the correction. This is easily done with four keys **h**, **j**, **k** and **l**.

h   moves the cursor one character to the left
l   moves the cursor one character to the right
j   moves the cursor down one line
k   moves the cursor up one line

The **j** and **k** commands maintain the column position of the cursor. For example, if the cursor is on the 7th character from the left, when you type **j** it goes to the 7th character on the new line. If there is no 7th character on the new line the cursor moves to the last character in the new line.

Instead of pressing a motion command key a number of times to move the cursor a corresponding number of spaces or lines, you can precede the command with the desired number. For example, to move two spaces to the right, you can press **l** twice or enter **2l**. You can move as many spaces, or lines as you want. If that place falls outside the current window that part will be scrolled. If that space or line does not exist **vi** will sound the bell.

Like most **vi** commands, the **h, j, k,** and **l** motion commands are silent; they do not appear on the screen as you enter them. The only time you would see characters on the screen on hitting keys is when you are in insert mode and are adding text to your file or when you are in ex command mode. If the motion command letters appear on the screen, you are still in the insert mode. Press the Esc key to return to command mode and try the commands again.

Adding Text

Let us now add some text to the end of the file. For this, first position the cursor on the last character in the file using the cursor movement keys discussed above. Next, hit an **a** to switch from command mode to text-input mode. The **a** here stands for append and it lets you add characters beyond the current cursor position. Type in some text so that your screen looks like this:

```
A clock in an office can never get stolen.
Too many employees watch it all the time.
Two stone-cutters were asked what they were doing. The first said, "I am
cutting this stone into blocks." The second replied, "I am on a team that is
building a temple." It's the attitude that matters!
Promise only what you can deliver.
Then deliver more than what you promised.
~
~
~
~
~
~
"tidbits"  9 lines  332 characters
```

Figure 6.2

Instead of adding new text at the end if you intend to add it in the middle, position the cursor where you wish to add text and then press **i** to indicate that you wish to insert the text before the current cursor position. As you type the new text it will appear on the screen to the left of the character on which you put the cursor. That character and all characters to the right of the cursor will move to the right to make room for your new text. The **vi** editor will continue to accept the characters you type until you press the Esc key. If necessary, the original characters will even wrap around onto the next line.

How to Delete Text

If you want to delete a character, move the cursor to that character and press the **x**. Watch the screen as you do so; the character will disappear and the line will readjust to the change. To erase three characters in a row, press **x** three times or press **3x**. You got the idea I believe. Let's put the whole thing more succinctly.

x   delete one character

nx   delete **n** characters, where **n** is the number of characters you want to delete.

Notice that **vi** adjusts the text so that no gap appears in place of the deleted string.

Overwriting Text

If you wish to overwrite the existing text then first position the cursor (using **h, j, k, l**) at the character from where you want overwriting to begin. Next hit a **R** (a capital R) to indicate that whatever you type next should overwrite the existing text at the current cursor position. Press Esc when you finish replacing text.

On Second Thoughts...

Having made changes in the text if you think you'd prefer the text the way it was before you made the changes you can undo the changes. Type an **u** and **vi** will undo the most recent change or deletion you made. If you type a capital U, **vi** undoes all changes to the current line since you moved the cursor to that line.

vi has very powerful undoing capabilities. It has more undo features than most jazzy word-processors available today. Obviously, the creator was aware that users were going to commit mistakes. These capabilities would be covered later in this chapter.

Quitting vi

Having made all the changes in the document you can finally save the document and quit out using **ZZ** in command mode or **:wq** in **ex** command mode. If you decide to quit and not save the changes you have made, type **:q!** in **ex** command mode and then press Enter. This means, "Leave **vi** and throw away my changes. I know what I'm doing".

Into The Murky Depths

Having seen how to type, edit and save a file let us now look deep down and explore what more features **vi** has to offer. Almost all letters, numbers, and symbols present on the keyboard are **vi** commands too, so watch what you type when you are in command mode. Instead of discussing each command in detail I think it would be more appropriate if we segregate the commands into logical groups like commands for cursor movement, commands for deleting text, commands for adding text etc.

Presented below are a few charts for these command groups. I hope these charts would also prove helpful whenever you forget a command and want a quick reference for it.

Commands for Positioning Cursor in the Window

Positioning by Character

Command	Function
h	Moves the cursor one character to the left.
Backspace	Moves the cursor one character to the left.
l	Moves the cursor one character to the right.
Space bar	Moves the cursor one character to the right.
0	Moves the cursor to the beginning of the current line.
$	Moves the cursor to the end of the current line.

Positioning by Line

Command	Function
j	Moves the cursor down one line from it's present position, in the same column.
k	Moves the cursor up one line from it's present position, in the same column.
+	Moves the cursor down to the beginning of next line.
-	Moves the cursor upto the beginning of previous line.
Enter	Moves the cursor down to the beginning of the next line.

Positioning by Word

Command	Function
w	Moves the cursor to the right, to the first character of the next word.
b	Moves the cursor back to the first character of the previous word.
e	Moves the cursor to the end of the current word.

Positioning in the Window

Command	Function
H	Moves the cursor to the first line on the screen, or "home".
M	Moves the cursor to the middle line on the screen .
L	Moves the cursor to the last line on the screen.

Commands for Positioning in the File

Scrolling

Command	Function
Ctrl f	Scrolls the screen forward a full window, revealing the window of text below the current window.
Ctrl b	Scrolls the screen back a full window, revealing the window of text above the current window.

Positioning on a Numbered Line

Command	Function
G	Moves the cursor to the beginning of the last line in the file.
nG	Moves the cursor to the beginning of the nth line in the file.

Commands for Inserting Text

Command	Function
a	Enters text input mode and appends text after the cursor.
i	Enters text input mode and inserts text at the cursor.
A	Enters text input mode and appends text at the end of current line.
I	Enters text input mode and inserts text at the beginning of current line.

o	Enters text input mode by opening a new line immediately below the current line.
O	Enters text input mode by opening a new line immediately above the current line.
R	Enters text input mode and overwrites from current cursor position onwards.

Commands for Deleting Text

Command	Function
x	Deletes the character at current cursor position.
X	Deletes the character to the left of the cursor.
dw	Deletes a word (or part of a word) from the cursor to the next space or to the next punctuation.
dd	Deletes the current line.
nx, ndw, ndd	Deletes **n** characters, **n** words or **n** lines.
d0	Deletes the current line from the cursor to the beginning of the line.
d$	Deletes the current line from the cursor to the end of the line.

Miscellaneous Commands

Command	Function
Ctrl g	Gives the line number of current cursor position in the buffer and modification status of the file.
.	Repeats the action performed by the last command.
u	Undoes the effects of the last command.
U	Restores all changes to the current line since you moved the cursor to this line.
J	Joins the line immediately below the current line with the current line.
~	Changes character at current cursor position from upper case to lower case or from lower case to upper case.
:sh	Temporarily returns to the shell to perform some shell commands. Type **exit** to return to **vi**.
Ctrl l	Clears and redraws the current window.

Commands for Quitting vi

Command	Function
ZZ	Writes the buffer to the file and quits **vi**.
:wq	Writes the buffer to the file and quits **vi**.
:w filename and :q	Writes the buffer to the file **filename** (new) and quits **vi**.
:w! filename and :q	Overwrites the existing file **filename** with the contents of the buffer and quits **vi**.
:q!	Quits **vi** whether or not changes made to the buffer were written to a file. Does not incorporate changes made to the buffer since the last write (:w) command.
:q	Quits **vi** if changes made to the buffer were written to a file.

Block Commands

Having been able to create files, add and delete text and save the text in a file let us now get into some advanced stuff. Something which will help you increase your efficiency when you work with **vi**. Block commands for instance. As their name suggests these commands work on a group of lines (a block of text) rather than an isolated line. For example, we may want to delete a group of lines from the file by using a single command. Or we may want to copy a group of lines from one part of the file to another. We can make block commands to work on single lines. But by doing so we would be under-utilising their power.

To be able to use block commands we must remember two things:

(a) All the block commands work in **ex** command mode.

(b) Line numbers should be associated with the text before we issue any block commands. This is so because block commands need to be told the line numbers on which they are supposed to operate.

For example, a block command like **:4,12d** indicates that lines 4 to 12 should be deleted from the file currently loaded in **vi**.

While issuing this command if the line numbers are displayed on the screen, we can promptly issue the command without having to take trouble to count the lines ourselves. Displaying line numbers is a simple matter.

You have to give a command **set number** in the **ex** command mode. You will recollect that in this mode, all commands begin with a colon (:). To display line numbers on the screen, first make sure you're in the Command mode. Then press the colon (:) key and notice how the cursor gets positioned at the last line of the screen. We had mentioned before that the last line of the **vi** screen is the command line. Now type in the command:

(Esc): set number   or   (Esc): set nu

Line numbers are instantly flashed onto the screen as shown in Figure 6.3.

```
     1     Congratulations on landing up with a job!
     2     As a new sales associate, just remember that true job of a
     3     salesman begins when the customer says "No".
     4     There is no limit to what you can achieve if you don't mind
     5     who gets the credit.
     6     To be bitter to somebody is to waste precious moments of a
     7     life that is too short already.
     ~
     ~
     ~
     ~
     ~
     ~
     "trial" [New file]
```
Figure 6.3

The lines in the file are numbered sequentially starting from 1. These line numbers get readjusted if you delete any existing lines of text or insert new ones. By displaying the line numbers in this way makes using block commands a whole lot easier.

Once the line numbers are displayed we can issue the following sample block commands.

:2,4d	Deletes line numbers 2 to 4
:5,8 co 15	Copies line numbers 5 to 8 after line number 15

Pretty simple! However you may note a point. While copying lines if the destination line number is greater than the number of the last line in the file, then **vi** will not be able to carry out the copying. Hence an error message will be displayed saying "Not that many lines in the buffer". So make sure that you give proper line numbers while issuing block commands.

Figure 6.4 shows the various block commands that you can perform in **vi**.

Command	Function
:nd	Deletes n^{th} line.
:m,n d	Deletes lines from **m** to **n**.
:n mo p	Moves line **n** after line **p**.
:m,n mo p	Moves lines **m** to **n** after line **p**.
:m co p	Copies line **m** after line **p**.
:m,n co p	Copies lines **m** to **n** after line **p**.
:m,n w filename	Writes lines **m** to **n** to a file.
:m,n w >> filename	Appends lines **m** to **n** to a file.
:r filename	Reads the contents of the file **filename** at current cursor position.
:r !command	Executes shell command and output of the command is read at the current cursor position.

Figure 6.4

When you are through with using the block commands and no longer want the line numbers to be displayed you can easily deactivate them by saying,

> (Esc): set nonumber   or   (Esc): set nonu

Search, Search Everywhere...

Like any text editor **vi** too is equipped with a mechanism to search strings in a file. These strings are more correctly known as patterns. The patterns can be searched from beginning to end or from end to beginning. A lot of variations can be made in building the pattern to be searched. For example, if we want to search for all occurrences of words 'pale', 'pile' and 'pole' in one scan of the file we can use the pattern **p[aio]le**. This indicates that the second character can be any character out of 'a', 'i' and 'o'.

Examine the following patterns to get a hang of the things:

Pattern   Meaning

^part   Will search for all lines which begin with the word 'part'.

part$ Will search for all lines which end with the word 'part'.

\<part   Will search for all strings which begin with the word 'part'. Thus 'partner' would qualify whereas 'depart' would not.

part\>   Will search for all strings which end with the word 'part'. Thus 'depart' would qualify whereas 'partner' would not.

\<part\>   Only the whole word 'part' will qualify for the search, whereas the words 'partner' and 'depart' would not.

[m-s]ing   Will search for strings which contain any character in the range 'm' to 's' and is followed by 'ing'.

[^p]art   Will search for all strings which contain the characters 'art', with 'art' being preceded by any character other than 'p'. Hence words like 'tart', 'cart' etc. will qualify for the search whereas 'part' will not.

wing*   All words which begin with characters 'wing' and end with any characters would qualify for the search.

The special characters that can be used in building patterns are shown in Figure 6.5.

Character	Meaning
*	Zero or more characters
[ ]	A set or a range of characters
^	If given at the beginning of a pattern, forces the match to succeed at the beginning of the line
$	If given at the end of a pattern, forces the match to succeed at the end of the line.
\<	Forces the match to occur only at the beginning of a word.
\>	Forces the match to occur at the end of a word.
.	Matches any single character except the newline character.

Figure 6.5

If any of the special characters mentioned above themselves occur in the pattern to be searched then they must be preceded by a backslash (\) if they are to be treated as ordinary characters.

The following figure summarises the commands available for pattern searching.

Command	Function
/pattern	Searches forward in the buffer for the next occurrence of the pattern of text. Positions the cursor under the first character of the pattern.
?pattern	Searches backward in the buffer for the first occurrence of the pattern of text. Positions the cursor under the first character of the pattern.
n	Repeats the last search command.
N	Repeats the search command in the opposite direction.

Figure 6.6

While searching a pattern you may want to search all occurrences of the word irrespective of whether it is in capitals or smallcase or any combination of these. In such an event you can arrange to ignore the case of the word while searching by issuing the following command.

(Esc) :set ignorecase   or   (Esc) :set ic

Find and Replace

Quite often having searched a pattern we want to replace it with another suitable pattern. **vi** provides a facility to carry out such tasks with ease. Using these commands we can carry out drastic changes in files in one stroke. Learning how to use these commands is crucial towards attaining efficiency.

Figure 6.7 shows the most frequently used combinations for search and substitute.

Command	Function
: s/str1/str2	Replaces first occurrence of **str1** with **str2** in current line.
: s/str1/str2/g	Replaces all occurrences of **str1** with **str2** in current line.
: m,n s/str1/str2/g	Replaces all occurrences of **str1** with **str2** from lines **m** to **n**.
: 1, $ s/str1/str2/g	Replaces all occurrences of **str1** with **str2** from 1st line to end of file.
: 1, . s/str1/str2/g	Replaces all occurrences of **str1** with **str2** from 1st line to current line.
: ., $ s/str1/str2/g	Replaces all occurrences of **str1** with **str2** from current line to end of file.

Figure 6.7

In all the commands in figure 6.7 the **g** stands for global and goes hand-in-hand with the substitute command **s**.

Delete and Paste

vi forgives the last nine deletions that the user makes. However it does not forget them. The user can review his last nine deletions and undo the changes. Now that's a lot more than the poor undo command (u) can handle.

We know that the undo command helps correct only the last change that we have made to a document. For example, if you have deleted 4 lines using the command **4dd** then we can bring these lines back by undoing the last delete operation using the command **u**. If we are to go beyond this and undelete the last but one deletion that we have made then the **u** command is of no help.

vi being a powerful editor it can undo the last nine deletions. **vi** maintains registers (buffers) in memory (I don't know why they are called registers) in which it remembers the user's changes and deletions. Using these registers it can retrieve the last nine deletions made by a user.

To recover the last deletion that you may have made you'll have to press **"1p**. The double quote at the beginning is mandatory. It is followed by the name of the buffer i.e. 1. The **p** command pastes the line from the buffer after the current line. Similarly, if you press **"2p**, the second last deletion you made will be recovered. You can carry on this process till **"9p** to recover the last nine deletions. To undo more than 9 deletions use the following:

Command	Function
"xdd	Deletes current line and copies it to a buffer named **x**. (**x** can be any alphabet).
"xndd	Deletes **n** lines from current line and copies them to a buffer named **x**.
"xdw	Deletes current word and copies it to a buffer named **x**.
"xndw	Deletes **n** words from current cursor position and copies them to a buffer named **x**.
"xp	Pastes contents of buffer **x** at current cursor position.

Figure 6.8

Yank and Paste

Unlike delete when you yank objects (word, line, group of words or a group of lines) **vi** copies these objects into buffers without removing them from the file. These objects can then be pasted to another location in the file or even to different files.

"Yank" means to extract or remove. However, this meaning of yank is misleading since on yanking the objects are certainly not removed from the file. This is another example in Unix where the words mean one thing and perform something else.

The yanking commands are similar to the deletion commands as Figure 6.9 would justify.

Command	Function
yw	Yanks word from cursor position.
yy	Yanks line from from cursor position.
y$	Yanks line from cursor position to end of line.
y0	Yanks line from cursor position to beginning of line.

Figure 6.9

To paste the matter present in the yank buffers use the following commands.

Command	Function
1p	Pastes last yanked buffer.
2p	Pastes last but one yanked buffer.

Figure 6.10

Nine such yanked buffers can be pasted. To yank and paste more than nine buffers, use the following:

Command	Function
"xyy	Yanks current line to a buffer named **x** (**x** can be any alphabet).
"xnyy	Yanks **n** lines from current line to a buffer named **x**.
"xyw	Yanks current word to a buffer named **x**.
"xnyw	Yanks **n** words from current cursor position to a buffer named **x**
"xp	Pastes contents of buffer **x** at current cursor position.

Figure 6.11

abbr is for Abbreviate

In commonly used editors like Wordstar there exist facilities for using shorthand characters for commonly required expressions. These shorthand commands can be invoked at the press of a single key for the user's convenience.

In **vi**, this can be achieved using the **abbr** command which stands for abbreviation. Suppose you are typing a C program in **vi**. You are required to use the word **printf** quite often in C programming. Hence we can think of abbreviating this word as **pr**. To get this done use the command:

    (Esc) :abbr pr printf

Now when you're typing the program and you press 'p' followed by 'r' they appear on the screen as they are. But now if you follow them with a 'space' or the 'Enter' they are instantly overwritten by the word 'printf'. By building such shorthand expressions (often known as macros) for commonly occurring text you can improve your productivity.

To see the entire list of macros that you have set you can issue the command:

    (Esc) :abbr

You can confirm that your recently set macro **pr** is indeed present in the list that is displayed. While abbreviating text you should take care not to use **to** or **at** or **in** or such commonly used words for shorthand expressions. Otherwise when you type them they would be promptly replaced by the text they have been abbreviated for.

You can set a long list of abbreviations using this command. These abbreviations however would be forgotten the moment you quit out of **vi**. Towards the end of this chapter we would see how **vi** can be made to remember these abbreviations when we quit out of **vi** or even when we log out.

When not required you can unabbreviate the macro using the following command:

(Esc) :una pr

And your abbreviation is forgotten.

Figure 6.12 has captured the essence of the abbreviation command.

Command	Function
:abbr <abbreviation> <longform>	An abbreviation is defined for a longform. When we type the abbreviation followed by a space, it is replaced by its longform.
:abbr	Lists currently defined abbreviations.
:una <abbr>	Unabbreviates the abbreviation.

Figure 6.12

Set Commands

We have seen two set commands so far. **set nu** and **set ic**. The first one was used to associate line numbers with the file you are currently working with. The second was used to ignore the case while searching a pattern in the file.

In addition to these two there are several other options that the user can **set** to customize the environment of **vi**. A thorough knowledge of the **set** options will help the user make the **vi** environment friendlier and more convenient to work with. The options are numerous, as always. To get a list of all the options available with **set**, use the command:

(Esc) :set all

Though the list is long there are only a few which are most commonly used. A list of these along with the effect of each is shown in Figure 6.13.

Command	Function
:set nu	Set display of line numbers on.
:set nonu	Set display of line numbers off (default).
:set eb	Beep the speaker when an error occurs (default).
:set noeb	Do not beep the speaker when an error occurs.
:set ai	Set auto indent on.
:set noai	Set auto indent off (default).
:set ic	Ignore case while searching a pattern.
:set noic	Do not ignore case while searching a pattern (default).
:set terse	Make messages terse.
:set noterse	Do not make error messages terse (default).
:set mesg	Permit receipt of messages from other terminals.
:set nomesg	Don't receive messages from other terminals (default).
:set show-mode	Display mode in which we are working.
:set noshow-mode	Do not display current working mode (default).
:set aw	Automatically write buffer contents to disk before switching to next file during multiple file editing.
:set noaw	Do not write buffer contents to disk before switching to next file during multiple file editing (default).

Figure 6.13

Customizing the *vi* Environment

Whenever you load **vi** it searches for a file called **.exrc** in your default working directory. This file is optional. It may be created by users to suite their convenience. If absent no error message is flashed. If present any set commands or abbreviations that you may have stored in this file become automatically effective in all your sessions with **vi**. Since its name begins with a '.' this file is treated as a hidden file. This file can be created using **vi** itself. Typical contents of this file are shown below:

```
set nu
set showmode
```

```
set ai
set nomesg
abbr ys "Yours Sincerely"
abbr re "Reference no.:"
```

When **vi** loads itself, it will execute all the commands in the **.exrc** file first and then display the current file on the screen. The **.exrc** file is a convenient way to customize the **vi** environment and like all good things you should put it to utmost use to improve your efficiency.

Multiple File Editing in *vi*

Multiple file editors became available under DOS platform in early nineties, whereas **vi** offered this facility from its early days. It permits you to load and edit several files simultaneously. For example, if we are to edit files **tidbits**, **letter** and **memo** simultaneously we can load all of them while invoking **vi** by saying,

$ vi tidbits letter memo

Once into **vi** the first file in the file list (**tidbits** in our case) is displayed for editing.

We can as well use metacharacters while mentioning the files to be edited. For example, we can load all C programs in the current directory by saying,

$ vi *.c

At any moment if we are to find out the files that have been loaded for editing we can do so by saying,

(Esc) :args

This displays the list of files with the name of the file being currently edited enclosed within square brackets [].

Having completed editing of a file we can go to the next file by simply typing,

(Esc) :n

Whether we would be able to go to the next file or not depends upon whether we have made changes to the current file or not. If we have not made any changes to the current file then we are taken to the next file. However, if we have made changes to the current file, **vi** prevents switching to the next file till you indicate whether you want to save the changes or abandon them.

If you want to save them use the usual method of Shift ZZ. And if you want to go to the next file by abandoning any changes made to the current file then say,

(Esc) :n!

Unlike **n** there is no command available for editing the file previous to the current file in the files loaded for editing. However, we can go back to the very first file in the file list by using the rewind command as shown below:

(Esc) :rew

Again, if we have made changes to the current file **vi** would refuse to go to the first file unless you decide what should be done with the changes. Either save the changes and then use **rew**, or use **rew!** to abandon the changes and rewind to the first file.

It's quite possible that when we mention the file list for editing we forget to include some filename in the list. If we now want to edit this left out file we can easily do so by saying,

(Esc):e document

vi instantly loads the file **document** on the screen. Note that this filename doesn't get added to the file list given while invoking **vi**. You can confirm this using the **args** command. Now you can edit the file **document**, save it and once again return to your original file list.

The commands required for carrying out multiple file editing are given in Figure 6.14.

Command	Function
$vi file1 file2 file3	Loads 3 files, **file1**, **file2**, **file3** into the **vi** buffer for editing.
:n	Permits editing of the next file in the buffer.
:n!	Permits editing of next file without saving the current file.
:rew	Permits editing of the first file in the buffer.
:rew!	Permits editing of the first file without saving the current file.
:args	Displays names of all files in the buffer in which name of current file is enclosed within [ ].
:f	Displays the name of the current file.

Figure 6.14

Command Line Options in *vi*

So far we have been invoking **vi** by mentioning one or more file names to be edited. However, there exist a few more ways for invoking **vi**. These are mentioned in Figure 6.15.

Command	Function
$ vi +100 file	Loads **file** and places cursor on the 100th line in the file.
$ vi +/pattern file	Loads **file** and places cursor on the first occurrence of the matching pattern.
$ view file	Displays **file** in the read-only mode of **vi**. Any changes made to the buffer will not be allowed to be written to the file.

Figure 6.15

In the end let me say that decor wise **vi** is not the best editor around. But it functions, and functions like none other. Only thing is you need to cleanse your bias, broaden your mind and spend time with it to get used to its cryptic one letter commands. Believe me it takes time to do so even for the best players in the game. But once you acquire the skills you would support **vi** all your life. Truly, **vi** is as much a part of Unix as the soul is of the body.

Exercise

[A]   Answer the following:

(a)   What are the 3 modes of operations of **vi**?
(b)   Other than **vi** which other editors are usually available under Unix?
(c)   What is the purpose of **.exrc** file?
(d)   Which commands in **vi** would you use to perform the following operations?
-    Block copy
-    Block move
-    Block delete
(e)   Two consecutive lines are to be combined into one. Which **vi** command would you use to do so?
(f)   Which **vi** command would you use to perform the following cursor movement operations?

-    3 words to the right
-    4 words to the left
-    Top of screen
-    Bottom of screen
-    Beginning of current line
-    End of current line
-    Beginning of file
-    End of file
-    goto 100th line in the file

(g)   How will you perform the following deletions in **vi**?

-     Character at the cursor
-     One word from current cursor position
-     Current line
-     Next 4 lines
-     Line to the left of cursor
-     Line to the right of cursor

(h)   What is the difference between the following **vi** commands?

    :w
    :q!
    :wq
    ZZ

(i)   What is the difference between yank and delete?

(j)   There are five files available. How would you replace all occurrences of the word 'printf' in these files with the word 'PRINTF'?

(k)   In the middle of a file being typed you want to import the output of **who** command. How would you do this?

(l)   While editing a file "file1" you want to read of the line nos. 10 to 20 from "file2". Can you do this?

(m)   What is the effect of the following commands? Where these commands should ideally be stored?

    set nu
    set ai
    set eb
    set ic

[B]   Type in the following text exactly as shown below and then perform on it the operations listed at the end.

In order for Unix to survive into nineties, it must get rid of its intimidating commands and outmoded jargon, and become compatible with the existing standards of our day. To this end, our technicians have come up with new version of Unix, System VI, for use by the PC - that is, the "Politically Correct." Here is a brief extract from the release notes:

The "man" pages are now called "person" pages.

To avoid casting aspersions on our feline friends, the "cat" command is now merely "domestic_quadruped."

The bias of the "mail" command is obvious, and it has been replaced by the more neutral "gender" command.

The "more" command reflects the materialistic philosophy of the modern era. System VI uses the environmentally preferable "less" command.

To avoid unpleasant, medieval connotations, the "kill" command have been renamed "euthanise."

The "nice" command was historically used by privileged users to give themselves priority over unprivileged ones, by telling them to be "nice". In System VI, the "sue" command is used by unprivileged users to get for themselves the rights enjoyed by privileged ones.

The "abort()" function is now called "choice()"

From now on, "rich text" will be more accurately referred to as "exploitative capitalist text". The term "daemons" is a Judeo-Christian pejorative. Such processes will now be known as "spiritual guides."

There will no longer be an invidious distinction between "dumb" and "smart" terminals. All terminals are equally valuable.

For far too long, power has been concentrated in the hands of "root" and his "wheel" oligarchy. We have instituted a democracy of the users. All system administration functions will be handled by the People's Committee for Democratically Organising the System (PC-DOS).

And finally, Unix itself will be renamed "PC" - for Procreatively Challenged.

Global searches and replacements to be made:

(a) Change all full stops to semicolons.
(b) Change all occurrences of the word the or (The) to THE.
(c) Replace one or more spaces with a single space.
(d) Replace one or more spaces following a full stop or a comma with two spaces.
(e) Delete all blank lines. A blank line may contain whitespace characters like spaces and tabs.
(f) Insert a > and a space at the start of every line in the file.
(g) Reverse the order of lines in the file.

7

Processes in Unix

U nix as we know is a multi-user, multi-tasking operating system. It means at any instant there might be several programs of several users running in memory. All these programs share the CPU's attention between them. Thus by ensuring that the CPU doesn't remain idle the overall efficiency of the computer is improved. There is a common misconcept that a program and a process are one and the same thing. They are very nearly so except for one subtle difference. A program is elevated to the status of a process when it starts executing. Thus a process can be defined as the instance of an executing program.

Though there might be several processes running in memory at any given moment, the CPU can cater to only one of these processes as the other processes await their turn. There is a program called 'scheduler' running in memory which decides which process should get the CPU attention and when. At any given moment a process in memory can be in one of the six states.

When you execute a program the scheduler submits your process to a queue called process queue. At this instant the process is said to be in **submit** state. Once submitted the process waits its turn in the queue for some time. At this stage the process is said to be in **hold** state. As the process advances in the queue at some instant it would become the next one in the queue to receive CPU attention. At this stage it is in **ready** state. Finally the process gets the attention of CPU and starts getting executed and thereby attains the **run** state.

In the middle of this execution it might so happen that the time slice allotted to this process gets over and the CPU starts running another process. At such times the old process is returned to the **ready** state and is placed back in the process queue. As the CPU diverts its attention to the new process all the necessary parameters of the old process are saved for retrieval when its next time slice arrives. The old process will now be in **ready** state waiting for its next time slice to arrive.

Some processes might be required to do disk input/output. Since I/O is a slow operation the CPU can't lie idle till the time I/O is over. Therefore, such processes are put in **wait** state until their I/O is over and are then placed in the **ready** state.

A process whose execution comes to an end goes into **complete** state and is then removed from the process queue.

What's Running Right Now

Should you want to see which processes are running at any instant just type **ps** and hit enter.

```
$ ps
PID    TTY    TIME    COMMAND
2269   3a     0:05    sh
2396   3a     0:00    ps
```

Unix assigns a unique number to every process running in memory. This number is called process ID or simply PID. The PIDs start with 0 and run upto a maximum of 32767. When the maximum number is reached it starts counting all over again from 0 onwards.

The output of **ps** shows the PIDs for the two processes being run by us when **ps** was executed. The output also shows the terminal from which the processes were launched, the time that has elapsed since the processes were launched and the names of the processes.

How come that only two processes are listed when there might as well be several users who have logged in right now? That's because **ps** is designed to display only the processes that are running at your terminal.

Observe carefully that the first process running at your terminal is **sh**. This stands for Bourne shell. This process is born the moment you login and dies only when you log out of the system. The other process that is running is **ps** itself. This process was obviously running when **ps** took the snapshot of memory to determine which processes were running.

Should you want to find out which processes are running for the other users who have logged in execute the **ps** command with the **-a** option, **-a** standing for processes of all the users.

```
$ ps -a
PID    TTY    TIME    COMMAND
2269   3a     0:05    sh
2396   3a     0:00    ps -a
2100   3b     0:00    sh
2567   3b     0:00    vi
```

If you want to see what a particular user is doing just say **ps -u user1** where **-u** stands for user and **user1** for his login name.

Don't you think that your security and privacy is getting violated if other users can find out what you are doing. True. But the kernel has decided to let anybody find out what's running in memory. So you will have to live with this small quirk.

Another useful option available with **ps** is **-t**. It lets you find out the processes that have been launched from a particular terminal. For example,

```
$ ps -t tty3d
```

would list all processes which have been executed from terminal **tty3d**. When the terminal file begins with the word 'tty' we are permitted to drop this word and just say **ps -t 3d** to get the same results.

Remember that **ps** always lists those processes which are in memory at the instant it was executed. It means that if some other user is working with a C program it may so happen that this process would not be listed by **ps -a** since at the instant **ps -a** took the snapshot of memory the user may just have completed the execution of the C program and returned to $ prompt. That's why the output of **ps** always contains **ps** itself as one of the running processes since it is obviously active when the snapshot is taken.

There's a lot of additional information that Unix stores about each running process. This information can be obtained by using the option **-f**, standing for full listing.

```
$ ps -f
UID    PID   PPID  C  STIME     TTY  TIME COMMAND
icit   288   1     1  09:32:25  02   0:01 -sh
icit   513   288   8  09:51:07  02   0:00 ps -f
```

A process is 'born' the moment it starts executing and is 'dead' once it terminates. For a process to be 'born' another process should give birth to it. In the Unix jargon the new process is called the 'child' whereas the process that starts it is called the 'parent'.

The child born out of a parent can then become a parent by giving birth to another child process. In the above output you can observe the field PPID which stands for the PID of the parent process. For example, the process **ps -f** in the above output has a PID 513, whereas its parent's PID is 288. Since **ps -f** was launched by the shell, PPID of **ps -f** is same as PID of **sh**. This way we can trace the ancestry of any process, right till the very first process, the **sched** who is the father of all.

Still More Processes

So far we have encountered only the processes associated with individual users. But there are several more running in memory which are necessary for the system to work. For example, there is a scheduler process running at all times in memory which schedules the CPU time and memory amongst all other processes and users. The following command would help you confirm this.

```
$ ps -e
  PID TTY  TIME    COMMAND
    0 ?    0:00    sched
    1 ?    0:01    init
    2 ?    0:00    vhand
    3 ?    0:00    bdflush
  487 01   0:01    sh
  288 02   0:01    sh
  289 03   0:00    getty
  100 ?    0:00    logger
  145 ?    0:00    cron
  290 04   0:00    getty
  151 ?    0:00    lpsched
  275 ?    0:00    deliver
  512 3h   0:00    vi
  514 02   0:00    ps
  295 05   0:00    getty
  296 06   0:00    getty
  297 07   0:00    getty
  298 08   0:00    getty
  299 09   0:00    getty
  300 10   0:00    getty
  301 11   0:00    getty
  302 12   0:00    getty
  303 ?    0:00    sdd
  304 3a   0:00    getty
  305 3b   0:00    getty
  306 3c   0:00    getty
```

307	3d	0:00	getty
308	3e	0:00	getty
309	3f	0:00	getty
310	3g	0:00	getty
311	3h	0:01	sh

Here, -e stands for every process running at that instant. Note the PID of the process **sched**. This is the scheduler that we talked about and is the first process that gets launched when the machine is booted. **sched** process gives birth to the initialiser process **/etc/init**. That's the reason why PPID of **/etc/init** would be 0. **init** is a file on disk present in the **/etc** directory. The **vhand** process is the 'virtual memory handler' and the task cut out for it is to swap active processes between memory and disk as they run or wait their turn in the queue to be processed by the system. Since **vhand** is launched after **init** its PID is 2. Another process of interest is **bdflush** standing for buffer to disk flush and is responsible for disk I/O. When we attempt to store something to the disk first it gets stored in a buffer in memory. When the buffer gets full its contents are then flushed (emptied) to the disk.

Since all these processes support the activities of the system and go about their task independent of what users are doing these processes are known as 'system processes'.

The processes such as **vhand**, **bdflush** and **sched** are housed in the kernel file **/unix** and are popularly known as 'daemons'. These processes are constantly running in the background. Daemon processes are characterised by the fact that they run without the user requesting them to do so. These processes are neither linked with a user nor with a terminal. These processes are created when the system boots up and remain active until the system is halted or shut down.

Background Processes

Most of the system processes run in the background, while the users execute their processes in the foreground. If the user so desires even he can run his processes in the background. Using this facility of Unix the user can run time-consuming tasks like sorting a huge file and storing the sorted output in a file in the background. This way he would not be required to wait till the sorting is over to be able to run the next process. He can immediately concentrate on another task the moment sorting process is submitted to run in the background.

To run a process in the background, Unix provides the ampersand (&) symbol. While executing a command, if this symbol is placed at the end of the command then the command will be executed in the background. When you run a process in the background a number is displayed on the screen.

This number is nothing but the PID of the process that you have just executed in the background. Let's understand this with an example.

```
$ sort employee.dat > emp.out &
17653
$
```

The task of sorting the file **employee.dat** and storing the output in **emp.out** has now been assigned to the background, letting the user free to carry out any other task in the foreground.

Though the facility to run processes in the background is of great advantage, it comes with a few limitations too. These are:

(a) On termination of a background process no success or failure is reported on the screen. Then how do we keep track of it? That's where the PID displayed on the screen (17653 in the above example) comes in handy. We can search for this PID in the output of **ps** to verify whether the process is still running or has been terminated.

(b) The output of a background process should always be redirected to a file. Otherwise you would get a garbled screen showing the output of the background process along with whatever you are doing in the foreground.

(c) With too many processes running in the background the overall system performance is likely to degrade.

(d) If you log out while some of your processes are running in the background all these processes would be abandoned halfway through. This is natural because all your processes are children/grandchildren/great grandchildren of your **sh** (shell) process. And when we log out the **sh** process dies along with all its children.

The *nohup* command

If we are to ensure that the processes that we have executed should not die even when we log out, the **nohup** command is the answer. Using this command we can submit the time consuming commands in the background, log out and leave the terminal and come next day to see our output ready. Appropriately, **nohup** stands for no hang ups.

The **nohup** command's usage is shown below:

```
$ nohup sort employee.dat > output.emp
17695
```

Now we can safely log out (without any hangups) without our process getting terminated on logging out. If all goes well with the sorting then our output would be ready in **output.emp** which can be verified when we log in next time.

Note that if we do not redirect the output of our background process the command acts intelligently and stores the output in the file 'nohup.out'.

```
$ nohup  sort  employee.dat
16779
Sending output to nohup.out
$
```

The 'nohup.out' file is always created in the current directory.

Another small issue. If the **nohup** command is used in a pipeline care should be exercised to precede every command in the pipeline by the word **nohup** as shown below. This would see to it that all the processes in the pipeline remain alive when the user logs out. If not done, the command which is not preceded by **nohup** will die when you log out. And if one process in the pipeline dies, the entire pipeline is bound to collapse as in the following command.

```
$ nohup cat employee.dat I nohup grep 'Nagpur' I sort  >  addresses &
12695
$
```

Killing A Process

Some of the reasons why you would like to terminate a process in the middle of its execution are mentioned below:

(a)   The terminal has hung. A typical example of this is when you attempt to **cat** a directory file.

(b)   The program which is running has gone in an indefinite loop and hence is not getting terminated.

(c)   The system performance has gone below acceptable limits because of too many processes running in the background. As a result, you may want to terminate a few time consuming processes.

In any of the above situations you would like to 'kill' the process. To carry out this killing we must first note the PID of the process to be killed using the **ps** command. Then we must employ this PID and the **kill** command to terminate the process. Here's an example.

```
$ cat employee.dat | grep 'Nagpur' | sort > output.dat &
6173
$
```

If the above background process is to be killed we must execute the following command.

```
$ kill 6173
6173 Terminated.
```

Let us understand how the **kill** command works. When invoked, it sends a termination signal to the process being killed. A signal is a mechanism to communicate with a process. These signals have been given numbers. In the above example we have not communicated the signal number to the process to be killed. Hence, the default signal number was sent to the process requesting it to terminate. This default signal is same as the one generated when you hit the Del key in the middle of a **ls** or **cat** command. This default signal however is not very powerful and may not be able to kill a process at all times. A good example is the **sh** process which cannot be terminated by this default signal. At such times we can employ signal number 9, the 'sure kill' signal to forcibly terminate a process as shown below:

```
kill -9 2316
```

How can you employ kill if your terminal has hung? Simple. Login once again through another terminal (yes a user can login from several terminals simultaneously). Then run the **who** command and **tty** command to figure out the number of the terminal which has hung. Next use the command **ps -t ttynumber** to find out the PID of the shell running on the hung terminal. Finally, using this PID number and the sure kill signal terminate the **sh** process. Next moment, the hung terminal would spring back to life and would once again show the login prompt.

There are processes which cannot be killed even by the sure kill signal. For example, the system processes like **sched** or **vhand** cannot be killed using the sure kill signal. This is quite reasonable, because if these processes get killed the entire Unix OS would collapse.

Another important point. You can kill only your processes and not those fired by other users. Superuser of course enjoys an altogether different status. He can kill any of the user's processes easily.

Changing Process Priorities

Though all processes are equal, some processes are more equal than others. They can be made so by increasing their priority. The processes with higher priority would obviously get a time slot earlier and would be fired earlier than the other processes in the queue.

The priority of a process is decided by a number associated with it. This number is called 'nice' value of the process. Though paradoxical, higher the nice value of a process lower is its priority. The nice value of a process can range from 0 to 39, with 20 as the default nice value of a process. Thus, a process with a nice value 25 would execute slower than the one with a nice value 20. Let's try to increase the nice value of one of our processes.

        $ nice cat employee.dat

This would increase the nice value of our **cat** process from 20 to 30. Since, we didn't specify the increment, an increment of 10 got assumed and the nice value got correspondingly incremented. If we so desire, we can specify the value of the increment.

        $ nice -15 cat employee.dat

Now the **cat** process will have a nice value 35 (20+15). Note that the increment can range from 0 to 19. By incrementing the nice value we are putting **cat** on a lower priority and hence it would be executed slower than what it does normally.

It sounds logical that if we can increase the nice value of a process we must as well be able to decrease it and thereby put our process on a higher priority. Wishful thinking. However hard we try, we as users can never decrease the nice value of our process. That's fair enough. Otherwise, every single user would try to put each of his processes on the highest priority. As you must have guessed, it's only the superuser who can put a process on a higher priority by reducing its nice value. That's another reason why you should try to maintain healthy relations with the superuser, so that at times you can request him to do you a favour by putting your process on a higher priority. The superuser can reduce the nice value of a process as shown below:

```
# nice --10 sort employee.dat > output.dat
```

When would the user like to increase the nice value of a process? After all, why would anybody wish to put his process on a lower priority! Remember a Unix user is expected to be reasonable and follow some ethics. If your process is going to be time consuming and is going to degrade the system performance, then you should always run the process in the background with a higher nice value.

Note that the priority of a process can be changed at the time of firing the process at command prompt. Once the process has been submitted to the process queue its priority cannot be changed.

You can see the nice values of the various processes running in memory using **ps -l**.

```
$ ps -l
 F  S  UID PID  PPID C  PRI NI  ....  TTY TIME CMD
20  S  214 290  1    1  30  20  ....  01  0:01 sh
20  O  214 363  290  7  63  20  ....  01  0:00 ps
```

In the above output the column with the heading NI indicates the nice value of a process.

Let's now seek some proof that a command with a higher nice value indeed runs slower than normal. For this we can employ the **time** command. It helps us to figure out the time taken to execute a command. Here's how it does so...

```
$ time ls -laR > dirlist.out
real 0.3
user0.0
sys 0.1
```

Note that in the above command we have redirected the output of **ls** so that it doesn't mix up with the output of the **time** command. The output of **time** command doesn't get redirected since the output of the **time** command is written to the standard error device, i.e. the screen.

The 'real' time in the above output represents the time taken by the command to execute since its initiation to its termination. The 'user' time represents the amount of time that the command/program took to execute its own code. For small programs which take milliseconds to execute, this time is often reported as 0.0, as in the above case. The 'sys' time represents the time taken by Unix to fire the command.

Let's now time the same command by executing it with a higher nice value.

```
$ time nice -19 ls -laR > directlist.out
real 0.6
user0.0
sys 0.2
```

Note that this time the process consumes a significantly higher time to execute. However, the time taken (user time) by the command to execute its own code has remained same.

Scheduling of Processes

Any multitasking OS must provide tools to permit scheduling of processes as per the user's/system's requirements. Unix is no exception to this. In fact Unix's understanding of time is marvellous, as you would soon realise. It can schedule processes to get executed within next few seconds to next few years. Once the user has submitted a process to Unix directing it to execute the process at a specified time and date in future, there onwards Unix takes over. Unix manages to remember the processes to be executed and goes about executing them whenever the time arises without needing any further directions from the user. That's the philosophy of scheduling processes. Now let us understand its mechanism.

Execute the following command:

```
$ ps -e | grep cron
147  ?  0:01    cron
```

Here the process **cron** stands for chronograph. This system process is responsible for scheduling the other processes. Neither user nor superuser can execute the executable file (**/etc/cron**) of this process directly. During booting Unix executes this file and displays the message 'cron started' on the host terminal. Once Unix launches this process there onwards **cron** is activated once every minute. When **cron** wakes up it checks whether any scheduled job is available for it to execute. If it is, it executes the job and goes back to sleep again, only to wake up the next minute to once again carry out the check. This cycle goes on till the Unix system isn't shut down on the host machine. There are three commands which make use of the **cron** daemon's scheduling capability. These are **at**, **batch** and **crontab**. Let's have a look at them one by one.

The *at* command

This command is capable of executing Unix commands at a future date and time. The Unix commands can be specified at the command prompt or can be stored in a file and the **at** command can use this file to execute the commands. Both these facilities are exemplified below.

```
$ tty
/dev/tty3c

$ date
Fri Jun 14 10:57:23 IST 1996

$ at 17:00
clear > /dev/tty3c
echo "It's 5 PM ! Backup your files and logout" > /dev/tty3c
Ctrl d
Job 803108760.a at Fri Jun 14 17:00:00 IST 1996
```

Observe that on pressing Ctrl d the **at** command displayed the job-id and the date and time we requested the two commands **clear** and **echo** to be executed. The job-id always terminates with a '.a' indicating that this job was submitted using the **at** command.

Once submitted this way, the message would be echoed on our terminal at 5.00 PM sharp. Is it necessary to redirect the output of **clear** and **echo** to our 'tty' file? Yes, otherwise the output of these commands would arrive as **mail** from the **cron** daemon. Let us see how.

```
$ at 17:00
echo "It's 5 PM! Backup your files and logout"
Ctrl d
Job 853158864.a at Wed Jun 14 17:00:00 IST 1996
```

At 5 PM in the evening you would see a message on your screen saying 'you have mail'. To examine what have you received in mail just type

```
$ mail
SCO System V Mail (version 3.2) Type? for help.
"/usr/spool/mail/icit": 1 message  1 new
1 cron        Wed Jun 14 11:50 14/405
&

message 1:
From cron Wed Jun 14 11:50:03 1996
From: cron@scosysv.UUCP (Cron daemon)
X-Mailer: SCO System V Mail (version 3.2)
To: user1
Date: Wed, 14 Jun 96 11:50:02 IST
Message-ID: <9607141150.aa00570@scostsv.UUCP
Status: R

It's 5.00 PM! Back up your files and logout.

Cron: The previous message is the standard output and standard
error of one of your cron commands.
$
```

That's a very comprehensive mail indeed! The last two lines clarify that this mail is in fact the standard output of commands executed by **cron**.

There are two options available with the **at** command which permit us to view the list of jobs submitted using **at** and to remove any unwanted jobs from this job queue. These options are **-l** for listing jobs and **-r** for removing jobs. While removing a submitted job its job-id should be mentioned. In fact, that's the reason why the jobs are given *ids* - for easy identification.

```
$ at  -r  853158864.a
```

would remove the job '853158864.a' from the job queue.

While specifying the time **at** command permits a lot of flexibility. Following are some of the specifications that can be used with **at**.

```
$ at  0915 am Mar 24
$ at  9:15 am Mar 24
$ at  now + 10 minutes
$ at  now + 1 day
$ at  7 pm Thursday next week
```

Let's now look at another way of executing the **at** command. Instead of specifying the commands at the prompt, here we would make **at** read them from a file and then execute them. Let's first create this commands file.

```
$ cat > cmdfile
clear
echo "Hi there! Do you never get bored with working?"
Ctrl d
```

Now we can ask the **at** command to read the commands from **cmdfile** as shown below.

```
$ at 5 PM < cmdfile
Job 853158870.a at Fri Jun 14 17:00:00 IST 1996
```

Now the **at** command will read the commands from **cmdfile** and execute them at 5 PM. Since we have not redirected the output to our terminal it would be mailed to us by **cron**.

The power of **at** command can be harnessed only by a select few and not by every Tom, Dick and Harry. These select few are decided by the System Administrator by placing their login names in a file **at.allow** present in the **/user/lib/cron** sub-directory. Only those users whose login name appears in this file are permitted to use the **at** command. If for some crooked reason your relations with the System

Administrator get strained then all that he has to do is delete your name from **at.allow** and include it in another file called **at.deny**. Having black-listed you this way, you would never be able to use the **at** command.

Needless to say, only the System Administrator can edit the files **at.allow** and **at.deny** to include or delete the login names.

Assuming that our login name appears in **at.deny** let us try the **at** command.

> $ at 5 PM
> at: you are not authorized to use at. sorry.

Moral is, you cannot afford to be on bad terms with the System Administrator.

The *batch* command

Instead of we specifying that our commands be executed at a precise moment in time sometimes we may let the system decide the best time for executing our commands. The way to achieve this is through a command called **batch**. When we submit our jobs using this command, Unix executes our job when it is relatively free and the system load is light. Since the time of execution of our commands is left for the system to decide we don't specify the time while executing the **batch** command.

> $ batch
> sort employee.dat | grep Nagpur > addresses.out
> Ctrl d
> job 692322435.b at Fri Jun 14 17:00:00 IST 1996

Once again note that the 'b' extension given to our job-id signifies that it has been submitted using the batch command.

The *crontab* command

Though **at** and **batch** are powerful tools for scheduling processes, both suffer from an obvious limitation. Once jobs submitted using these commands have been executed, the jobs will have to be rescheduled if they are to be carried out again. For example, if we want to backup all our C program files at the end of the day then we may do so as follows

```
$ at 5 PM
cp *.c ./cbackup
```

However, we must remember to issue such an **at** command every morning to be able to take backups every evening without fail. What if we forget to issue the **at** command some day? The backups won't be taken. It's as simple as that.

This is where the **crontab** command excels over **at**. It can carry out a submitted job every day for years together, without needing any prompting from us. The jobs can be carried out on a regular basis using the **crontab** command as shown below:

```
$ crontab  cmdfile
```

However, this time **cmdfile** should not only contain commands which we wish to get executed but also the details of date and time in a specific format. This format is shown below:

```
Minute   Hour  Day of Month   Month of year  Day of week  Command
```

Using this format let us create our **cmdfile**.

```
$ cat > cmdfile
30 10  1   *   *    echo "Work hard on first day of the month"
0   0  17  11  *    mail aa2 < confi.letter
Ctrl d
$
```

Let us understand the commands that we have given in our **cmdfile**. The first one would be used to echo the message at 10:30 am on first day of every month. The second message would mail the contents of the file **confi.letter** to the user **aa2** on 17th November of every year.

Note that each field in **cmdfile** is separated either by a space or a tab. For the 'Month of year' and 'Day of week' fields we have used a '*'. A '*' means all possible values. Another thing to note is that Sunday is represented as 0 in the 'Day of week' field.

When we execute the **crontab** command using the **cmdfile**

> $ crontab cmdfile

the contents of **cmdfile** are automatically transferred to the **/user/spool/cron/crontabs** directory where they are stored in a file which has the same name as your login name. There onwards the **cron** daemon will read this file and execute the commands present in it on a regular basis.

As with the **at** command we can view the commands that we have submitted by using the **-l** option with the **crontab** command.

> $ crontab -l

Likewise, to remove the submitted job we can use

> $ crontab -r

Here we are not required to specify the job-id since using **crontab** we can submit only one command file. If we want to schedule a few more jobs we need to edit the **cmdfile** in our home directory and then resubmit it using

> $ crontab cmdfile

Once again **cmdfile**'s contents would be transferred to **/usr/spool/cron/crontabs** directory and would be stored in a file with our login name. Obviously, the earlier file with this name would be overwritten.

As with **at**, here also there are two files **cron.allow** and **cron.deny** which decide which users are permitted and which are prevented from using the **crontab** command.

Exercise

[A]   Answer the following:

(a)   What do the terms UID, PID and PPID stand for? For a particular process which is currently executing how can you obtain these values?

(b)   How will you terminate a process which has gone in an infinite loop?

(c)   Which are the different states in which a process can be?

(d)   What are the advantages and disadvantages of running a process in the background?

(e)   Having run a process in the background if you log out what would happen to the process? How would you overcome this problem?

(f)   What do you mean by a 'Daemon'? How will you kill a Daemon?

(g)   If the nice value of a process is increased, what would be the effect on the speed of execution of the process?

(h)   Can we change the nice value of a process which is already present in memory?

(i)   How will you find out how much time is required to execute a particular process?

(j)   What are the contents of the file **/usr/lib/cron/at.deny**? Can an ordinary user modify its contents?

(k)   Where would be the output of following command stored?

nohup sort aaa bbb ccc

(l) Which processes cannot be killed using the **kill** command?
(m) How would you decrease the priority of a particular process?
(n) How will you find out which jobs have been submitted for execution? Can you remove a job which has been submitted for execution? If yes, how?
(o) How will you find out which processes have been launched from a specific terminal?
(p) What's the difference between scheduling processes using **batch** command and using **at** command?
(q) How will you schedule a process which should wish you happy birthday on each of your birthday throughout the rest of your life?

[B] What would the following commands do?

(a) at 0915am Mar 24
echo "Good Morning"
date
Ctrl d

(b) at 18:32 tomorrow
echo "Happy Birthday"
Ctrl d

(c) at now + 15 minutes
clear
ls -l
Ctrl d

(d) at 6pm wednesday next week
who
uptime
Ctrl d

(e)   at now + 1 week < atfile

(f)   batch
       sort * > bigfile &
       Ctrl d

(g)   batch < batchfile

(h)   nohup cat * | sort -d &

(i)   nohup cat bigfile &

8 Communication - Unix Style

A social creature that man is, the urge to communicate is inherent and integral to human nature. Back in the days of the tom-toms, who would have thought that some day men would take in their stride talking to someone on the other side of the earth? Clearly, someone did. Trust the human brain to materialise what it has the power to imagine. While the universe is expanding, the world is shrinking with the electronic media bridging all distances. Quite naturally computer the sagest of all electronic devices got into the act too. And as man started communicating through computers Unix OS running on the computers led the way, armed with ingenious software that took advantage of the almost total hardware independence achieved by it. A direct application of a network system, communication is handled expertly by Unix. Let us examine one by one what tools it offers.

The *write* Command

The write command can be used by any user to write something on someone else's terminal, provided the recipient of the message permits communication.

```
$ write  user2
Hey there! I am back from Paris.
Just wanted to say Hello!
- Your favourite Chimp
Ctrl d
```

On executing this command the message would be relayed to the user whose login name is **user2**. He would hear a beep on his terminal, followed by the message:

> Message from user1 on unix (tty3a) [Thu Oct 15 17:13:58]....
> Hey there! I am back from Paris.
> Just wanted to say Hello!
> - Your favourite Chimp
> (end of message)

Now "user2" may respond as follows:

> $ write user1
> Alas! I was hoping you would fall off the Eiffel Tower.
> Anyway, now that you have come let's celebrate.
> - Your Ethnic beauty
> Ctrl d

There are two prerequisites for a smooth **write** operation:

(a)   The recipient must be logged in, else an error message is inevitable.

(b)   The recipient must have given permission for messages to reach his or her terminal. This is done by saying at the $ prompt

> $ mesg -y

If you are expecting nothing of consequence and do not wish to be disturbed by social trivia like the one we just saw, you can deny write permission to your terminal by saying

> $ mesg -n

A superuser however can write to any terminal, irrespective of whether **mesg** has been set to **-y** or **-n**. For all lesser mortals, it is a good idea to first ascertain who all are logged in and who allow messages to be written to their terminals and then run the **write** command. There are two ways to do so. **finger** is one command that tells you which users are connected and which, if any, can receive messages. It displays a list of all those who have logged in and places a * next to those terminals where **mesg** is set to **-n**.

```
$ finger -i
Login    TTY        When              Idle
veena    *tty01     Fri Oct 13 17:25  8 minutes 12 seconds
prafull  tty3f      Fri Oct 13 17:21  49 seconds
user3    tty3a      Fri Oct 13 16:59
user2    *tty3c     Fri Oct 13 14:46
user1    *tty3e     Fri Oct 13 13:59
```

Another command that may be used for the purpose is **who -T**. The **who** command lists all the users who are currently logged in. When used with the **-T** option, it places a '+' next to the users who have allowed messages and a '-' sign beside others.

```
$ who -T
veena   - tty01   Oct 13 17:25
prafull + tty3f   Oct 13 17:21
user3   + tty3e   Oct 13 16:59
user2   - tty3a   Oct 13 14:46
user1   - tty3c   Oct 13 13:59
```

Let's now try to write to somebody who has set **mesg** to **n** on his terminal.

```
$ write user3
Permission denied.
$
```

Suppose we decide to send message to a user who has set **mesg** to **y**, whereas you have set it to **n** at your terminal. Let's see what happens if in such a case we decide to send message from our terminal.

```
$ write user2
```

Imagine the progress that man has made in communication since the days of smoke signals and carrier pigeons!
Warning: You have your terminal set to "mesg -n". No reply possible.

The warning is quite self-explanatory.

Let us imagine another variation. Suppose a user has logged in at more than one terminal and you want to send a message only to one terminal. In such a case you need to specify which particular terminal you want the message to go to as shown below:

```
$ write  user2  tty3c
Had I known grandchildren are so much fun I would have had them
first!
Ctrl d
```

Thus, even if **user2** has logged in at **tty3a** and **tty3b** apart from **tty3c**, the message will only go to **tty3c**. What if we do not mention the terminal to which the message should be sent?

```
$ write  user2
user2 is logged on at more than one place
You are connected to "tty3a"
Other locations are :
tty3b
tty3c
The greatest accomplishments have been made by individuals acting
alone. There is never a statue dedicated to a committee.
Ctrl d
```

Let us try to understand what exactly happened. The **write** command found that **user2** has logged in at more than one place. So it connected you to the terminal **tty3a** since this is decided by a precedence of port connections of a terminal. This is **write** command's own solution in case of confusion - quite smart, you would agree.

The *wall* Command

This command can only be used by the superuser. Among the various privileges enjoyed by him is the ability to write to any user on the network. **wall** enables the superuser to 'write to all' irrespective of whether the users have given write permission to their terminals or not. The superuser, or the system administrator can take a number of such liberties, and not without reason. If the Unix system is going to be shutdown in say 10 minutes time, it is upto the system administrator to warn all connected users and notify them to save whatever they are working on. He does so using **wall**. The **wall** command must be given as:

```
# /etc/wall
System shutting down in 10 minutes.
You are advised to take the required backups.
Ctrl d
```

All users who are logged in, will hear a beep and see a message flashed on their screens as follows:

```
Broadcast Message from root (tty01) on unix May 15 9:37 1996
System shutting down in 10 minutes.
You are advised to take the required backups.
```

The **wall** program resides in **/etc** directory and since this directory is not in our path we have to give the command as **/etc/wall** rather than just **wall**. Observe that the command prompt is shown as # and not the usual $, as that is the prompt the superuser works at.

Why not pose ourself as superuser and try to post messages to everybody's terminal.

```
$ /etc/wall
You don't have to look far to see a miracle. Here I am, posting mes-
sages to you even when I am not a superuser.
Ctrl d
```

Broadcast Message from (user1) on scosysv Apr 19 18:30 1996...
You don't have to look far to see a miracle. Here I am, posting messages to you even when I am not a superuser.
Cannot send to user6 on /dev/tty01
open: Permission denied
Cannot send to prafull on /dev/tty3f
open: Permission denied
Cannot send to user3 on /dev/tty3e
open: Permission denied
Cannot send to aa5 on /dev/tty3a
open: Permission denied

The above messages indicate we have been able to broadcast the
message to nobody except ourselves. Unix seems to have made a
correct estimate of our smartness.

What's The News Today

The system administrator is the sole person who can make news under
the Unix OS. He types the information which he wants everyone on
the network to know of in different files in **/usr/news** directory.
Whenever we log in if any fresh news has come in since we logged
out last time then a message is displayed on our terminal saying,

news: rally tennis appeal

where **rally**, **tennis** and **appeal** are the names of the files in which
the news items are available.

We may either choose to ignore it, or if any news item interests us
we may decide to peruse the same. To read the news, we have to say
at the dollar prompt:

$ news
rally (root) Sat Apr 19, 17:45:56 1996

Leander Paes has reached the Wimbledon finals and was having a very loooonnnggggg rally with Pete Sampras when this news item was posted.

tennis (root) Sat Apr 19, 15:54:53 1996

World Tennis Association in its annual general meeting has decided that points in tennis would be counted as 1, 2, 3 etc. rather than from 15, 30, 40 etc. Another resolution was passed that the day an Asian wins a grand slam event it would be declared as World Tennis Day.

appeal (root) Sat Apr 19, 13:25:33 1996
The Prime Minister has asked us to rededicate ourselves towards achieving this goal. He has also declared that children of all schools in the country would be given mid day meals every day and a tennis ball every month such that children would come to school at least to have a ball. He opined that the day is not far when India will have a Wimbledon champion not only in every metro but also in every city, district, town, village etc. What a ball!

And yes, Leander won that rally!

Note that the news items are displayed in such a manner that the most recent item is displayed first. Once the news is read by a user, a file **.news_time** gets created in the user's home directory. This file is of zero bytes and its time of creation is used to find out when the user accessed the news. The next time the user says **news** at the dollar prompt, Unix compares the time at which the news item was posted and the creation time of **.news_time** file. Only if the news item has been posted after the time that is recorded with **.news_time** will anything be displayed on the screen, else Unix refuses to display stale news. We can get around this by using the **-a** option with **news. news -a** shows 'all' the news, stale or new (in such a case the time recorded with **.news_time** is not updated). Another option could be to delete the file **.news_time**. If this file is absent then news always gets displayed.

When there are multiple news items, the **news** command tends to display them all at a time, and the messages often scroll off the screen very fast. To prevent fast scrolling it would be a good idea to pipe the output of **news** to **more** so that you can read the news more comfortably.

If you want to peruse only a particular item from the several items then you can say,

> $news rally
> rally (root) Sat Apr 19, 13:45:56 1996
>
> Leander Paes has reached the Wimbledon finals and was having a very loooonnnggggg rally with Pete Sampras when this news item was posted.

If you decide to peruse all the news items and as the news is being displayed on your terminal you come across an item in which you are not interested just hit the delete key. Immediately that news item would be abandoned and it would start displaying the next item. If you hit the delete key twice in close succession then the first delete key would abandon the news item being displayed and the second one would return you to the dollar prompt.

There are two more options available with the **news** command. The **-n** option only lists the names of the news items from the **/usr/news** directory that have not yet been read by you.

> $ news -n
> news: teleconf urgentnote chitchat

Instead of this list if you wish to find out only the number of news items that have not been read by you then you may use the **-s** option which provides a count of the unread new items in the **/usr/news** directory.

> $ news -s

5 news items.

If you try **news -s** after you have gone through all the news item it promptly displays the message 'No news'.

motd is for Message of The Day

The 'message of the day' like the news, is typed by the superuser in the file **/etc/motd**. In case of the **news** command it is entirely the user's discretion whether to read the news or not. As against this the user doesn't have a choice whether to read the message of the day or not. Reading the message of the day is mandatory, as it is displayed as soon as you login. As soon as you login a file **/etc/profile** file gets executed. This file contains a command **cat /etc/motd.** As a result the contents of **/etc/motd** are bound to get displayed on the screen. When I logged in I found the following message on my screen.

The air-conditioning system needs a maintenance check! Hence the system would be down between 2.00 to 5.00 PM. See you at 5.00.

The **/etc/profile** is like our good old AUTOEXEC.BAT of DOS. It gets executed every time the user logs in. In addition every user has his own **.profile** file in his home directory using which he can customize his working environment. The sequence of execution of these files is **/etc/profile** followed by **.profile**.

As you must have guessed it is only the superuser who can change the contents of the file **/etc/motd**.

Mail: The Basis of Unix Communication

Using **mail** you can quickly and efficiently circulate memos and other written information to your co-workers, including directions for the out of town party this Saturday and the latest meanderings. You can even send and receive mail from people outside your organization, if you and they use networked computers.

write requires that the user to whom the message is to be sent not only to be logged in, but also open to messages. Unlike this, mail can be sent to users who have logged in currently or even to users who haven't logged in currently. In case the user has logged in at several terminals the moment mail is sent to this user it becomes available at all the terminals.

Sending Mail

This is pretty simple. We have to pick up the logname of the recipient of the mail and say:

```
$ mail  user2
Subject: Unix course
It is overheard that the system administrator plans to conduct a 4 day
crash course in Unix. Don' join it. Between you and me, nothing
crashes like a crash course. After all nothing worthwhile is ever learnt
in 10 easy lessons.
Ctrl d
```

As shown above you are prompted for the subject or the header to be attributed to the message. Having given the subject, you type in your message and end it by hitting Ctrl d.

If in one go you want to send the same mail to more than one user, you can say

```
$ mail  user2  user3  user4
Subject: Think over it!
Yesterday I visited a hospital. There was a sign above the patient's
bed. It read "I have cancer but the cancer doesn't have me". I was so
touched. I thought about it all night.
Ctrl d
```

If you are to mail a program written by you then you of course cannot be expected to type in the program after you have issued the **mail** command as in the above cases. In such cases you can use input redirection as shown below:

```
$ mail user2 user3 veena < myprog.c
```

Now the contents of the file **myprog.c** would be promptly mailed to **user2**, **user3** and **veena**.

Handling Incoming Mail

The incoming mail received by a user is stored in a mailbox. Each user is given a mailbox whose name is same as the logname of the user. For example, for user **aa1** the filename would be **aa1** and it would be present in **/usr/spool/mail** directory. All mail received from different sources is appended to this mailbox file. However while viewing mail the messages are shown separately as if they are being read from separate files.

When mail is sent to you there are two possibilities: either you are logged in at that moment or you are not. If you haven't logged in when the mail was received then a message 'you have mail' is displayed on your screen as soon as you log in. Suppose you have logged in and are working with some program and at that moment somebody sends a mail to you. In such a case also the message 'you have mail' is displayed on the screen.

At what precise moment such a message would be displayed depends upon the value of a Unix variable called MAILCHECK.

Generally the value of this variable is kept 600. This tells Unix to check every 600 seconds whether any mail has arrived, and if it has, then the message 'you have mail' is flashed. If you want you can set this variable to have some other value.

To read the mail that has been received we simply say **mail** at the shell prompt.

```
$ mail
SCO System V Mail (version 3.2) Type? for help.
"/usr/spool/mail/user1": 3 messages 1 new 2 unread
>   N   3   prafull   Sat Oct 14   11:05   9/233   Unix course
    U   2   veena     Sat Oct 14   09:30   5/413   tidbits
    U   1   raka      Fri Oct 13   11:42   4/391   reminder
&
```

The output shows that there are 3 messages in our mailbox of which 1 has been received since we logged in whereas 2 were lying in the mailbox unread even before we logged in. The N or a U in the first column indicates just this. Each message present in the mailbox is given a number. These numbers are shown in the second column. The > sign indicates that the current message is message number 3. Followed by this is the logname of the person who sent the mail, the date and time when the mail was received as well as the subject of each message.

Observe the **&** displayed at the bottom. This is known as the mail prompt. We can issue several commands at this prompt. If you want to know which, you can type a ? and obtain help on these commands. Let us now view the third message. Just type a 3 at the **&** prompt.

```
&3
N 1 user1    Wed Oct 14 11:50 14/405
Unix course
& message 3:
From prafull Sat Oct 14 11:05:32 1995
From: prafull@scosysv.UUCP ( )
X-Mailer: SCO System V Mail (version 3.2)
To: aa12
Subject: Unix Course
Date: Sat, 14 Oct 95 11:05:32 IST
Message-ID: <9506141150.aa00805@scosysv.UUCP>
Status: R
It is overheard that the system administrator plans to conduct a 4 day
crash course in Unix. Don' join it. Between you and me, nothing
```

crashes like a crash course. After all nothing worthwhile is ever learnt in 10 easy lessons.
&

My god! What's all this junk at the beginning of the message? Any mail message has a header that the mail program creates automatically. The message consists of the following pieces:

- The To address (the person to receive the mail)
- The From address (the person who has sent the mail)
- The message number
- The date and time when the mail was sent and when it was read
- The subject

Don't worry too much about the header. You would get used to it. Likewise we can type the message numbers of whichever message we want to view. Finally, we can exit from the **mail** command by typing **q** at the **&** prompt.

```
&q
Saved 2 messages in /usr/aa12/mbox
held 1 message in /usr/spool/mail/aa12
```

This implies that out of the three messages we have received we have gone through 2 messages hence they have been removed from our primary mailbox file **usr/spool/mail/aa12** and appended to the secondary mailbox file **/usr/aa12/mbox.** One message which remains unread is still lying in the primary mailbox file. If we invoke mail once again we would be shown only the one unread message. What if we want to review the messages transferred to the secondary mailbox? Simply invoke the mail command as shown below:

```
$ mail  -f
```

This now starts displaying the messages which were stored in the secondary mailbox file **mbox**. If you have saved the mail in some other file then the **-f** option should be followed by that filename.

Messages in the secondary file can be read or otherwise processed using the same commands as in the primary mailbox. The file **mbox** can get pretty big if you don't edit it now and then, since messages remain in it until forcibly removed.

The mail program understands lots of commands given at the **&** prompt. A few important ones are listed in Figure 8.1.

Customizing mail

The way there is a hidden file **.exrc** which permits us to customize our **vi** environment, there exists a file called **.mailrc** which permits customization of mail. For example, if you are required to frequently send mail to users **aa1**, **aa2**, **aa3** and **aa4** then you can given some alternative name to this set of users using the **alias** command shown below.

        alias salesrep aa1 aa2 aa3 aa4

This command can of course be given at the **&** prompt. However it makes more sense in typing this command in **.mailrc** since the command given at the **&** prompt is effective only for the current session of **mail**. As soon as we quit out from the **&** prompt the effect is gone. Next time we again invoke **mail** we would be required to retype the **alias** command. Instead, if given in **.mailrc** the command would come into effect every time **mail** command is invoked since the **.mailrc** file gets called every time we invoke the **mail** command.

The other popular settings that can be made in **.mailrc** file are given in Figure 8.2.

Command	Description
h	Displays headers of mail received in descending order by time at wich they were received.
.	Displays the current message.
z	Displays message headers page by page if there are too many to fit on one screen.
+	Displays the next message, if it exists.
Enter	Displays the next message, if it exists.
n	Displays the next message, if it exists.
-	Displays the previous message, if it exists.
n	Displays the nth message, where **n** stands for the message number.
^	Displays the first message.
$	Displays the last message.
=	Prints current message number.
?	Help about commands that can be given at the **&** prompt.
d	Deletes current message.
d 1 2 3	Deletes specified messages.
u	Undeletes last deleted message.
u 1 2 3	Undeletes specified messages.
v	Permits editing of current message with vi.
f logname	Forwards the current mail message to the specified user.
l 1 2 3	Prints specified mail on line printer.
s 1 2 file	Appends the specified messages to file for later use.
r	Sends a reply to current message's sender.
r 4	Sends a reply to sender of message number 4.

Figure 8.1

Command	Description
set askcc	Asks whether carbon copies of the mail are to be sent to anybody.
set asksubject	Asks subject while mailing messages.
set nosave	Prevents aborted messages from being appended to a file **dead.letter** in home directory. By default messages are saved in the file **dead.letter** in case of an untimely interrupt.

Figure 8.2

That's the **mail** command for you. In fact **mail** is too exhaustive to be called a command. You would agree that it is nothing short of a full-fledged application.

Exercise

[A] Answer the following:

(a) List 5 commands which are available in Unix to communicate with other users.

(b) With reference to **mail** command, what is the meaning of the following:
f aaa
d 1 2 3
u 1 2
v
=
^
$
r

(c) What would the following settings achieve with reference to the **mail** command? Where should these settings be ideally stored?

```
set askcc
set mchron
set asksubject
set nosave
```

(d) How would you mail a letter to 5 different users through one command.

(e) If you do not want to be disturbed by messages from other users while you are working, what would you do?

(f) Using which two commands can you find out whether you have a write permission to a particular terminal or not.

(g) Can we communicate using **write** command with a user who hasn't currently logged in? If not, what is the solution?

(h) Out of the following which commands can be used only by superuser?
write   mail wall news

(i) How will you send mail through a single command to all users who have currently logged in?

(j) How will you send mail to all users who belong to a particular group?

(k) You have already logged in and somebody sends mail to you. In such an event when would you receive the message 'you have mail'?

(l) What would you do to ensure that you are prompted with the message 'you have mail' as soon as somebody sends the mail to you?

(m) What is the purpose of the command **alias** in relation with the **mail** command?

9

Shell Programming - The First Step

S o far we have familiarised ourselves with the Unix operating
system, its commands and its means of handling data. Making
use of all the knowledge gained so far, we can now graduate to
Unix Shell programming. What we did up till now was like studying
the alphabet towards learning the programming language. We have
seen that the Unix commands are executed when they are typed in at
the shell prompt. A shell program is nothing but a series of such
commands. Instead of specifying one job at a time, we give the shell
a to-do list - a program - that carries out an entire procedure. Such
programs are known as 'shell scripts'. The shell scripts offer new
horizons to our computing prowess, combining the collective power
of various commands and the versatility of programming language.
In time we shall see for ourselves the tremendous scope allowed by
shell programming to develop anything from simple routines to
full-fledged, custom-made software applications.

As we know, the Unix shell is an interface between the user and the
operating system itself, and forms one of the major components of
the Unix operating system. The Shell also incorporates a powerful
programming language that enables the user to exploit the full power
and versatility of Unix. The shell programming language incorporates most of the features that most modern day programming
languages offer. For example, it has local and global variables,
control instructions, functions, etc. So if you already know a programming language you would find many familiar concepts in shell
programming. If we are to execute a shell program we don't need a
separate compiler. The shell itself interprets the commands in the
shell program and executes them.

Since a shell script contains a variety of valid Unix commands this and the rest of the chapters would put to test our knowledge of all the diverse Unix commands that we have dealt with so far.

However, while writing shell programs we would be using these commands in a slightly different light. Instead of using them to perform an isolated task we will combine them effectively (using the shell programming language features) to perform complex tasks.

Shell programming is so powerful that several tasks like system shutdown, checking how much disk space is available etc. are carried out by Unix using nothing but the shell scripts. The commands **dfspace** and **shutdown** are nothing but shell scripts.

Incidentally there are at least 280 shell scripts that come with the Unix operating system. How did I find this out? By writing a shell script, what else. That should put the whole thing in the right perspective. Once we learn some basic concepts of shell programming you too would be able to put together such a script.

Before We Start...

We had a brief glimpse at the Unix Shells in Chapter 1. Just to reiterate, the three most widely used Unix shells are the Bourne Shell, the C Shell and the Korn Shell. All the shells support processes (both foreground and background), pipes, filters, directories, and other similar standard features of Unix.

Each shell has merits and demerits of its own. Moreover the shell scripts written for one shell may not work with the other shell. This is because different shells use different mechanisms to execute the commands in the shell script. Also, the keywords available in one shell to implement the control instructions would not be available in the other shell. In this book all the shell scripts would be discussed with reference to the Bourne shell since it is one of the most widely used Unix shells in existence today.

Almost all Unix implementations offer the Bourne Shell as part of their standard configuration. It is smaller than the other two shells and therefore more efficient for most shell processing. However, it lacks some features offered by the C and the Korn shell.

All shell programs written for the Bourne shell are likely to work with the Korn Shell. The reverse however may not be true. This is so since the facilities like arrays, command aliasing and history mechanism available in the Korn shell are not supported by the Bourne shell. However, it may still be a good idea to first learn the Bourne shell programming and then graduate to the Korn shell. You will find migration to the Korn Shell simple and smooth.

The C shell programming language resembles the C language and is quite different from the language of the Bourne shell. Only the very basic shell scripts will run under both the C and the Bourne shell; a vast majority will not. C shell keeps track of the commands as you enter them (history) and allows you to go back and execute them again without typing the command. Or, if you want to, you can recall them, make modifications, and then execute the new command.

The C shell also offers command aliasing, which allows the user to create alternatives for command names. The C Shell also offers greater control over background (behind the scenes) and foreground (at the terminal) tasks. In the Bourne shell, if you start a command in background or foreground, it stays there until it ends. In the C shell, you can move commands from foreground execution to background execution as required.

When to Use Shell Scripts

Since a user cannot interact with the kernel directly, shell programming skills are a must to be able to exploit the power of Unix to the fullest extent. Shell programs can be used for a variety of tasks some of which are mentioned below:

(a)   Customizing your work environment. For example, every time you log in if you want to see the current date, a welcome message and the list of users who have logged in you can write a shell script for the same.

(b)   Automating your daily tasks. For example, you may want to back up all your programs at the end of the day. This can be done using a shell script.

(c)   Automating repetitive tasks. For example, the repetitive task of compiling a C program, linking it with some libraries and executing the executable code can be assigned to a shell script. Another example could be that of producing sales reports every month.

(d)   Executing important system procedures like shutting down the system, formatting a disk, creating a file system on it, mounting the file system, letting the users use the floppy and finally unmounting the disk.

(e)   Performing same operation on many files. For example, you may want to replace a string **printf** with a string **myprintf** in all the C programs present in a directory.

You should not use shell programming when the task:

-       is too complex, such as writing an entire billing system.
-       requires a high degree of efficiency.
-       requires a variety of software tools.

The First Shell Script

Without any more preamble let us now begin with our first shell script.

```
# SS1
# Usage: SS1
ls
who
pwd
```

This straightforward, five line script marks the beginning of our association with Unix shell programming. The first line begins with a #. This is the symbol which marks the beginning of a comment. What follows it, **SS1** is the name of the file in which we will type this shell script. You know what **ls, who** and **pwd** do. The shell is told to first give a list of all files in the current directory, then a list of all users who have logged in and finally print the working directory. To execute the shell script we type **SS1** at the shell prompt and hit the Enter key.

```
$ SS1 (Enter)
SS1: execute permission denied
```

Let that not put you off. The 'execute permission denied' from the shell is no bad omen at the very outset of our programming trip. The reason is, by default every file is to get created with the permissions 666, i.e. **rw-rw-rw-**. These permissions, as we know, are further modified by a **umask.** To know your current **umask** enter **umask** at the shell prompt.

```
$ umask
0022
```

This is an octal number which signifies what permissions are 'masked' from the file. Our file **SS1** got created with the permissions 666 - 022 which equals 644. Thus, we as owners have the permission to read and write to the file, but not to execute it. The remedy to this is the **chmod** command.

```
$ chmod 744 SS1
```

This command changes the mode or the permissions available with a file. The new permissions for **SS1** are therefore 744, or **rwxr--r--**. Again execute **SS1** and you would get the expected results.

```
$ SS1
a.out
ascii.c
calender.c
dance.c
file1
matter
newcal
ss1
tree
aa11        tty01      Nov 06 08:34
aa12        tty3a      Nov 06 09:41
veena       tty3b      Nov 06 10:06
aa10        tty3c      Nov 06 09:12
/usr/veena
```

Let us now see how the shell script got executed. So far we have been executing commands at the dollar prompt. When we execute a shell script instead of accepting the commands from the dollar prompt the shell accepts them from our shell script. However there is a small difference here.

When we execute commands at the dollar prompt they are executed (unless otherwise specified) in the shell that was invoked when we logged in. As against this, when we execute a shell script, the login shell creates a new shell, a new command interpreter and waits idly in the background while the new shell executes our shell script. When all the commands in our shell script have been completed, the new shell terminates and our login shell once again takes over the control.

Note that any task that can be accomplished via a shell script can be accomplished at the dollar prompt and vice-versa. Then why write shell scripts at all? Because if the task that you wish to carry out is repetitive then if we are to get the task done at the command prompt we will have to every time type in the commands necessary to achieve the task at the command prompt. Thus, the basis of shell programming rests on the fact that the Unix shell can accept commands not only from the keyboard but also from a file.

Interactive Shell Scripts

The script **SS1** was a very elementary affair. A worthwhile program needs to talk to the user, and in turn requires a language. Two very basic words in the shell vocabulary are **read**, to accept input, and **echo**, to display output. The script **SS2** given below illustrates how these work.

```
# SS2
# Usage: SS2
# An interactive shell script

echo What is your name\?
read name
echo Hello $name. Happy programming.
```

Remember that **SS2** too has the default file permissions of 644, so we must change its mode before executing it. Having done that when you enter **SS2** at the shell prompt, what ensues is this:

```
$ SS2
What is your name?
Mandar
Hello Mandar. Happy programming.
```

Your eagle-eye must have noticed the '\' just before the question mark at the end of the first **echo** statement in the script. This is an escape sequence which takes away the special significance the '?' symbol has been assigned. Being a metacharacter, the question mark must be preceded by a backslash to convey to the shell that here the

'?' is to be treated as an ordinary character. If not preceded by a '\',
for the shell the '?' stands for all files in the current directory whose
names are one character long.

Another way of specifying the arguments to **echo** is by including
them within double quotes. The backslash may now be omitted, as
the shell treats the contents within " " as a single string to be
displayed.

The name entered is read by the shell, and **name** is a variable wherein
it is collected. Notice how **$name** figures in the last **echo** statement.
This means extract the value of the variable **name** and echo it on the
screen.

Having used a variable in our program let's now examine the different
types of variables available under Unix, which play a prominent role
in our understanding of the system.

Shell Variables

Shell variables are an integral part of shell programming. They
provide the ability to store and manipulate information within a shell
program. The variables you use are completely under your control.
You can create and destroy any number of variables as needed to
solve the problem at hand.

The rules for building shell variables are as follows:

(a)   A variable name is any combination of alphabets, digits and
       an underscore ('_').
(b)   No commas or blanks are allowed within a variable name.
(c)   The first character of a variable name must either be an
       alphabet or an underscore.
(d)   Variables names should be of any reasonable length.

(e) Variable names are case-sensitive. That is, Name, NAME, name, NAme are all different variables.

Here are a few sample variable names:

```
si_int
m_hra
pop_e_89
```

Since there is no limit on the length of a variable name, an enormous number of variable names can be constructed using the aforementioned rules. It is a good practice to exploit this enormous choice in naming variables by using meaningful variable names.

Thus, if we want to calculate simple interest, it is always advisable to construct meaningful variable names like **prin**, **roi**, **noy** to represent Principle, Rate of interest and Number of years rather than using the variables **a**, **b**, **c**.

Shell Keywords

Keywords are the words whose meaning has already been explained to the shell (or in a broad sense to the computer). The keywords **cannot** be used as variable names because if we do so we are trying to assign a new meaning to the keyword, which is not allowed by the shell. Some implementations of the shell allow you to construct variable names which exactly resemble the keywords. However, it would be safer not to mix up the variable names and the keywords. The keywords are also called 'Reserved words'. Following is the list of keywords available in Bourne shell, given here for your ready reference. A detailed discussion of each of these keywords would be taken up in later chapters wherever their use is relevant.

echo	if	until	trap
read	else	case	wait
set	fi	esac	eval
unset	while	break	exec
readonly	do	continue	ulimit
shift	done	exit	umask
export	for	return	

Figure 9.1

Another Way of Assigning Values to Variables

Instead of assigning a value to a variable by supplying the value to a **read** statement as was done in SS2 above, we can assign values to shell variables using a simple assignment operator. For example,

```
name=mandar
age=20
dirname=/usr/aa5
```

Note that while assigning values to variables using the assignment operator '=', there should be no spaces on either side of =. If you leave a space the shell will try to interpret the value being assigned as a command to be executed.

While carrying out the assignment if the variable does not exist it will be created and the value would be assigned to this variable. On the other hand if the variable already exists it will store the new value, replacing the old value that the variable contains. A variable may be set to a value once or many times in a program or at the command prompt. Likewise, the variable can be referenced to extract the value that it contains as many times as needed.

Variables in Unix are of two types:

(a)   Unix-defined variables or System variables:

These are standard variables which are always accessible. The shell provides the values for these variables. These variables are usually used by the system itself and govern the environment we work under. If we so desire we can change the values of these variables as per our preferences and customize the system environment.

(b)   User-defined variables:

These are defined by us and are used most extensively in shell programming.

Unix-defined or System Variables

The Unix OS has defined these variables for its own use. The **$** prompt that we see is the default value of the Unix-defined variable **PS1** standing for system prompt 1. We may assign a different value to **PS1** if we want the prompt to be something else other than the **$** .

```
$ PS1="What next"
What next
```

So now every time the system prompts you, it displays not the **$** but **What next**.

Some of the commonly used system variables and their meaning is given in Figure 9.2.

Variable	Meaning
PS2	The system prompt 2, default value is ">"
PATH	Defines the path which the shell must search in order to execute any command or file.
HOME	Stores the default working directory of the user. On entering just a **cd**, the system understands that **HOME** is where we want to go and we are back to our default directory.
LOGNAME	Stores the login name of the user.
MAIL	Defines the file (along with the path) where the mail of the user is stored.
MAILCHECK	Defines the duration after which the shell checks whether the user has received any mail. By default its value is 600 (seconds).
IFS	Defines the Internal Field Separator, which is a space, a tab or a newline.
SHELL	Defines the name of your default working shell.
TERM	Defines the name of the terminal on which you are working.
TZ	Defines the name of the time zone in which we are working.

Figure 9.2

The list of all system variables and their values can be displayed by saying at the $ prompt,

```
$ set
HOME=/usr/veena
HZ=100
IFS=

LOGNAME=veena
MAIL=/usr/spool/mail/veena
MAILCHECK=600
OPTIND=1
```

```
PATH=/bin:/usr/bin:/usr/veena:/bin:.
PS1=$
PS2=>
SHELL=/bin/sh
TERM=vt100
TZ=IST-5:30
```

User-defined Variables

The variable length can be of any reasonable length and may constitute alphabets, digits and underscores. However the first character must be an alphabet or an underscore.

```
$ a=20
```

This statement has defined a variable **a**, and has assigned a value **'20'** to it. The shell may be made to display the value of the variable using **echo**.

```
$ echo $a
20
```

The **$** as mentioned earlier, causes the value of **a** to get displayed. Omitting the **$** would simply treat **a** as a character to be echoed.

```
$ echo a
a
```

Tips and Traps

Having seen the different types of shell variables a few tips are in order.

(a)   All shell variables are string variables. In the statement **a=20**, the '20' stored in **a** is treated not as a number, but as a string of characters **2** and **0**. Naturally, we cannot carry out arithmetic operations on them unless we use a command called **expr**.

(b)   A variable may contain more than one word. In such cases, the assignment must be made using double quotes.

```
$ c="Two words"
$ echo $c
Two words
```

(c)   We can carry out more than one assignment in a line. So also, we can echo more than one variable's value at a time.

```
$ name=Johny age=10
$ echo $name $age
$ Johny 10
```

We can even be more elaborate while echoing the name and age.

```
$ echo Name of the boy is $name, and his age is $age.
Name of the boy is Johny, and his age is 10.
```

(d)   All variables defined inside a shell script die the moment the execution of the script is over.

(e)   A variable which has been defined but has not been given any value is known as a null variable. A null variable can be created in any of the following ways.

```
$ d=""
$ d=''
$ d=
```

(f)   On echoing a null variable, only a blank line appears on the screen.

```
$ a=""
$ echo $a

$
```

(g)   If a null variable is used anywhere in a command the shell manages to ignore it. For example,

```
$ var1=""
$ var2=""
$ wc -l $var1 $var2 file1
110
```

Since **var1** and **var2** were null variables the shell promptly eliminated them from the command line and displayed the number of lines present in the file **file1**.

(h)   Not only the system variables but also the user-defined variables defined at the $ prompt or in a shell script can be displayed using the **set** command.

Unchanging Variables

In some applications a need may arise for variables to have a constant or fixed value. For instance, if we want that **a**'s value should always remain 20 and not changed, we can achieve this by saying,

```
$ a=20
$ readonly a
```

When the variables are made **readonly**, the shell does not allow us to change their values. All such variables can be listed bv entering **readonly** at the $ prompt.

Wiping Out Variables

Variables can be made to cease existing. If we want the shell to forget about a variable altogether, we use the **unset** command.

```
$ unset b
```

On issuing the above command the variable **b** and with it the value assigned to it are simply erased from the shell's memory. However we can't try such stunts indiscriminately. For instance, saying

```
$ unset PS1
```

is not allowed. Quite naturally so, since if **PS1** is unset then there would be no system prompt left for you to issue any commands at.

Positional parameters

On many occasions we need to convey information to a program. A very convenient way of doing this is by specifying arguments at the command line. But how does the shell script know what has been passed to it? For this, the shell uses something called 'Positional Parameters'. These can be thought of as variables defined by the shell. They are nine in number, named **$1** through **$9**.

Consider the following statement, where **SS** is any executable shell script file and the remaining are the arguments.

```
$ SS Pro is to Con as Progress is to Congress
```

On entering such a command, each word is automatically stored serially in the positional parameters. Thus, **$0** would be assigned **SS**, **$1** would be assigned 'Pro', $2 'is' and so on, till 'Congress', which is assigned to **$9**. These are available to the shell script to use as need be. This is an extremely useful feature, as we now proceed to demonstrate.

Passing Command Line Arguments

The knowledge of positional parameters opens up a wider scope to programming, at the same time makes things easier. Say for instance we have to write a shell script which accepts two file names from the command line, copies the first file to the second and then displays it. SS3 is the answer:

```
# SS3
# Usage: SS3 <source filename> <target filename>

cp $1  $2
cat $2
```

To make it executable, we would change its mode using **chmod** and then execute it thus:

```
$ SS3  machine  machine_copy
I really hate the dammed machine,
I wish that they would sell it,
It never does quite what I want,
But only what I tell it!
```

Well, those were the rantings of some woebegone programmer under a cloud, which were stored in the file **machine**. Hope he found the silver lining soon.

The statement **cp $1 $2** is translated by the shell as **cp machine machine_copy**, as **$1** collected the first argument and **$2**, the second. Hence **machine** is copied to **machine_copy**, (which gets created if not already present) and then **cat $2** displays its contents.

Here is another example. There's no way you can create a file which gives the owner the execute permission. That's the reason why we reminded you every time to change the mode of a shell script before executing it. It's a bit of a nuisance, saying **chmod** first then executing any new script. We can substitute the two commands by writing a shell script for new files, which by itself makes the file executable as well as execute it. Like all good ideas, even this script is a short and sweet one.

```
# SS4
# Usage: SS4 <filename>

chmod 744 $1
$1
```

Now, for a newly created file, or for any file which does not grant executable permission to that owner, **SS4** can be used as shown below:

```
$ SS4 AnyScript
```

Whatever the permissions of **AnyScript**, rest assured that you won't get the 'execute permission denied' message. **$1** is replaced by the shell by **AnyScript**, it's mode is set to 744, and lastly simply saying **$1** calls **AnyScript** for execution. Just as files can be executed from the shell prompt, so also can they be from the shell script.

Setting Values of Positional Parameters

Though we have compared the positional parameters with variables, they are in essence quite different. For instance you can't assign values to **$1, $2**.. etc. as we do to any other user-defined variables, or system variables for that matter. Saying **a=10** or **b=alpha** is fine but **$1=dollar** or **$2=100** is simply not done. We have already seen how positional parameters are set up by the command line arguments. There is one more way to assign values to the positional parameters - using the **set** command.

```
$ set Friends come and go, but enemies accumulate
```

The above command sets the value **$1** with 'Friends', **$2** with 'come' and so on. To verify, we use the **echo** statement to display their values.

```
$ echo $1 $2 $3 $4 $5 $6 $7
Friends come and go, but enemies accumulate
```

On giving another **set** command, the old values of **$1, $2**, etc. are discarded and the new values get collected.

```
$ set Do you want credit or results
$ set A smiling face is always beautiful
$ echo $1 $2 $3 $4 $5 $6
A smiling face is always beautiful
```

Had we echoed the values of $1 through $6 before issuing the second **set** command obviously the results would have been different.

Let us now see another way of setting values in positional parameters. Suppose we have typed the line 'Give luck a little time and it will surely change' in a file called 'lucky'. We can make **set** take the values to be assigned to positional parameters from this file by saying,

```
$ set 'cat lucky'
$ echo $1 $2 $3 $4 $5
Give luck a little time
```

Whenever the quoting metacharacters ' ' are used the command given within ' ' is replaced by the output of the command. In our case 'cat lucky' got replaced by **Give luck a little time and it will surely change**. Hence **set** used this sentence to set up the positional parameters as the output of the **echo** command would justify. The characters ' ' are called reverse quotes or more correctly 'accent graves'. The following shell script gives another illustration of their use with **set**.

Suppose we want to write a script that reads a filename from the command line and changes the name to **filename.aa1** where **aa1** is the logname of the user. Here is the shell script...

```
# SS5
# Usage: $SS5 <filename>
# Renames any file aaa to aaa.aa1, where aa1 is the user login name.

name=$1
set 'who am i'
mv $name $name.$1
```

SS5 first collects the supplied filename in a variable called **filename** through the statement **name=$1**. This is necessary, as in the next statement, **set** is going to be executed which will store new values in $1, $2, etc., causing us to lose what was earlier present in $1.

The command **who am i**, we know, gives the information about the user himself. If you check it out, you will see that the first field in its output gives the logname. That is, $1 is assigned the logname. Rest is taken care of by a simple **mv** command.

Displaying Date in Desired Format

The **date** command by default displays the current date and time in the following format:

Fri Apr 19 11:30:45 IST 1996

To display the information in any other order say this:

Fri 19 Apr 1996

we can use the **set** command as shown in **SS6**.

```
# SS6
```

```
# Usage: SS6
# Displays date in desired format

set 'date'
echo $1 $3 $2 $6
```

All we have done is juggled the position of the various positional parameters.

To find out how many positional parameters were set - either by **set** command or by command line arguments - there is a special parameter $#. The following script gives the total number of files supplied at the command line.

```
# SS7
# Usage: SS7
# Gives number of files supplied as arguments

echo Total number of files = $#
```

The usage of the script would be like this:

```
$ SS7 file1 file2 file3
Total number of files = 3
```

We know that in Unix the metacharacter * can represent all the files when given as argument. The same can be used to find out the total number of files in the current directory.

```
$ SS7 *
Total number of files = 18
```

So our current directory has 18 files. How come 18 positional parameters were reported to be set when there exist only 9 - $1, $2 ... $9 ? Fact is, we can supply any number of arguments, but can access only nine of them at a time ($0 contains the name of the file being executed). The next section deals with how to tackle the rest.

Using Shift on Positional Parameters

We have used the **set** command to set upto 9 words. But we can use it for more.

> $ set You have the capacity to learn from mistakes. You will learn a lot in your life.
> $ echo $1 $2 $3 $4 $5 $6 $7 $8 $9 $10 $11
> You have the capacity to learn from mistakes. You You0 You1

Observe the last two words in the output. These occurred in the output because at a time we can access only 9 positional parameters. When we tried to refer to **$10** it was interpreted by the shell as if you wanted to output the value of **$1** and a 0. Hence we got **You0** in the output. Same is the story with **$11**. Does that mean the words following the ninth word have been lost? No. If not, then where have they gone? They are very much there, safe with the shell. But to reach them we must do the following.

> $ shift 7
> $ echo $1 $2 $3 $4 $5 $6 $7 $8 $9
> mistakes. You will learn a lot in your life.

Now where have the first seven words gone? They have been shifted out. Each word vacated a position for the one on its right with the first word getting lost in the bargain. This occurred 7 times, hence we find the last 9 words in $1 through $9. The first seven are lost for ever, as we did not take the precaution to store them elsewhere. So that was one thing we learnt from the loss. What we should have done is:

> $ set You have the capacity to learn from mistakes. You will learn a lot in your life.
> $ a=$1
> $ b=$2
> $ c=$3
> $ d=$4

```
$ e=$5
$ f=$6
$ g=$7
$ shift 4
$ echo $a $b $c $d $e $f $g $1 $2 $3 $4 $5 $6 $7 $8 $9
You have the capacity to learn from mistakes. You will learn a lot in
your life.
```

Instead of going through this rigmarole, we can employ an easier method.

```
$ set You have the capacity to learn from mistakes. You will learn a lot
in your life.
$ echo $*
You have the capacity to learn from mistakes. You will learn a lot in
your life.
```

Here $* stands for all positional parameters, including those beyond $9. This means that using $* we can access all the parameters taken together but not individually. The following example would further clarify this concept.

```
# SS8
# Usage: SS8
# Example of positional parameters and shift command

set If you are headed in the wrong direction, God allows U turns.
echo $*
shift 1
echo $*
shift 1
echo $*
shift 1
echo $*
shift
echo $*
```

And here is the output you would get when you execute it...

> If you are headed in the wrong direction, God allows U turns.
> you are headed in the wrong direction, God allows U turns.
> are headed in the wrong direction, God allows U turns.
> headed in the wrong direction, God allows U turns.
> in the wrong direction, God allows U turns.

Observe the last **shift** command in the program. Here we have not mentioned the number of parameters to be shifted. When we do not do so, by default 1 parameter is shifted.

Arithmetic in Shell Script

So far we have seen how to assign values to variables. Let us now see how we can operate upon these values. You may recall that all shell variables are string variables. If we are to carry out arithmetic operations on them we have to use the command **expr** which is capable of evaluating an arithmetic expression. The following program shows the various arithmetic operations that can be carried out using **expr**.

```
# SS9
# Usage: SS9
# Example of arithmetic operations

a=20     b=10
echo 'expr $a + $b'
echo 'expr $a - $b'
echo 'expr $a \* $b'
echo 'expr $a / $b'
echo 'expr $a % $b'  # modular division, returns remainder
```

On execution of this script we get the following output...

30

```
10
200
2
0
```

There are several things that should be noted in this program:

(a)   Comment about the program should be preceded with a #. Moreover, any number of comments can be given at any place in the program.

(b)   A comment cannot be split over more than one line, as in,

```
# This is
 a jazzy
 comment
```

A comment split over multiple lines must have a # at the beginning of each line.

(c)   Although a lot of comments are probably not necessary in this program, it is usually the case that programmers tend to use too few comments rather than too many. Comments should be used at any place where there is a possibility of confusion.

(d)   More than one assignment can be done in a single statement. Hence we have initiated variables **a** and **b** in the same line.

(e)   In addition to the normal addition, subtraction, multiplication and division the **expr** command can also perform a modular division operation. The symbol used to do so is %. It returns the remainder obtained on dividing the first number by the second. The remainder always takes the sign of the numerator.

(f)   The multiplication symbol must always be preceded by a \. Otherwise the shell treats it as a wildcard character for all files in the current directory.

(g)   Terms of the expression provided to **expr** must be separated by blanks. Thus, the expression **expr 10+20** is invalid.

(h)   While evaluating an expression **expr** performs the various arithmetic operations according to the following priorities.

     /, *, %   - First priority
     +, -   - Second priority

(i)   In case of a tie between operations of same priority, preference is given to the operator which occurs first. For example, in the expression **$a * $b + $c / $d**, **$a * $b** would be performed before **$c / $d** since * appears prior to the / operator.

(j)   To force one operation to be performed earlier than the other we have to enclose that operation within a pair of parentheses. For example, in the expression **$a * \($b + $c \) / $d**, since the operation **$b + $c** has been parenthesized it would be evaluated earlier than the multiplication or division. Observe that the parentheses have been preceded by a '\' to take away their special meaning.

(k)   Within a parentheses, the same hierarchy as mentioned earlier is operative. Also, if there are more than one set of parentheses, the operations within the innermost parentheses will be performed first, followed by the operations within the second innermost pair and so on.

(l)   We must always remember to use pairs of parentheses. A careless imbalance of the right and left parentheses is a common error.

(m)   Since the **expr** command has been put within accent graves it is substituted with the output of **expr**, which is then promptly displayed by the **echo** statement on the screen.

(n)   **expr** is capable of carrying out only integer arithmetic. To carry out arithmetic on real numbers it is necessary to use the **bc** command as shown in the following program.

```
# SS10
# Usage: SS10
# Example of floating point arithmetic operations

a=10.5
b=3.5
c='echo $a + $b | bc'
d='echo $a - $b | bc'
e='echo $a \* $b | bc'
f='echo $a / $b | bc'
echo $c $d $e $f
```

expr $a + $b is a legal expression whereas **bc $a + $b** isn't. Hence we have piped the result of **echo** to **bc**. Thus, **bc** went to work on 10.5 and 3.5, carried out the addition operation and accent graves ensured that instead of displaying the result on the screen it got stored in the variable **c**.

read and *echo* Revisited

So far we have used the **read** and **echo** statements in their simplest garb. Below the outwardly simple appearance these statements have lot more to offer, especially the **echo** statement. Let us first tackle the **read** statement. Let us consider a very simple shell script given below:

```
# SS11
# Usage: SS11

echo Enter the values of a, b and c
read a b c
echo $a $b $c
```

Suppose during execution we supply the values 'one', 'two' and 'three' to the **read** statement. As a result, 'one' would be assigned to the variable **a**, 'two' to variable **b** and 'three' to variable **c**. The **echo** statement would then promptly display these values. What do you think would happen if we supply only 'one' and 'two'? Now the variable **c** would not receive any value and would be treated as a null variable. Let us imagine another situation. Suppose we supply the values 'one', 'two', 'three' and 'four' to the **read** statement. This time the variable **c** would be assigned the value 'three four'. This means that if we supply more values than the number of variables, the **read** statement starts assigning values to the variables on a one to one basis and the moment it finds that it has come across the last variable and there are still more than one value left to be assigned, it assigns rest of the values to the last variable in the list.

So much about the **read** statement. Let us now take a closer look at the **echo** statement.

By default every **echo** statement echoes the output on a fresh line. If we want that output of a single **echo** statement should be split across lines we can use the newline escape sequences as shown below:

```
$ echo "I like work...\n I can sit and watch it for hours."
I like work...
I can sit and watch it for hours.
```

The sequence **\n** is called the newline character. It sends the cursor to the beginning of the next line. Hence after printing 'I like work...' the cursor is positioned at the beginning of the next line and the tail piece gets printed on this line.

There are a few more escape sequences available. These are in fact carried forward from the C language, in which most of the Unix OS is written. Note that when escape sequences are used, the string to be displayed should be enclosed within double quotes. The remaining escape sequences are discussed below.

The Carriage Return

The **\r** sequence is called the carriage return. It causes the cursor to be positioned at the beginning of the current line.

```
$ echo "I like work...\r I can sit and watch it for hours."
I can sit and watch it for hours.
```

Seems like the first part never got printed? But that isn't the case. The shell had faithfully printed it, but the **\r** placed the cursor back where the 'I' was displayed. Having done so, the work done prior to the **\r** was undone as 'I can sit...' was written over 'I like work...'

The Tab and The Backspace

The function of the tab key is emulated by the sequence **\t**, and that of the backspace, by **\b**. Thus, **\t** takes the cursor a predetermined number of columns ahead while **\b** moves the cursor one column back.

```
$ echo "There is always one more \b\b\b\b\b bug. \t\t -By Law."
There is always one bug.     -By Law.
```

In the above **echo** statement, the word 'more' and the space after it were overwritten, as the 5 backspaces positioned the cursor at 'm' of 'more' and then **echo** proceeded to display the remaining part of the message there. The two tabs pushed '-By Law' towards the end of the line.

Positioning The Cursor

By default, after an **echo** statement, the cursor is placed at the beginning of the next (or new) line. We may wish the cursor to wait at the end of the **echo**ed line, say while asking the users choice from a presented menu. The trick to do this is by saying **\c** at the end of the statement.

```
$ echo "Enter your choice...\c"
Enter your choice...
```

The cursor waits after the ellipsis, and not on the next line.

Beep, Beep...

Another escape sequence is for the bell, usually sounded to alert the user.

```
$ echo "\07"
$
```

Nothing on the screen, but you'll hear a beep from your machine.

Bold and Beautiful

Escape sequence also allow you to control the manner in which characters are displayed on the screen.

```
$ echo "\033[1m This is Bold "
This is Bold.
```

You'll notice that the letters are thicker than usual. The Martian looking **\033[1m** is an escape sequence, which tells the shell that the following string is to be written is bold letters.

```
$ echo "\033[7m This is Bold and Reverse."
This is bold and reverse
```

With this second sequence, we obtain what is called reverse video. Counter intuitive to real life writing practices, light colored letters on dark background are taken to be the regular or normal mode. That's because this is how the writing on the computer usually looks. When you have dark letters on a light background, you are seeing reverse video. The last **echo** statement resulted in bold letters on a light background, though only the sequence for reverse video was included in it. The reason for this is the previous **echo** statement, which set the mode to bold letters. Until we reset the mode to normal, the letters will continue to be displayed bold, in reverse video. To return to the plain, normal mode, we have yet another sequence.

```
$ echo "\033[0m"
```

No you won't see anything new on the screen, as this **echo** statement was not passed any string to display. But it has done its job, which was to restore the normal viewing mode. Whatever you type now will be devoid of any fancy effects.

The following figure summarises these escape sequences.

Escape Sequence	Meaning
\033[0m	Normal characters
\033[1m	Bold characters
\033[4m	Underlined characters
\033[5m	Blinking characters
\033[7m	Reverse video characters

Figure 9.3

The *tput* Command

Other than **echo** there is a command called **tput** using which we can control the way the output is displayed on the screen. Since Unix permits usage of different terminal types it maintains a database which contains useful information about these terminal types. This database has a name **termcap** (short for terminal capabilities) and is present in the **/etc** directory. Different terminals may use different escape sequences for effects like blinking, reverse video etc. The

terminfo database defines escape sequences for different terminal types.

Suppose we use the **tput** command to display a message in bold. Let us see what happens now. Remember the TERM system variable? When we issue the **tput** command it reads the value of the TERM variable and looks up the escape sequences for that particular terminal type in the **terminfo** database. It then sends this escape sequence to the terminal followed by the message which is to be displayed in bold.

In the **echo** statement discussed above we have used the escape sequences for a terminal whose type is ANSI. These escape sequences may not work for some other terminal type. In that sense **tput** is more powerful since it can send the desired escape sequence for different terminal types.

Let us now see how to use the **tput** command's capabilities in a shell script.

```
# SS12
# Usage: SS12
# Demonstration of tput command

tput bel
tput clear
echo "Total no. of column on screen = \c"
tput cols

echo "Total no. of rows = \c"
tput lines

echo "This is a normal message"

tput blink
echo "This is a blinking message"

tput bold
```

```
echo  "This is a bold message"

tput  cup  10  20   # positions cursor at 10 th row, 20 th column
echo  "Testing of tput"

tput  smso    # start stand cut (bold) mode
echo  "The bold has begun..."
tput  rmso    # end stand out mode

tput  smul    # start mode underline
echo  "So also has underline"
tput  rmul    # end mode underline
```

The meaning of each option used in this shell script is given in Figure 9.4.

Option	Action
clear	clear the screen
cup r c	move cursor to row r and column c
bold	bold display
blink	blinking display
rev	reverse video (black on white) display
smul	start mode underline
rmul	end underline mode
bel	echo the terminal's "bell" character
lines	echo number of lines on the screen
cols	echo number of columns on the screen
ed	clear to end of the display
el	clear to end of the line

Figure 9.4

Control Instructions in Shell

As the name suggests the 'Control Instructions' enable us to specify the order in which the various instructions in a program are to be executed by the computer. In other words the control instructions determine the 'flow of control' in a program. There are four types of control instructions in shell. They are:

(a) Sequence Control Instruction
(b) Selection or Decision Control Instruction
(c) Repetition or Loop Control Instruction
(d) Case Control Instruction

The Sequence control instruction ensures that the instructions are executed in the same order in which they appear in the program. Decision and Case control instructions allow the computer to take a decision as to which instruction is to be executed next. The Loop control instruction helps computer to execute a group of statements repeatedly.

Three important aspects of any language are the way it stores data, how it accomplishes input and output, and the operators it uses to transform and combine data. In this chapter we examined all these aspects. Of course, in a single chapter we can't present every aspect of each of these topics; much will remain to be said in the later chapters. However, what we have covered here will be enough to at least get you off the ground. In the following chapters we will put these building blocks to use while exploring the control instructions of the language: decision, loop and case. Try your hand at the Exercise presented on the following pages before proceeding to the next chapter, which discusses the decision control instruction.

Exercise

[A] Indicate whether the following variable names are valid or invalid. If invalid, state the reason for the same.

```
number of years
si-int
AVERAGE
percent%
457
SaLaRy
#regpay
variable
expr
_newvar
```

[B] Point out the errors, if any, in the following statements:

(a)   t = 562

(b)   yrsofworking=expr today - dateofjoining

(c)   3.14 * $r * $r = area

(d)   k='expr a * b'

(e)   m_inst='expr $rate * $amount'

(f)   tput cup $row $col

(g)   message=happy holi

(h)   a='3.14 + $r + $c I bc'

(i)   cmd='34'

(j)   z=echo $a + $b | bc

(k)   readonly a
       a=100

(l)   a=100
      readonly a
      unset a

[C]   State True or False:

(a)   You can execute a shell script once it has been typed.

(b)   In **a=1235**, **a** is a numeric shell variable.

(c)   Shell variables are case sensitive.

(d)   Programs written for Bourne shell are compatible with C shell.

(e)   Programs written for Bourne shell are compatible with Korn shell.

(f)   While executing a shell script the shell acts as a compiler.

(g)   There is no restriction on the length of a shell variable.

(h)   Variables declared in a shell script can be displayed at the dollar prompt using the **set** command.

(i)   **expr** can handle only integers whereas **bc** can handle both integers as well as floats.

(j)   Any shell script by default gets executed in the current shell.

(k)   **echo** statement's output cannot be redirected to a file.

(l)   Comments can be split over multiple lines if each line is preceded by a #.

(m)   A shell variable cannot hold negative values.

[D]   Pick up the correct alternative for each of the following questions:

(a)   The escape sequence \033[4m is used to
        (1) Underline characters
        (2) Mark them as bold
        (3) Display them in reverse video
        (4) None of the above

(b)   Which of the following assignments is illegal?
        (1) a='ls'
        (2) b='ls -l'
        (3) c='1972'
        (4) d='who | grep aa1'

(c)   Which of the following assignments is illegal?
        (1) a='cat file'
        (2) a=100 b=50
        (3) age = 25
        (4) All the above

(d)   A null variable **a** can be created using
        (1) a=
        (2) a=''
        (3) a=""
        (4) All the above

(e)   The shell metacharacter $# represents
        (1) Number of arguments supplied to the shell script
        (2) Total number of files in the current directory
        (3) Total number of users who have logged in
        (4) Total number of processes running in the background

(f)   When we are executing a shell script the shell acts as
      (1) An interpreter
      (2) A compiler
      (3) An operating system
      (4) None of the above

(g)   On executing a statement **set -3 + 1**
      (1) $1 would be -3
      (2) $1 would be -
      (3) $1 would be set
      (4) This command would result into an error

(h)   On executing the command **shift $v**
      (1) The positional parameters would be shifted by the value of
          the variable **v**.
      (2) The positional parameters would be shifted by 1
      (3) The positional parameters would not be shifted at all
      (4) This command would result into an error

(i)   Which of the following is NOT a shell keyword
      (1) shift
      (2) readonly
      (3) unset
      (4) ls

(j)   To the statement **read v1 v2 v3** we can supply
      (1) Maximum 3 values
      (2) Only 1 value
      (3) Exactly 3 values
      (4) Any number of values

(k)   The metacharacter **$*** represents
      (1) Number of parameters supplied at the command prompt
      (2) Parameters supplied at the command prompt
      (3) Value of the variable *
      (4) All files in the current directory

(l)   A shell variable cannot start with
        (1) An alphabet
        (2) A number
        (3) A special symbol other than an underscore
        (4) Both (2) & (3) above

(m)   Which of the following shows the correct hierarchy of arith-
        metic operations in shell
        (1) ( ), **, * or /, + or -
        (2) ( ), **, *, /, +, -
        (3) ( ), **, /, *, +, -
        (4) ( ), /, % or *, - or +

(n)   Which of the following statement is correct
        (1) a=expr $b + $c
        (2) a='expr $b * $c'
        (3) a='expr $b * ($c + $d)'
        (4) a='expr $b * \($c + $d \)'

(o)   Which of the following is allowed in an arithmetic statement
        involving **expr** instruction
        (1) [ ]
        (2) { }
        (3) ( )
        (4) None of the above

(p)   The statement z='expr 5 / 2' would store in **z** a value
        (1) 2.5
        (2) 3
        (3) 2
        (4) 0

(q)   The expression, **expr -7 % 2** evaluates to
        (1) 1
        (2) -1
        (3) -3.5
        (4) 0

(r) The expression, **expr -2 % 7** evaluates to
   (1) 2
   (2) -2
   (3) 0
   (4) 0.285

(s) Hierarchy decides which operator
   (1) is most important
   (2) is used first
   (3) is fastest
   (4) operates on largest numbers

[E] Answer the following:

(a) What do the following Unix system variables signify?

   HOME   PS1   PS2   PATH   TERM   MAILCHECK

(b) How will you find out using two different ways whether the value you assigned to a variable has been stored in it or not?

(c) What will be the output of the following commands?

```
a=*
echo $a
echo "$a"
```

(d) If a shell script called SS1 is executed at command prompt by saying,

   $SS1 ??

   What will be the values of $0, $1, $2, $#, $*

(e) Can we write the following statements in a shell script?

   $3="Hello"

```
echo $3
```

(f)   If values "Hi" and "Hello" are supplied to the following state-
      ment, what will be the output?

```
read n1 n2 n3 n4
echo $n1 $n2 $n3 $n4
```

(g)   If values "Hi", "Hello", "Bye" and "Goodbye" are supplied to
      the following statements, what will be the output?

```
read n1 n2
echo $n1 $n2
```

(h)   How will you find the number of files present in the current
      directory without using **wc** command?

(i)   Make a list of all shell metacharacters that you know (mini-
      mum 10).

(j)   What will be the output of the following statements?

```
a="*"
b=a
echo $b
```

(k)   What will be the output of the following shell script

```
set Only God is in a position to look down upon someone.
echo $10 $11 $*
```

(l)   What would be the output of following statements if they are
      executed at the $ prompt and if they are executed through a
      shell script.

```
set You have two choices for dinner. Take it or leave it.
echo $0
```

(m)   What would be the output of following statements?

```
set who am i
echo $*
set "who am i"
echo $*
set 'who am i'
echo $*
```

[F]   Write shell scripts for the following:

(a)   Ramesh's basic salary is input through the keyboard. His dearness allowance is 40% of basic salary, and house rent allowance is 20% of basic salary. Write a program to calculate his gross salary.

(b)   The distance between two cities (in km.) is input through the keyboard. Write a program to convert and print this distance in meters, feet, inches and centimeters.

(c)   The length & breadth of a rectangle and radius of a circle are input through the keyboard. Write a program to calculate the area & perimeter of the rectangle, and the area & circumference of the circle.

(d)   If a five digit number is input through the keyboard, write a program to calculate the sum of its digits.

(Hint: Use the modulus operator '%')

(e)   The file **/etc/passwd** contains information about all the users. However it is difficult to decipher the information stored in it. Write a shell script which would receive the logname during execution, obtain information about it from **/etc/passwd** and display this information on the screen in easily understandable format. (Hint: Use **cut** command)

(f)   Write a shell script which will receive either the filename or the filename with its full path during execution. This script should obtain information about this file as given by **ls -l** and display it in proper format.

10 *Taking Decisions*

In the programs written in Chapter 9 we have used sequence control structure in which the various steps are executed sequentially, i.e. in the same order in which they appear in the program. In fact to execute the instructions sequentially, we don't have to do anything at all. By default the instructions in a program are executed sequentially. However, a serious program is rarely a straight-forward list of things to do. Most of the times you need the program to do one thing under some circumstances and a different thing in another situation. For this it is essential to have control over the order of execution of the commands in the program. The Bourne shell offers four decision making instructions. They are:

(a)   The **if-then-fi** statement
(b)   The **if-then-else-fi** statement
(c)   The **if-then-elif-else-fi** statement
(c)   The **case-esac** statement

Let us learn each of these and their variations in turn.

The *if-then-fi* Statement

Like most programming languages, shell too uses the keyword **if** to implement the decision control instruction. The simplest form of the **if** statement looks like this:

```
if control command
      command 1
fi
```

If you are familiar with any high level language you must have used some form of an **if** statement. The Unix shell **if** statement is different from others at least on one count. In most high level languages the **if** statements are usually concerned with the values of variables - is age greater than 20, is answer equal to yes or some such condition.

Unlike this the **if** statement of Unix is concerned with the exit status of a command. The exit status indicates whether the command was executed successfully or not. The exit status of a command is 0 if it has been executed successfully, 1 otherwise. For example, if the **cp** command when executed is able to copy the files(s) successfully then its exit status would be 0. Likewise, if **grep** is unable to locate the pattern it was searching for, then its exit status would be 1.

In the form of the **if** statement shown above the control command can be any valid Unix command. The keyword **if** tells the shell that what follows, is a decision control instruction. If the control command, whatever it is, returns an exit status 1, then the command 1 is executed. If the exit status is 1 then command 1 is not executed; instead the control skips past it. Note that every **if** statement has a corresponding **fi** which indicates where the **if** statement ends.

Here is a more concrete example.

```
# SS13
# Usage: SS13

Enter source and target file names
read source target

if cp $source $target
then
      echo File copied successfully
fi
```

Having read the source and target file names supplied from the keyboard, **cp** proceeds to copy the contents of source file into target file. If it is able to do so successfully it would return an exit status of 0. In such a case the **echo** statement would get executed. If for some reason **cp** is unable to carry out the copying job successfully an exit status of 1 would be returned. This would transfer the control beyond the **fi** without executing the **echo** statement. As you must have guessed, the **if** statement allows you to place several commands between the **then** and the **fi** keywords if required.

The *if-then-else-fi* Statement

The **if** statement by itself will execute a single command, or a group of commands, when the exit status of the control command is 0. It does nothing when the exit status is 1. Can we execute one group of commands if the exit status is 0 and another group if the exit status is 1? Of course. This is what is the purpose of the **else** statement, which is demonstrated in the following shell script.

```
# SS14
# Usage: SS14

Enter source and target file names
read source target

if cp $source $target
then
     echo File copied successfully
else
     echo Failed to copy the file
fi
```

As you can see the response of this program depends on how the **cp** procedure went. If the control command (**cp** in this case) executes successfully, then the **echo** between **then** and **else** gets executed, otherwise the **echo** between **else** and **fi** gets executed.

A few points worth noting...

(a)   The **if** statement can be represented by a block diagram as
       shown below.

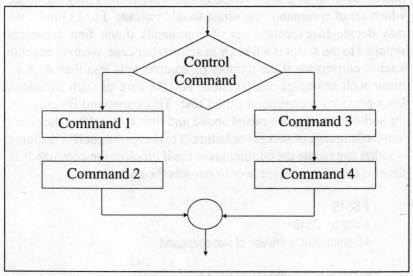

Figure 10.1

(b)   The group of commands between the **then** and **else** is called
       an 'if block'. Similarly, the commands between the **else** and **fi**
       form the 'else block'.

(c)   Notice that the **else** is written exactly below the **if**. The state-
       ments in the if block and those in the else block have been
       indented to the right. This formatting convention is followed
       throughout the book to enable you to understand the working
       of the program better.

(d)   Unlike languages like C or Pascal, even if there is only one
       command to be executed in the if block the **fi** cannot be
       dropped.

The test Command

As we know the working of **if** depends upon the exit status of the control command. But quite often this status is not the only matter of interest to us or to a shell script. Some other factors may influence which set of commands the script should execute. For example, we may decide to execute a set of commands if the first argument supplied to the script is a file. Or in some other case, we may execute a set of commands if the number of arguments is less than 4. A lot many such examples can be cited. To take care of such situations Unix provides a command called **test**. This command investigates the sort of tests that we raised above and then it translates the result into the language of success or failure. This helps the shell in deciding whether to execute the commands in the if block or the commands in the else block. Let us see how to put this theory to work.

```
# SS15
# Usage: SS15
# Demonstrates the use of test command

echo Enter a number from 1 to 10
read num

if test $num -lt 6
then
    echo I used to think I was indecisive, but now I am not so sure
    echo - Anonymous
fi
```

A sample run of the program would be like this.

```
$ SS15
Enter a number from 1 to 10
4
I used to think I was indecisive, but now I am not so sure
- Anonymous.
```

No wonder we don't know who said that, if he was so indecisive. Here, we have used **test** to carry out a test whether the value of **num** is less than 6. You may recall that all shell variables are string variables. Still when we use **test** in conjunction with operators like **-lt** the numeric value of the string stored in **num** is used for comparison.

The **test** command can carry out several types of tests. These are:

(a)   Numerical tests
(b)   String tests
(c)   File tests

As the name suggests, numerical tests are used when comparisons between values of two numbers is to be done. They allow us to compare two values to see whether they are equal to each other, unequal, or whether one is greater than the other. In our program we have used the operator **-lt**. The other operators that can be used for numerical test are shown in Figure 10.2.

Operator	Meaning
-gt	greater than
-lt	less than
-ge	greater than or equal to
-le	less than or equal to
-ne	not equal to
-eq	equal to

Figure 10.2

To make you comfortable with the usage of numerical test in a program one more example has been given below. Study it carefully before reading further.

Example 10.1: In a company an employee is paid as under:

If his basic salary is less than Rs. 1500, then HRA = 10% of basic salary and DA = 90% of basic. If his salary is either equal to or above Rs. 1500, then HRA = Rs. 500 and DA = 98% of basic salary. If the employee's salary is input through the keyboard write a program to find his gross salary.

```
# SS16
# Usage: SS16
# Example of numeric test
# Calculation of gross salary

echo Enter basic salary
read  bs

if [  $bs -lt 1500 ]
then
        hra='echo $bs \* 10 / 100 | bc'
        da='echo $bs \* 90 / 100 | bc'
else
        hra=500
        da='echo $bs \* 98 / 100 | bc'
fi

gs='echo $bs + $hra + $da | bc'
echo Gross salary = Rs. $gs
```

Here is some sample interaction with the program.

```
$ SS16
Enter Basic salary 1200
Gross salary = Rs. 2400


$ SS16
Enter Basic salary 2000
Gross salary = Rs. 3960
```

Note that in the **if** statement instead of explicitly mentioning the word **test** we have placed the condition within **[ ]** which is allowed.

File Tests

The **test** command has several options for checking the status of a file. These are shown in Figure 10.3. Using these we can find out whether the specified file is an ordinary file or a directory, or whether it grants read, write or execute permissions, so on and so forth.

Option	Meaning
-s file	True if the file exists and has a size greater than 0
-f file	True if the file exists and is not a directory
-d file	True if the file exists and is a directory file
-c file	True if the file exists and is a character special file
-b file	True if the file exists and is a block special file
-r file	True if the file exists and you have a read permission to it
-w file	True if the file exists and you have a write permission to it
-x file	True if the file exists and you have an execute permission to it
-k file	True if the file exists and its sticky bit is set

Figure 10.3

Here is how we can use a file test in a shell script.

```
# SS17
# Usage: SS17

Enter file name
read fname
if [ -f $fname ]
then
```

```
        echo you indeed entered a file name
else
        echo what you entered is not a file name
fi
```

Observe the **if** statement carefully. Instead of using the **test** command we have enclosed the file test within [ ]. This is permissible and it avoids typing of **test** every time we wish to perform a test. However, care should be exercised while using []. There should always be a space immediately after '[' and immediately before ']'. Thus the test **[-f $file]** would be invalid.

Let us write another program on similar lines. This one checks whether the user has a write permission to a file. If yes, it prompts the user to type a message which then gets appended to the mentioned file.

```
# SS18
# Usage: SS18

echo Enter file name
read filename

if [  -w  $filename ]
then
        echo Type matter to append. To stop type Ctrl D.
        cat >> $filename
else
        echo No write permission.
fi
```

If the user has a write permission to the filename supplied from the keyboard, the matter typed by the user is read by the **cat** command and then using redirection operator (>>) gets appended to the desired file. When the user hits Ctrl d the **cat** command comes to an end.

String Tests

Another set of tests that the **test** command can handle are the string tests. The checks that we can carry out using these tests are shown in Figure 10.4

Condition	Meaning
string1 = string2	True if the strings are same
string1 != string2	True if the strings are different
-n string	True if the length of string is greater than 0
-z string	True if the length of the string is zero
string	True if the string is not a null string

Figure 10.4

Here is a program which puts these string tests into action.

```
# SS19
# Usage: SS19

str1="Good"
str2="Bad"
str3=

[ $str1 = $str2 ]
echo $?

[ $str1 != $str2 ]
echo $?

[ -n $str1 ]
echo $?
```

```
[ -z "$str3" ]
echo $?

[ -z $str3 ]
echo $?

[ "$str3" ]
echo $?
```

There is a lot of new material in this program. Let us examine it more carefully. To begin with you can observe that nowhere have we used an **if** statement to carry out the tests. This brings about the fact that **test** is really an independent command. Only thing is we have been using it as a control command in association with an **if**. Then how do we know whether the two strings being compared are identical or not, or whether length of a string is zero or non-zero? That's the time the metacharacter **$?** comes to help. This metacharacter contains the success or failure of the last command that has been executed (the **test** command in this case). That's the reason we have used a separate **echo** statement after each test. Each **echo** statement reports the success (0) or failure (1) of the test preceding it. Here is the output of the program...

```
1
0
0
0
test: argument expected
```

The output of the first three **echo** statements is straight-forward. Why did we get the error **test: argument expected**? Because **str3** is a null string and as we know a null string is ignored by the shell. Hence **test** gets to work on [**-z**], hence the error. This situation can be avoided as shown in the fourth test. This time we have enclosed **str3** within "". Therefore this time the **test** command gets to work with [**-z** ""], which returns a 0 since "" indeed represents a zero length string. How come the output of last **echo** statement did not get displayed? Did anything go wrong with the test? No, the test is quite correct, but it never got a chance to get evaluated. This is because any time an error occurs in a shell script the shell abandons the rest of the program.

Observe that while carrying out the equality test there is a space on either side of '='. This is necessary. Devoid of spaces it would become a simple assignment.

Can you figure out what would be the output of the following program?

```
# SS20
# Usage: SS20

str1="Good morning"
str2="Good bye"

[ $str1 = $str2 ]
echo $?
```

And here is the output of the program...

```
test: unknown operator morning
```

Surprised to get an error? Well, let us analyse it. Since two word strings are being assigned to variables **str1** and **str2** we have taken care to enclose the strings within a pair of double quotes. Still the test failed. Look at the error message and you would be able to understand the reason. The **test** command went to work with **[Good morning = Good bye]**. Naturally, **morning** was treated as an operator, hence the error. If you write the test as shown below the error would vanish.

```
[ "$str1" = "$str2" ]
```

Nested *if-else*s

It is perfectly all right if we write an entire **if-else-fi** construct within either the body of the **if** statement or the body of an **else** statement. This is called 'nesting' of ifs. This is shown in the following program.

```
# SS21
# Usage: SS21
# A quick demo of nested if-else

echo Enter either 1 or 2
read  i

if [ $i -eq 1 ]
then
      echo You would go to heaven!
else
        if [ $i -eq 2 ]
        then
              echo Hell was created with you in mind
        else
              echo How about mother earth!
        fi
fi
```

Note that the second **if-else** construct is nested in the first **else** statement. If the test in the first **if** statement fails, then the test in the second **if** statement is performed. If it is false as well, the final **else** statement is executed.

You can see in the program how each time a structure is nested within another structure, it is also indented for clarity. Inculcate this habit of indentation, otherwise you would end up writing programs which nobody (you included) can understand easily at a later date.

In the above program an **if-else** occurs within the **else** block of the first **if** statement. Similarly, in some other program an **if-else** may occur in the **if** block as well. There is no limit on how deeply the **if**s and the **else**s can be nested.

Forms of *if*

The **if** statement can take any of the following forms:

(a)   if control command
      then
          do this
          and this
      fi

(b)   if control command
      then
          do this
          and this
      else
          do this
          and this
      fi

(c)   if control command
      then
          do this
      else
          if control command
          then
               do this
          else
               do this
               and this
          fi
      fi

(d)   if control command

```
then
        if control command
        then
                do this
        else
                do this
                and this
        fi
else
        do this
fi
```

Use of Logical Operators

Shell allows usage of three logical operators while performing a test. These are:

(a)   -a (read as AND)
(b)   -o (read as OR)
(c)   ! (read as NOT)

The first two operators, **-a** and **-o**, allow two or more conditions to be combined in a test. Let us see how they are used in a program. Consider the following problem.

Example 10.2: The marks obtained by a student in 5 different subjects are input through the keyboard. The student gets a division as per the following rules:

        Percentage above or equal to 60 - First division
        Percentage between 50 and 59 - Second division
        Percentage between 40 and 49 - Third division
        Percentage less than 40 - Fail

Write a program to calculate the division obtained by the student.

Here is the program...

```
# SS22
# Usage: SS22

echo "Enter marks in five subjects \c"
read  m1  m2  m3  m4  m5

per=`expr \( $m1 + $m2 + $m3 + $m4 + $m5 \) / 5`

if [ per -ge 60 ]
then
        echo First division
fi

if [ per >= 50  -a  per < 60 ]
then
        echo Second division
fi

if [ per >= 40  -a  per < 50 ]
then
        echo Third division
fi

if [ per < 40 ]
then
        echo Fail
fi
```

As can be seen from the second **if** statement, the **-a** operator is used to combine two conditions. 'Second division' gets printed if both the conditions evaluate to true. If one of the conditions evaluate to false then the whole thing is treated as false.

So far we have used only the logical operators **-a** and **-o**. The third logical operator is the NOT operator, written as **!**. This operator reverses the value of the expression it operates on; it makes a true expression false and a false expression true. Here is an example of the NOT operator.

```
[ ! -d $dirname ]
```

This test is treated as true if **dirname** contains something other than a directory name.

Let us see another example of logical operators.

```
# SS23
# Usage: SS23

echo "Enter any file name \c"
read fname

if [ ! -z "$fname" ]
then
     if [ -r $fname -a -w $fname -a -x $fname ]
     then
          echo You have a read, write and execute permissions to $fname
     else
          echo Read, write and execute permissions denied
     fi
else
     echo Improper file name
fi
```

Note how we have used the ! operator. It lets the **if** block of the first **if** get executed only if **fname** contains a string of non-zero length. If the file name is correct then the script proceeds to check whether you have read, write and execute permissions to the file and displays an appropriate message.

Hierarchy of Logical Operators

Since we have now added the logical operators to the list of operators we know, it is time to review these operators and their priorities. Figure 10.5 summarizes the operators we have seen so far. The higher an operator is in the table, the higher is its priority.

Operators	Type
!	Logical Not
-lt, -gt, -le, -ge, -eq, -ne	Relational
-a	Logical And
-o	Logical Or

Figure 10.5

If you want to override any priority while carrying out a test use parentheses. Do not forget to precede the parentheses with a \. This is necessary since parentheses themselves are shell metacharacters. What do they exactly do we would find out in Chapter 12. Following example shows how to parenthesize the expressions.

```
[ $age -gt 10 -a \( -r $fname -o -w $fname \) ]
```

Looking at the hierarchy of operations shown in Figure 10.5 can you imagine how the test would be interpreted by the shell if the parentheses are omitted from the above expression.

else + *if* Equals *elif*

The **if** statement can take one more form. It permits you to group together several alternatives (multiple **else**s) one after the other. This is possible through a keyword **elif** which is a short form of **else if**. Given below are two shell scripts. The first doesn't use the keyword

elif whereas the second one does use it. Go through them and then we would discuss which form is better.

```
# SS24
# Usage: SS24
# Example of nested else's without using the elif clause

echo "Enter the adapter name \c"
read adapter

if [ "$adapter" = MA ]
then
     echo you have a monochrome adapter
else
     if [ "$adapter" = CGA ]
          echo You have a colour graphics adapter
     else
          if [ "$adapter" = EGA ]
          then
               echo You have an enhanced graphics adapter
          else
               if [ "$adapter" = VGA ]
               then
                    echo You have a video graphics adapter
               else
                    echo You have a super video graphics adapter
               fi
          fi
     fi
fi
```

```
# SS25
# Usage: SS25
# Example of nested else's using the elif clause

echo "Enter the adapter name \c"
```

```
read adapter

if [ "$adapter" = MA ]
then
      echo you have a monochrome adapter
elif [ "$adapter" = CGA ]
then
      echo You have a colour graphics adapter
elif [ "$adapter" = EGA ]
then
      echo You have an enhanced graphics adapter
elif [ "$adapter" = VGA ]
then
      echo You have a video graphics adapter
else
      echo You have a super video graphics adapter
fi
```

I don't suppose the shell script SS24 needs any explanation. So let us concentrate on SS25. If the first test is satisfied then the if block is executed and the control reaches the **fi**. If the first test fails then the control goes to the first **elif** where it performs a test. If this test is satisfied then the **echo** statement is executed following which again the control reaches **fi**. The same thing takes place for other **elif**s as well. If all the tests fail then the control reaches the **else** block and executes the **echo** statement within it.

Does this program offer any advantage over SS24? Yes. Two in fact.

(a)   Even though there are multiple tests being carried out only one **fi** is required.

(b)   In SS24 any time an **if** is encountered the statements following it are indented to the right to keep the program readable. As a result, more the number of tests more is the level of indentation. As against this **elif** maintains the level of indentation at a manageable level and the program doesn't creep to the right even if several tests are carried out.

The Case Control Structure

Another way of controlling the sequence of execution is using the case control structure. Though **if-else** constructs can be nested, an abundance of conditions may make tracing the control in a program difficult. Hence, for a program where we are required to select from several alternatives a case control structure is the answer. The general form of the case control instruction is given below (Also refer Figure 10.6).

```
case value in
    choice1)
        do this
        and this
        ;;
    choice2)
        do this
        and this
        ;;
    choice3)
        do this
        and this
        ;;
    *)
        do this
        ;;
esac
```

The "do this" and "and this" lines in the above form represent any valid Unix command. Also, **choice1**, **choice2** and **choice3** are labels which identify the potential choices of action. What happens when we run a program containing a case control structure? Firstly, the expression following the **case** keyword is evaluated. The value that it yields is then matched, one by one against the potential choices (**choice1**, **choice2** and **choice3** in the above form). When a match is found, the shell executes all commands in that case upto ;;. This pair of semicolons placed at the end of each choice are necessary. They

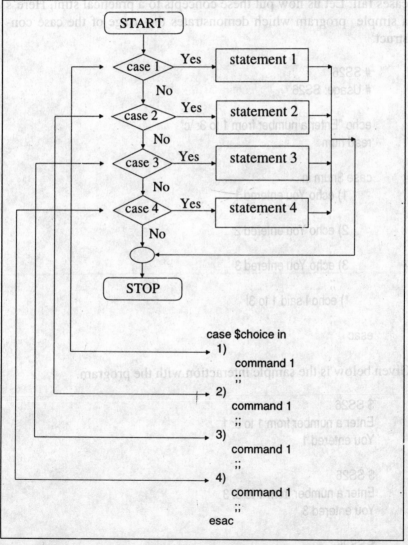

Figure 10.6

mark the end of statements within that choice. On encountering semicolons the control is transferred to **esac** (**case** spelt backwards), the keyword denoting the end of a case. If we omit the semicolons an error results. Observe the last case '*)'. This represents the default clause of the case control instruction. It gets executed when all other cases fail. Let us now put these concepts to a practical stint. Here's a simple program which demonstrates the usage of the case construct.

```
# SS26
# Usage: SS26

echo "Enter a number from 1 to 3: \c"
read num

case $num in
    1) echo You entered 1
       ;;
    2) echo You entered 2
       ;;
    3) echo You entered 3
       ;;
    *) echo I said 1 to 3!
       ;;
esac
```

Given below is the sample interaction with the program.

```
$ SS26
Enter a number from 1 to 3: 1
You entered 1

$ SS26
Enter a number from 1 to 3: 3
You entered 3

$ SS26
```

Enter a number from 1 to 3: 6
I said 1 to 3!

The Tips and Traps

Let us jot down a few useful tips about the usage of **case** and a few pitfalls to be avoided:

(a)   The earlier program which used the **case** control instruction may give you a wrong impression that you can use only cases arranged in ascending order, 1, 2, 3 and default. This is not so. You can in fact put the cases in any order you please. Here is an example of scrambled case order:

```
# SS27
# Usage: SS27

echo "Enter any number \c"
read num

case $num in
    121) echo I am in case 121
        ;;
    7) echo I am in case 7
        ;;
    22) echo I am in case 22
        ;;
    *) echo I am in default
        ;;
esac
```

(b)   The value portion of the **case** statement can be a shell variable, a shell script argument or output of a command. For example, the shell script SS28 given below uses the shell script argument in the value portion of the **case**. Likewise,

```
case 'who am i | cut -f1' in
```

would also be a valid beginning of a **case** statement.

```
# SS28
# Usage: SS28 dog/cat/parrot

case $1 in
        cat) echo You supplied cat at command line
                ;;
        dog) echo You supplied dog at command line
                ;;
        parrot) echo You supplied parrot at command line
                ;;
        *) echo You supplied an incorrect argument at command line
                ;;
esac
```

Notice that the choice labels in this program are entire words; we are not limited to using single digits or letters while checking the choices.

(c)   If we want to execute the same set of statements if any of the two choices are made we can combine the options using the or (|) operator as shown in the following program.

```
# SS29
# Usage: SS29 dog or cat / parrot or crow / whale or shark

case $1 in
        cat | dog) echo You supplied name of animal at command line
                ;;
        parrot | crow) echo You supplied name of a bird at command line
                ;;
        whale | shark) echo You supplied name of a fish at command line
                ;;
        *) echo You supplied an incorrect argument at command line
```

```
    ;;
esac
```

If we supply 'dog' or 'cat' to this script the same message would be echoed. Note that the | operator used here has got nothing to do with the piping symbol. Depending upon the context in which the | symbol has been used the shell carries out an appropriate action.

(d)   We can use shell's pattern matching abilities in the choice labels. In fact we have used one example already, when we used *) to match any pattern. In addition we are permitted to use the ? and [ ] shell metacharacters. They are used for pattern matching in the same way as they are used in matching filenames. The following script shows how to use them.

```
# SS30
# Usage: SS30

echo Enter any character
read char

case $char in
    [a-z]) echo You entered a small case character
    ;;
    [A-Z]) echo You entered a capital letter
    ;;
    [0-9]) echo You entered a digit
    ;;
    ?) echo You entered a special symbol
    ;;
    *) echo You entered more than one character
    ;;
esac
```

The program asks the user to enter a character and then determines whether the user entered a smallcase letter, a capital

letter, a digit or a special symbol. You may recall that both **?**
and **[ ]** represent one character, the difference being **?** represents any character, whereas **[ ]** represents the range or group
of characters mentioned within **[ ]**. The ***)** once again represents
the default case and in our program the control reaches here if
more than one character is supplied to the **read** statement.
Using this pattern matching ability of **case** we can build
complicated patterns like the ones shown in the following
program.

```
# SS31
# Usage: SS31

echo Enter any word
read word

case $word in
    [aeiou]*) echo The word begins with a small case vowel
        ;;
    [AEIOU]*) echo The word begins with a capital vowel
        ;;
    *[0-9]) echo The word ends with a digit
        ;;
    ???) echo You entered a three lettered word
        ;;
esac
```

(e) Even if there is a single command in a case it is necessary to
     follow it with ;;. Actually, the ;; after the final choice in the
     case is not compulsory. At the same time it causes no harm
     even if we use it in the last case.

(f) If we have no **default** case, and no case is satisfied then nothing
     is done and the program simply moves on to whatever comes
     after the **case-esac** statement.

(g)   Ideally, we should write the default choice '*)' as the last choice. Making it the first choice would cause the first choice to match any value, and the **case** would not be searched any further.

(h)   Is **case** a replacement for **if**? Yes and no. Yes, because it offers a better way of writing programs as compared to **if**, and no because in certain situations we are left with no choice but to use an **if**. The disadvantage of **case** is we cannot have a choice in **case** which looks like...

$i -lt 20)

All that we can have as a choice is a specific alternative or a group of alternatives.

The advantage of **case** over an **if** is that it leads to a more structured program and the level of indentation is more manageable.

(i)   In principle, a **case** may occur within another, but in practice it is rarely done. Such statements would be called nested **case** statements.

(j)   The **case** statement is very useful while writing menu driven programs. This aspect of switch is discussed in the exercise at the end of this chapter.

Exercise

if, *if-else*, Nested *if-else*s, *elif*

[A]   What will be the output of the following programs:

(a)   a=300
       [-n $a]

```
        echo $?
        [ -z $a ]
        echo $?

(b)     b=
        [ -n $b ]
        echo $?
        [ -z $b ]
        echo $?

(c)     [ -n $name ]
        echo $?
        [ -z $name ]
        echo $?

(d)     x=3  y=5  z=10
        if [ \( $x -eq 3 \)  -a \( $y -eq 5  -o  $z -eq 10 \) ]
        then
              echo $x
        else
              echo $y
        fi

(e)     x=3
        y=3.0
        if [ $x -eq $y ]
        then
              echo x and y are equal
        else
              echo x and y are not equal
        fi

(f)     x=3
        y='[ $x -eq 10 ]'
        z='[ $x -lt 10 ]'
        echo x=$x  y=$y  z=$z
```

(g) k=35
     echo '[$k -eq 35]' '[$k -eq 50]'

(h) i=4 z=12
     if [$i = 5 -o $z -gt 50]
     then
          echo Sonata
     else
          echo Sonnette
     fi

(i) i=4 z=12
     [$i = 5 -a $z -gt 5]
     echo $?

(j) i=4 j=-1 k=0
     [$i -o $j -o $k]
     echo $?
     [$i -a $j -a $k]
     echo $?
     [$i -a $j -o $k]
     echo $?

(k) i=3
     if [! -z $i]
     then
          echo Thoughts thunk while writing this
     else
          echo Thoughts cannot be thunk
     fi

(l) if [! -z $code -a ! $flag]
     then
          echo macinations on the mac
     fi

[B] Point out the errors, if any, in the following programs:

(a)
```
a=12.25  b=12.52
if [ a=b ]
then
      echo "\na and b are equal"
fi
```

(b)
```
j = 10  k = 12
if test [ k -ge j ]
then
      k=j
      j=k
fi
echo $j $k
```

(c)
```
j = 10  k = 12
if [ k >= j ]
then
      k=j
      j=k
fi
echo $j $k
```

(d)
```
x=10
if [ x -ge 2 ]
then
      echo x
fi
```

(e)
```
x=10
if [ $x -ge 2 ]
      echo $x
fi
```

(f)
```
x=10  y=15
if [ $x % 2 -eq $y % 3 ]
then
      echo Barnie
fi
```

(g)
```
x=10  y=15
if [ 'expr $x % 2' = 'expr $y % 3' ]
then
      echo "\nCarpathians"
fi
```

(h)
```
a=10  b=15  c=20
if [ $a -ge 5  and  $y -ge 10  or  $c -ge 20 ]
then
      echo "\nThe desert thunder"
fi
```

(i)
```
a=Sameer
if [ $a = Sameer ] then echo "\nThe carribeans" fi
```

(j)
```
Echo Enter filename
read fname
if [ -rwx $fname ]
then
      echo You have read, write and execute permissions to the file
fi
```

(k)
```
a=10
if [$a -ge 5]
then
      echo "\nStormy petrel"
fi
```

(l)
```
# This script demonstrates
```

the use of Logical operators
```
i=2 j=5
if [ i -eq 2 -a j -eq 5 ]
then
        echo Satisfied at last
fi
```

(m)
```
read filename
if ( ! -s $filename )
then
        echo Size of files is 0 bytes
fi
```

(n)
```
i=Amay j=Ajay
if [ ( $i = Amay ) -a ( $j = Ajay ) ]
then
        echo Good day!
fi
```

(o)
```
i=4
y=`expr `expr $i + 5` + 5`
if [ -n $y ]
then
        echo $y
fi
```

[C] if x=11, y=6 then find the exit status of the expressions in the following table:

Expression	Value
[$x -gt 9 -a $y -ne 3]	0
$x -eq 5 -o $y -ne 3	
[! $x -gt 14]	
[! $x -gt 9 -a ! $y -ne 23]	
[$x -eq 11 -a $y -ne 8]	

[D]   Attempt the following:

(a)   If cost price and selling price of an item is input through the keyboard, write a program to determine whether the seller has made profit or incurred loss. Also determine how much profit was made or loss incurred.

(b)   Any integer is input through the keyboard. Write a program to find out whether it is an odd number or even number.

(c)   Write a shell script which receives any year from the keyboard and determines whether the year is a leap year or not. If no argument is supplied the current year should be assumed.

(d)   Write a shell script which receives two filenames as arguments. It should check whether the two file's contents are same or not. If they are same then second file should be deleted.

(Hint: Use the **cmp** command to compare files)

(e)   Write a shell script which will automatically get executed on logging in. This shell script should display the present working directory and report whether your friend whose logname is **aa10** has currently logged in or not. If he has logged in then the shell script should send a message to his terminal suggesting a dinner tonight. If you do not have a write permission to his terminal or if he hasn't logged in then such a message should be mailed to him with a request to send confirmation about your dinner proposal.

(f)   While executing a shell script either the LOGNAME or the UID is supplied at the command prompt. Write a shell script to find out at how many terminals has this user logged in.

(g)   A shell script can receive an argument 'one', 'two' or 'three'. If the argument supplied is 'one' display it in bold, if it is 'two' display it in reverse video and if it is 'three' make it blink on the screen. If a wrong argument is supplied report it. Use an **elif** statement.

(h) Any year is entered through the keyboard, write a program to determine whether the year is leap or not. Use the logical operators **-a** and **-o**.

[E] What will be the output of the following programs:

(a)
```
suite=3
case $suite in
    1) echo Diamond ;;
    2) echo Spade ;;
    3) echo Heart ;;
    *) echo I thought one wears a suite
esac
```

(b)
```
terminal=vt100
case $terminal in
    VT100) echo Dec terminal ;;
    vt200) echo Old terminal ;;
    ansi) echo Commonly used terminal ;;
    v*) echo vt series terminal ;;
    *) echo Any terminal ;;
esac
```

(c)
```
read dirname
case $dirname in
    *) echo any directory name ;;
    c*) echo Cobol directory name ;;
    f*) echo Fortran directory name ;;
esac
```

(d)
```
ch=a
case "$ch" in
    a | b | c ) echo One of the first three alphabets ;;
```

```
            [A-Z]) echo Some capital letter ;;
            [e-ir-z]) echo Some character between e to i or r to z ;;
        esac
```

(e)   i=" "
```
      case $i in
            " ") echo 1 space ;;
            "  ") echo 2 spaces ;;
            "   ") echo 3 spaces ;;
            "    ") echo 4 spaces ;;
            *) echo no space ;;
      esac
```

[F]   Point out the errors, if any, in the following programs:

(a)   suite=1
```
      case suite in
            0) echo Club ;;
            1) echo Diamond
      esac
```

(b)   read temp
```
      case $temp in
            temp <= 20) echo Ooooooohhhh! Damn cool! ;;
            temp > 20) echo Rain rain here again! ;;
            \*) echo Good old nagpur weather ;;
      esac
```

(c)   a=3.5
```
      case $a in
            0.5) echo 20000 leagues under the C ;;
            1.5) echo The C calisthenics ;;
            *) echo Simply c ;;
      esac
```

(d)   a=

```
        case $a in
            A) echo I C C U ;;
            a I b) echo I C C U ;;
            *) echo I see see you ;;
        esac
```

(e)   read name
        case $name in
            *.c) echo It is a C program file
            *.for) echo It is a Fortran program file
            *) echo Can't say for sure
        esac

[F]   Attempt the following:

(a)   A shell script can receive an argument 'one', 'two' or 'three'. If the argument supplied is 'one' display it in bold, if it is 'two' display it in reverse video and if it is 'three' make it blink on the screen. If a wrong argument is supplied report it. Use a **case** control instruction.

(b)   Write a shell script which gets executed the moment the user logs in. It should display the message "Good Morning"/"Good Afternoon"/"Good Evening" depending upon the time at which the user logs in.

(c)   Write a menu driven program which has following options:

      1.   contents of /etc/passwd
      2.   List of users who have currently logged in
      3.   Present working directory
      4.   Exit

      Make use of **case** statement. The menu should be placed approximately in the centre of the screen and should be displayed in bold using the **tput** statement.

11 The Loop Control Structure

The Loop Control Structure

The programs that we have developed so far used either a sequential or a decision control structure. In the first one, the commands were executed in a fixed order, while in the second, an appropriate set of instructions was executed depending upon the outcome of the condition being tested (or a logical decision being taken).

These programs were of limited nature, because when executed, they always performed the same series of actions, in the same way, exactly once. Almost always, if something is worth doing, it's worth doing more than once. In real life programming we are frequently required to perform an action over and over, often with variations in the details each time. The mechanism which meets this need is the 'loop', and loops is the subject of this chapter.

Loops

A loop involves repeating some portion of the program either a specified number of times or until a particular condition is being satisfied. There are three methods by way of which we can repeat a part of a program. They are:

(a) Using a **for** statement
(b) Using a **while** statement
(c) Using an **until** statement

Each of these methods are discussed in the following pages.

The *while* Loop

It is often the case in programming that you want to do something a fixed number of times. The **while** loop is ideally suited for such cases. Let us look at a simple example which uses a **while** loop. The flowchart shown below would help you to understand the operation of the **while** loop.

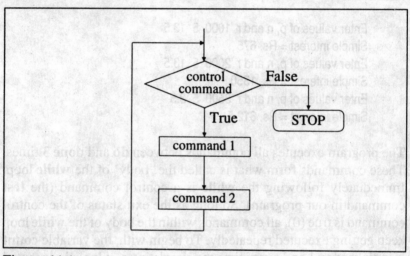

Figure 11.1

Let us now try a program which makes use of a **while** loop. Suppose we want to calculate simple interest for three sets of principal, number of years and rate of interest. Here is the program which shows how this can be done.

```
# SS32
# Usage: SS32
# Calculation of simple interest for 3 sets of p, n and r

count=1
while [ $count -le 3 ]
do
        echo "\nEnter values of p, n and r \c"
```

```
                    read p n r
                    si='echo $p \* $n \* $r / 100 | bc'
                    echo Simple interest = Rs. $si

                    count='expr $count + 1'
            done
```

And here are a few sample runs...

```
        Enter values of p, n and r  1000  5  13.5
        Simple interest = Rs. 675
        Enter values of p, n and r  2000  5  13.5
        Simple interest = Rs. 1350
        Enter values of p, n and r  3500  5  3.5
        Simple interest = Rs. 612.5
```

The program executes all commands between **do** and **done** 3 times. These commands form what is called the 'body' of the **while** loop. Immediately following the **while** is a control command (the **test** command in our program). So long as the exit status of the control command is true (0), all commands within the body of the **while** loop keep getting executed repeatedly. To begin with, the variable **count** is initialised to 1 and every time the simple interest logic is executed the value of **count** is incremented by one. The variable **count** is many a times called either a 'loop counter' or an 'index variable'.

Tips and Traps

The general form of **while** is as shown below:

```
        while control command
        do
              command 1
              command 2
        done
```

Note the following points about **while**...

- The statements within the **while** loop would keep on getting executed till the exit status of the control command remains true. When the exit status of the control command turns out to be false, the control passes to the first command that follows the body of the **while** loop (i.e. the first command after **done**).

- The control command can be any valid Unix command. Some examples of control commands are shown below.

```
while [ $# -le 5 ]
while who I grep $logname
while [ -r $file -a -w $file ]
```

- The statements within the loop may be a single command or a group of commands. In either case it is necessary to put them between **do** and **done**.

- As a rule the **while** must have a control command that will eventually return an exit status 1 (false), otherwise the loop would be executed forever, indefinitely.

```
# SS33
# Usage: SS33

count=1
while [ $count -le 10 ]
do
        echo $count
done
```

This is an indefinite loop, since **i** remains equal to 1 forever. The correct form would be as under:

```
count=1
while [ $count -le 10 ]
```

```
        do
                echo $count
                count='expr $count + 1'
        done
```

- Instead of incrementing a loop counter, we can even decrement it and still manage to get the body of the loop executed repeatedly. This is shown below:

```
# SS34
# Usage: SS34

count=10
while [ $count -ge 1 ]
do
        echo $count
        count='expr $count - 1'
done
```

- It is not necessary that a loop counter must only be an integer. It can even be a float.

```
# SS35
# Usage: SS35

count=10.0
while [ $count -le 20.0 ]
do
        echo "\nRaindrops on roses..."
        echo "...and whiskers on kittens"
        count='echo $count + 0.1 | bc'
done
```

Even floating point loop counters can be decremented. Once again the increment and decrement could be by any value, not necessarily 1.

What do you think would be the result of the following test:

```
a=3.5
[ $a  -eq  3.7 ]
echo $?
0
```

The fact that the exit status is being reported as 0 means the test was satisfied. This is because while comparing real numbers using **-eq** the fractional part is ignored and only the integer part is used to carry out the comparison.

Friend, Where are You...

Let us now see a practical example of the **while** loop. Suppose a friend of yours has promised to log in at a particular time. However, he has not kept the promise. You want to contact him as soon as he logs in. Let us write a shell script which checks after every one minute whether your friend has logged in or not. The script should report whenever he logs in along with the amount of time he was late in logging in. The logname should be supplied to the shell script at the command prompt.

```
# SS36
# Usage: SS36 username

if [ $# -lt 1 ]
then
        echo Improper usage
        echo Correct usage is: $0 username
        exit
fi

logname=$1
time=0
```

```
while true
do
        who I grep "$logname" > /dev/null
        if [ $? = 0 ]
        then
                echo $logname has logged in.
                if [ $time -ne 0 ]
                then
                        echo He is $time minutes late.
                fi
                exit
        else
                time='expr $time + 1'
                sleep 60
        fi
done
```

Shown below are two runs of this program.

```
$ SS36 &
32105
Improper usage
Correct usage is: $0 username
$ SS36 aa10 &
32654
aa10 has logged in
He is 12 minutes late.
```

Let us digest the new concepts incorporated in this script a step at a time. To begin with, the **if** checks whether correct number of arguments have been supplied at the command prompt while running the shell. During the first run of the program an error resulted. This so happened because the username was not supplied when the script was executed for the first time. You should note two things here.

(a)   While indicating the correct usage we have used the command echo Correct usage is: $0 username

Here instead of using SS36 we have used **$0**. This is more sensible since tomorrow if the file (SS36) which holds this shell script is renamed to say NEWSS36 the message flashed would be

Correct usage is: NEWSS36 username

(b) After flashing the message indicating the correct usage the execution of the script should be terminated. This is achieved by the **exit** statement. Whenever the shell comes across an **exit** statement in a script it immediately terminates the execution of the script.

If the control reaches beyond the first **if** statement it means the usage of the script is correct. Hence the login name supplied as the argument is collected in the variable **logname**. Now we must check whether this user has logged in or not. This can be done by scanning the output of **who** using the **grep** command. So far so good. But why the **while true** has been used? Because we wanted to execute the loop an infinite number of times since we are unsure when our friend would log in and we would like to search for him every minute. **true** does nothing except returning a zero exit status. Likewise, **false**, **true**'s counterpart does nothing except returning a non-zero exit status.

First time through the loop when we search for our friend by scanning the output of **who** using **grep**, the output of **grep** is redirected to **/dev/null**. Whenever the output of any command is redirected to this file the output is ignored. This is necessary, otherwise the output would appear on the screen, something the script is not planning. Whether **grep** has been able to locate our friend or not can be verified from the exit status of **grep** using our normal **$?**. Note that whenever commands are used in a pipeline **$?** reports the exit status of the last command in the pipeline (**grep** in our case). If **grep** is successful we promptly display the message that the user has logged in along with the time. If the user has not logged in then we reach the **else** block.

Here we encounter the command **sleep 60**. This command postpones the execution of the next command by 60 seconds. Of course in place of 60, **sleep** can take any other argument. Once 60 seconds are over the program resumes its work. That is, the control goes to **fi**, **done** and finally back at the beginning of the **while** loop. This continues to happen till our friend doesn't log in.

It is important to run this script in the background. If we do not do this and our friend doesn't log in for hours together the control would remain within the infinite **while** loop waiting for our friend to log in.

The IFS Thing

Remember IFS? It stands for Internal Field Separator and is one of the system variables. By default its value is space, tab and a new line. It signifies where in a line does one field (word) end and another begin.

What would be the output of the following program segment?

```
set The Unix Operating System
echo $1 $2 $3 $4
```

Obviously, $1 would echo 'The', $2 would echo 'Unix' and so on. How come **set** managed to assign a value 'The' to $1 and 'Unix' to $2. That's where the IFS comes in. Since one of the default values of IFS is a space the space after 'The' was taken as end of the word. Would the results change if IFS has a different value? Of course, as the following program's output would justify.

```
# SS37
# Demo of IFS

IFS=:
set The Unix Operating System
echo $1
```

```
echo $2 $3 $4
```

And here is the output...

```
The Unix Operating System

$
```

Note that this time the entire 'The Unix Operating System' got assigned to $1 since no words were separated by a ':'. Naturally, $2, $3 and $4 are null variables, hence a blank line is outputted when we attempt to echo them.

But when would we like to change the value of IFS? Whenever the fields are separated by some separator other than a space or a tab. For example fields in the file **/etc/passwd** which stores information about all users are separated by a ':'. So if we are to access these fields separately we will have to set the IFS to : before accessing individual fields. Once the fields have been accessed the value of IFS should be reset to original. The program to achieve this is given below.

```
# SS38
# Usage: SS38 username

if [ $# -lt 1 ]
then
      echo "Improper usage: $0 username"
fi

logname=$1
line='grep $logname /etc/passwd'

oldifs="$IFS"
IFS=:
set $line

clear
```

```
tput cup 10 20
echo User = $1

tput cup 11 20
echo User ID = $3

tput cup 12 20
echo Group ID = $4

tput cup 13 20
echo Comment about the user = $5

tput cup 14 20
echo Default Working Directory = $6

tput cup 15 20
echo Default working shell = $7
```

Here, firstly the user name supplied at the command prompt is picked up in the variable **logname**. Next the line containing this logname is extracted from the file **/etc/passwd** using **grep**. This line is stored in the variable **line**. In our case the value of **line** turned out to be

```
aa10:x:203:50:This is working account of aa10:/usr/aa10:/bin/sh
```

Now the original value of **IFS** is stored and the new value is set to ':'. When **set** operates on this line it sets **$1** with 'aa10', **$2** with 'x' etc. These values are then promptly displayed on the screen.

Reading from A File

So far we have used the **read** statement to read strings from the keyboard. We can use the same **read** statement to carry out the reading from a file. The following program reads each line in a file and displays it on the screen.

```
# SS39
# Usage: SS39

echo Enter file name
read fname

terminal='tty'
exec < $fname

while read line
do
      echo $line
done

exec < $terminal
```

To begin with the program asks for the filename whose contents are to be displayed. The name supplied is picked up as usual using the **read** statement. Here onwards reading should take place from the file. This is achieved by the statement **exec < $fname**. This statement ensures that the input for the **read** statement now comes from the file and not from the keyboard. The **read** statement continues to read each line from the file and display it. When the end of file is reached and there are no more lines left to read the **read** statement again attempts to read a line. This time an exit status of 1 is returned by the **read** statement, hence the **while** loop is terminated. Having read the entire file now the standard input should be reset back to the terminal. Since different users would be working at different terminals we should set back the standard input properly. Hence before using **exec** we have preserved the terminal name (file) in the variable **terminal**. Once the **while** loop is terminated, using the value stored in **terminal** the standard input is reset back to original.

We can write a similar program which counts the number of lines and words present in a file. If no filename is supplied at the command prompt then the input is taken from the keyboard. Here is the program...

```
# SS40
# Usage: SS40 [filename]
# Count number of lines and words supplied at standard input

if [ $# -eq 1 ]
then
    terminal='tty'
    exec < $1
    flag=1
fi

nol=0
now=0

while read line
do
    nol='expr $nol + 1'
    set -- $line
    now='expr $now + $#'
done

echo "Number of lines = $nol"
echo "Number of words = $now"

if [ "$flag" = 1 ]
then
    exec < $terminal
fi
```

If filename is supplied at the command prompt while executing the script, then the input is redirected from this file using **exec**. However, if filename is not supplied then **read** carries out the reading from the keyboard. The **flag** variable is used to keep track of whether the filename was supplied or not. Each line as it is read is counted and then using **set** and $# the number of words in it are counted.

We can force the **read** statement to alternately read from the file and from the keyboard. This is how it can be done.

```
# SS41
# Usage: SS41

echo Enter filename
read fname

terminal='tty'
exec < $fname

while read line
do
        echo $line
        echo Press any key...
        read key < $terminal
done

exec < $terminal
```

Here once the standard input is set to the filename (using **exec**) the control reaches the **while** loop. The **read line** command now reads a line from the file and echoes it on the screen. A message 'Press any key...' is now displayed and the program waits for the user to supply a key press. Note that here the **read** statement should carry out the reading from the keyboard and not from the file. One way of achieving this could be by using the **exec** statement twice as shown below:

```
echo Press any key...
exec < $terminal
read key
exec < $fname
```

Instead of this, we can continue to let the file act as standard input and we can collect the keypress using the statement,

```
read key < $terminal
```

This avoids setting and resetting of the standard input time and again inside the loop.

The *until* Loop

An **until** loop looks like this:

```
until control command doesn't return true
do
        this
        and this
        and this
        and this
done
```

The statements within the **until** loop keep on getting executed till the exit status of the control command remains false (1). When the exit status becomes true (0), the control passes to the first command that follows the body of the **until** loop (i.e. the first command after **done**).

There is a minor difference between the working of **while** and **until** loops. The **while** loop executes till the exit status of the control command is true and terminates when the exit status becomes false. Unlike this the **until** loop executes till the exit status of the control command is false and terminates when this status becomes true. This difference is brought about more clearly by the following programs.

```
# SS42
# Usage: SS42
# Prints numbers from 1 to 10 using while

i=1
while [ $i -le 10 ]
do
```

```
        echo $i
        i='expr $i + 1'
done


# SS43
# Usage: SS43
# Prints numbers from 1 to 10 using until

i=1
until [ $i -gt 10 ]
do
        echo $i
        i='expr $i + 1'
done
```

Did you notice the difference in the way the loops have been written in the two programs given above. The **while** loop continues its job till the test remains true and terminates when the test fails. Unlike this, the **until** loop continues till the test remains false and terminates when the test becomes true.

Apart from this peculiarity the **while** and the **until** loops behave exactly identically. Can you now attempt to rewrite the program SS36 using an **until** loop.

Note the following points about **until**...

-       The control command can be any valid Unix command. Some examples of control commands are shown below.

```
        until [ $i -le 5 ]
        until who | grep $logname > /dev/null
        until [ -s $file -a -r $file ]
```

- The statements within the **until** loop may be a single command or a group of commands. In either case it is necessary to put them between **do** and **done**.

- As a rule the **until** must have a control command that will eventually return an exit status 0 (true), otherwise the loop would be executed forever, indefinitely.

The *for* Loop

The **for** loop is more frequently used as compared to the **while** and the **until** loops. Its working is also different than the other two loops. The **for** allows us to specify a list of values which the control variable in the loop can take. The loop is then executed for each value mentioned in the list.

The general form of **for** statement is as under:

```
for control-variable in value1 value2 value3 ...
do
      command 1
      command 2
      command 3
done
```

Here the **for** loop would execute the same sequence of commands for values mentioned in the list following the keyword **in**. Here is a simple example of the **for** loop.

```
# SS44
# Usage: SS44

for word in High on a hill was a lovely mountain
do
      echo $word
done
```

Before explaining this script, let's see what it does when it is executed.

```
$ SS44
High
on
a
hill
was
a
lovely
mountain
```

The **word** in the for loop is known as a control variable. The words mentioned after **in** are values the variable **word** takes in succession as the shell executes the **for** loop. That is, firstly the instructions between **do** and **done** are executed with **word** set to a value 'High'. Then **word** is set to the next value 'on', and the instructions between **do** and **done** are executed again. Each time while executing the **echo** statement **$word** represents the current value of the variable **word**. This continues until all the values in the list are used. Note that the statements between **do** and **done** have been indented. Though this is not necessary, it is desirable since it makes it easier to see where the loop starts and where it ends.

Using *for* with Command Line Arguments

Instead of mentioning the list of values explicitly after the **in**, a **for** loop can take values from command line arguments. Here is a modified version of SS44 which uses command line arguments to provide values to the variable **word**. Recall that $* stands for all command line arguments following the name of the script.

```
# SS45
# Usage: SS45 [ arg1 arg2 arg3 arg4 ... ]
```

```
for word in $*
do
      echo $word
done
```

Let us see what happens when we execute this program.

```
$ SS45 Merry go round and Tora Tora Tora
Merry
go
round
and
Tora
Tora
Tora
```

Now the variable **word** takes in turn each of the arguments supplied at command prompt and **echo** echoes these values.

We are so frequently required to use the form

```
for word in $*
```

that Unix accepts the abbreviation

```
for word
```

This means we can rewrite SS45 as follows:

```
# SS46
# Usage: SS46 [ arg1 arg2 arg3 arg4 ... ]

for word
do
      echo $word
done
```

This program would work similar to SS45, using each argument given to the script in turn while executing the **for** loop.

Let us now write another program using **for**. Suppose we want to print names of all sub-directories present in the current directory.

```
# SS47
# Usage: SS47

for entry in *
do
      if [ -d $entry ]
      then
            echo $entry
      fi
done
```

This program illustrates another way of giving values to the control variable in the **for** loop. Instead of using $*, here we have used *, which represents all files in the current directory. Within the loop we check whether the entry in question is a directory. If it is so, then we display its name, otherwise we go to the next entry in the list.

Creating Nested Directories

Having seen how the **for** loop works let us put it to a more practical use. Suppose a full path like **dir1/dir2/dir3/mydir** is supplied during execution of a shell script. Here **dir1**, **dir2**, **dir3** and **mydir** are directory names. Let us write a shell script which creates these directories (if they do not already exist) and change to the last directory in the list. We would also check for the possibility that there might exist a filename with the same name as any of the directory names present in the supplied path. The shell script is given below.

```
# SS48
# Usage: SS48 pathname
```

```
if [ $# -lt 1 ]
then
        echo "Improper Usage: $0 pathname"
fi

oldifs="$IFS"
IFS=/

for arg in $*
do
    if [ -d $arg ]   # if the argument is an existing directory
    then
        cd $arg
    else
        if [ -f $arg ]   # if the argument is a file
        then
            echo $arg is a file
            exit
        else
            mkdir  $arg   # create directory
            cd  $dir   # and go into it
        fi
    fi
done

IFS="$oldifs"
```

Having discussed scripts which change the value of IFS earlier, I would leave this one for you to figure out on your own.

Generating Values for a *for* Loop

Several ways exist to give values to the control variable in a **for** loop. Some of these ways we have already seen. Let us enumerate them here for easy remembrance. A few new ways are also exemplified here.

(a) Mention the values that the control variable should take immediately after the keyword **in** as shown below:

```
for var in Moderation is for marks
```

(b) Take the values from shell script arguments, as in

```
# SS49
for var in $*
```

or its equivalent short-form

```
# SS49
for var
```

While executing a script which contains such a **for** loop the arguments should be supplied at the command prompt while executing the script as shown below:

```
$ SS49 Goosy Goosy Gander
```

(c) Take filenames from a directory as values for the control variable as shown below:

```
for file in *.c
do
    mv $file $file.cpp
done
```

This loop would pick up all C program files from the current directory and add the extension '.cpp' at the end of each such file.

All the following forms are acceptable to the shell.

```
for file in mydir/letters/*.let
for var in mydir/a??
for entry in ../../??.*
```

At this stage you should appreciate the difference between the forms

```
for var in *
```

and

```
for var in $*
```

The first form represents all files in the current directory, whereas the second represents all command-line arguments.

(d)   The control variable can take values from a shell variable as shown below:

```
phrase="to stay out of trouble"
for word in $phrase
do
    echo $word
done
```

On execution the control variable would take values 'to', 'stay', 'out' etc. in turn. This would so happen because the **for** statement would become

```
for word in to stay out of trouble
```

The control variable now gets assigned each word from this list, one at a time. Thus, each iteration through the loop would print just one word.

(e)   The control variable can take values from the output of a command as shown in the following example:

```
for cmd in 'cat commandlist'
do
        man $cmd >> helpfile
done
```

Remember the effect of back-quotes? They ensure that the command within the back-quotes is replaced with the output of the command. Hence here the **'cat commandlist'** would be replaced with the list of commands that may be present in the file **commandlist**. Then these command names would be used as successive values for the variable **cmd**. The manual pages for each of these commands are then appended to the file **helpfile**.

Each of the above mentioned ways are needed while using **for** loops in different programming situations.

Nesting of Loops

The way **if** statements can be nested, similarly **whiles**, **untils** and **fors** can also be nested. To understand how nested loops work, look at the program given below: .

```
# SS50
# Usage: SS50
# Demonstration of nested loops

r=1
while [ $r -le 3 ]  # outer loop
do
    c=1
    while [ $c -le 2 ]  # inner loop
    do
        sum='expr $r + $c'
        echo r = $r c = $c sum = $sum
        c='expr $c + 1'
```

```
            done
            r='expr $r + 1'
      done
```

When you run this program you will get the following output:

```
      r = 1 c = 1 sum = 2
      r = 1 c = 2 sum = 3
      r = 2 c = 1 sum = 3
      r = 2 c = 2 sum = 4
      r = 3 c = 1 sum = 4
      r = 3 c = 2 sum = 5
```

Here, for each value of **r** the inner loop is cycled through twice, with the variable **c** taking values from 1 to 2. The inner loop terminates when the value of **c** exceeds 2, and the outer loop terminates when the value of **r** exceeds 3.

As you can see, the body of the outer **for** loop is indented, and the body of the inner **for** loop is further indented. These multiple indentations make the program easier to understand.

Instead of using two statements, one to calculate **sum** and another to print it out, we can compact this into one single statement by saying:

```
      echo r = $r c = $c sum = 'expr $r + $c'
```

The way **while** loops have been nested here, similarly, two **until** loops or two **for** loops can also be nested. Not only this, a **for** loop can occur within a **while** loop, or a **while** within a **for** or any such combination.

The *break* Statement

We often come across situations where we want to jump out of a loop instantly, without waiting to get back to the control-command. The keyword **break** allows us to do this. When the keyword **break** is encountered inside any loop, control automatically passes to the first statement after the loop. A **break** is usually associated with an **if**. As an example, consider the following problem.

Example 11.1: Write a program to count and report the number of entries present in each sub-directory mentioned in the path which is supplied as a command-line argument.

The following program implements this logic.

```
# SS51
# Usage: SS51 pathname

pathname=$1
oldifs="$IFS"
IFS=/
flag=no

set $pathname
for dir in $*
do
      if [ ! -d $dir ]
      then
            echo $dir is not a directory... hence breaking out
            flag=yes
            break
      else
            num='ls | wc -l'
            echo $dir has $num entries
      fi
done

if [ flag = yes ]
then
      echo Abrupt end to the for loop
fi
```

IFS=$oldifs

In this program the moment the condition **[! -d $dir]** fails (i.e. the value stored in **dir** is not a directory entry) the message "not a directory... hence breaking out" is echoed and the control breaks out of the **while** loop. Why does the program require the **if** statement after the **while** loop at all? Well, there are two ways the control could have reached outside the **while** loop:

(a)   It jumped out because all the values taken by the **for** loop have exhausted.

(b)   The loop came to an end on execution of **break**.

To keep track of whether the loop was terminated because of the second case cited above we have used the variable **flag**. It is set to a value 'yes' if we come across an entry which is not a directory.

The keyword **break**, breaks the control only from the **while** in which it is placed. Consider the following program which illustrates this fact.

```
# SS52
# Usage: SS52

i=1 j=1

while [ $i -le 100 ]
do
      while [ $j -lt 200 ]
      do
          if [ $j -eq 150 ]
          then
              break
          else
              echo $i $j
          fi
```

```
            j='expr $j + 1'
        done

            i='expr $i + 1'
    done
```

In this program when **j** equals 150, **break** takes the control outside the inner **while** only, since it is placed inside the inner **while**. If we were to take the control outside the outer **while** when **j** equals 150 we should have said

```
    break 2
```

Likewise, if we have three nested loops then to take the control from the innermost loop to the statement outside the outermost loop we should use the statement:

```
    break 3
```

The *continue* Statement

In some programming situations we want to take the control to the beginning of the loop, bypassing the statements inside the loop which have not yet been executed. The keyword **continue** allows us to do this. When the keyword **continue** is encountered inside any loop, control automatically passes to the beginning of the loop.

A **continue** is usually associated with an **if**. As an example, let's consider the following program.

```
    # SS53
    # Usage: SS53

    i=1
    while [ $i -le 2 ]
    do
```

```
j=1
while [ $j -le 2 ]
do
     if [ $i -eq $j ]
     then
           j='expr $j + 1'
           continue
     fi

     j='expr $j + 1'
     echo $i $j
done
i='expr $i + 1'
done
```

The output of the above program would be...

```
1 3
2 2
```

Note that when the value of **i** equals that of **j,** the **continue** statement takes the control to the **while** loop (inner) bypassing rest of the statements pending execution in the **while** loop (inner).

break and **continue** can be used with **until** and **for** loops just as they are in a **while** loop. Note that a **break** takes you out of the loop bypassing all commands within the loop. A **continue** sends you straight to the control command at the beginning of the loop.

Also, as with the **break** statement a number can be associated with the **continue** statement. Thus, if we have three nested loops and we use **continue 3** in the innermost loop it would take the control to the to the outermost loop.

Exercise

while and *until* Loop

[A] Point out the errors, if any, in the following programs:

(a)
```
j=1
while [ $j -le 10 ]
do
      echo $j
      j = j + 1
done
```

(b)
```
while who I grep aa12 I wc -l
do
      echo hello
done
```

(c)
```
while false
do
      echo false
done
```

(d)
```
until=1
while [ $until = 1 ]
do
      echo until cannot be used as a variable name
done
```

(e)
```
IFS=P
set -P PParrots are Pretty
echo $*
```

(f)
```
exec < mydir/myfile
echo enter your name
read name < 'tty'
```

[B] Answer the following:

(a) What will be the output of the following program:

```
IFS=+
set economists+are+seldom+right
echo $3 $4 $#
```

(b) From where the **read** statement would read if following state-ments are executed:

```
exec < file1
exec < file2
exec < file3
read line
```

(c) Choose the correct answer:

Your shell script has a name **ls**. If you execute **ls**

1. Your script would get executed.
2. The **ls** command would get executed.
3. Whether script is executed or command is executed depends upon the value of PATH.
4. Both **ls** and the script would get executed one after another.

[C] Attempt the following:

(a) Write a program to calculate overtime pay of 10 employees. Overtime is paid at the rate of Rs. 12.00 per hour for every hour worked above 40 hours. Assume that employees do not work for fractional part of an hour.

(b) Write a program to find the factorial value of any number entered through the keyboard.

(c) Two numbers are entered through the keyboard. Write a program to find the value of one number raised to the power of another.

(d) Write shell scripts which works similar to the following Unix commands:

      head   tail   more

Try to incorporate as many options as possible that are available with these Unix commands.

(e) Write a shell script which reports names and sizes of all files in a directory (directory would be supplied as an argument to the shell script) whose size is exceeding 1000 bytes. The filenames should be printed in descending order of their sizes. The total number of such files should also be reported.

(f) A friend of yours has promised to log in at a particular time. However, he has not kept the promise. You want to contact him as soon as he logs in. Write a shell script which checks after every one minute whether your friend has logged in or not. The logname should be supplied to the shell script at command prompt. Use **until** loop.

for, break, continue

[D] What will be the output of the following programs:

(a)
```
# Assume that the command line arguments are dog parrot cuckoo
for argument in $*
do
    echo $argument
done
```

(b)
```
# Assume that the command line arguments are dog parrot cuckoo
for argument in "$*"
```

```
            do
                echo $argument
            done
```

(c)   # Assume that the command line arguments are dog parrot cuckoo
```
        for argument in *
        do
            echo argument
        done
```

(d)   # Assume that the command line arguments are dog parrot cuckoo
```
        for argument in "*"
        do
            echo $argument
        done
```

(e)
```
        for i in a b c d e
        do
            echo $i
        done
```

(f)
```
        for i in 'a b c d e'
        do
            echo $i
        done
```

(g)
```
        i=1
        for [ i -le 10 ]
        do
            echo $i
            i='expr $i + 1'
        done
```

(h)
```
        i=1 j=1 k=1
        while [ $i -lt 10 ]
        do
```

```
        while [ $j -lt 10 ]
        do
            while [ $k -lt 10 ]
            do
                echo $i $j $k
                k='expr $k + 1'
                break 3
            done
            j='expr $j + 1'
        done
        i='expr $i + 1'
done
echo out at last
```

[E] Answer the following:

(a) State true or false:

Using a **for** loop we can calculate factorial value of a number.

(b) State true or false:

If in a script the value of IFS is changed to ':', after execution of the script the value of IFS is automatically set back to the original value.

(c) The **break** statement is used to exit from:

1. an **if** statement
2. a **for** loop
3. a program
4. None of the above

(d) An **until** loop ensures that the statements within the loop get executed:

1. Only once

2. At least once
3. Not even once
4. None of the above

[F] Attempt the following:

(a) Write a program to print all prime numbers from 1 to 300. (Hint: Use nested loops, **break** and **continue**)

(b) Write a program to generate all combinations of 1, 2 and 3 using **for** loops.

(c) Write a shell script for renaming each file in the directory such that it will have the current shell PID as an extension. The shell script should ensure that the directories do not get renamed.

(d) A file called **wordfile** consists of several words. Write a shell script which will receive a list of filenames, the first of which would be **wordfile**. The shell script should report all occurrences of each word in **wordfile** in the rest of the files supplied as arguments.

(e) Write a shell script which deletes all lines containing the word **unix** in the files supplied as arguments to this shell script.

(f) The word **unix** is present in only some of the files supplied as arguments to the shell script. Your shell script should search each of these files in turn and stop at the first file that it encounters containing the word **unix**. This filename should be displayed on the screen.

(g) A shell script receives even number of filenames. Suppose four filenames are supplied then the first file should get copied into second file, the third file should get copied into fourth file, and so on. If odd number of filenames are supplied then no copying should take place and an error message should be displayed.

(h)   Write a shell script which displays a list of all files in the current directory to which you have read, write and execute permissions.

(i)   Write a shell script which will receive any number of filenames as arguments. The shell script should check whether every argument supplied is a file or a directory. If it is a directory it should be appropriately reported. If it is a filename then name of the file as well as the number of lines present in it should be reported.

(j)   Write a shell script which will receive any number of filenames as arguments. The shell script should check whether such files already exist. If they do, then it should be reported. If these files do not exist then check if a sub-directory called **mydir** exists in the current directory. If it doesn't exist then it should be created and in it the files supplied as arguments should get created. If **mydir** already exists then it should be reported along with the number of files that are currently present in **mydir**.

(k)   Suppose a user has renamed some files in current directory using a command like **mv filename filename.$$**. Write a shell script to search all such files and rename them such that they do not contain the shell PID.

12   *Shell Metacharacters*

Filename Substitution Metacharacters
I/O Redirection Metacharacters
Process Execution Metacharacters
    Conditional Execution Using && and ||
Quoting Metacharacters
Positional Parameters and Special Parameters
    Oh! I Forgot...
    Debugging a Script
    $* And $@
Exercise

T he shell has a big family of metacharacters which are special characters to which special significance has been given. These characters are accorded a VIP treatment by Unix. Sometimes metacharacters are also called 'regular expressions'. Though we have met some of them in different contexts earlier, their importance is such that they warrant a separate chapter devoted to them. In this chapter we would take a closer look at these royal members of the Unix family. All metacharacters can be classified as shown if Figure 12.1.

Type	Metacharacters
Filename sbstitution	? * [...] [!...]
I/O Redirection	> < >> << m> m>&n
Process execution	; ( ) & && ‖
Quoting metacharacters	\ " " ' ' ' '
Positional parameters	$1..$9
Special characters	$0 $* $@ $# $! $$ $-

Figure 12.1

Filename Substitution Metacharacters

We are familiar with these. These are used for matching filenames in a directory. Let us quickly revise them.

*   A wild card character, it can represent any combination of any number of characters. A null or no character at all may also qualify for representation by a *****. When mentioned at the command line or with command like **ls**, it yields a complete list of all files in the current directory, except hidden files that start with a period (.).

?   Stands for any one character.

[..]   Gives the shell a choice of any one character from the enclosed list.

[!..]   Gives the shell a choice of any one character except those enclosed in the list.

Here are a few examples:

ls a*   Lists all files beginning with character 'a'.

ls ??   Lists all files whose names are 2 characters long.

ls a?b?   Lists all 4 character filenames whose first character is 'a' and third character is 'b'.

ls [kdgp]*   Lists all files whose first character is 'k', 'd', 'g' or 'p'.

ls [c-fmrv-z]*   Lists all files whose first character is 'm' or 'r' or is in the range c to f or v to z.

ls [!d-m]*   Lists all files whose first character is anything other than an alphabet in the range d to m.

I/O Redirection Metacharacters

These special characters specify from where input is to be picked up and where the output is to be sent.

     $ cat mypaper > out_there

The above command causes the output of the **cat** command to go to a file called **out_there** instead of the standard output, the screen, where it would ordinarily have gone.

On similar lines is **>>**, which along with indicating an output destination, instructs the shell to append the output to the file if it is already present.

    $ cat poem >> out_there

The above command ensures that **out_there** is not overwritten, but contents of **poem** are added after the contents of **out_there**.

In the case of input redirection, **<** is used to specify the standard input, which by default is the keyboard. The above command may also have been written as

    $ cat < poem >> out_there

The result would have been same. This is because the way **cat** functions, input is taken from **poem** even in the absence of **<**, but then the official input, is still the keyboard. This is evident when **cat** is executed followed by no argument at all. It waits for you to type the input and sends it to the standard output, the screen, until you terminate it by saying Ctrl d.

    $ cat
    Sample text : Whatever I say.
    Ctrl D
    Sample text : Whatever I say.
    $

With the next operator, **<<**, you can select the input from the specified source.

    $ cat << optimist

The above command will continue to read from the standard input only till the word 'optimist' is not fed in on a fresh line. **cat** will terminate if it encounters a fresh line containing 'optimist' as shown below. Note that the word 'optimist' when it is embedded in a sentence doesn't terminate the **cat** command.

```
$ cat << optimist
It is impossible for an optimist to be pleasantly surprised.
optimist
It is impossible for an optimist to be pleasantly surprised.
$
```

The two redirection operators remaining are:

m> filename   Makes **filename** the output of **m**

m>&n   Merges the standard output and standard error if m=1 and n=2. Here **m** and **n** denote file descriptors. They can take the values 0, 1 or 2 representing standard input, standard output and standard error respectively.

The best use of **m>filename** is when we want to redirect all our error messages to some file. Say we want to run some shell script and study the error messages that come with it at leisure. This would do the trick:

```
$ SS40 2> errors
```

The file descriptor 2 signifies the standard error, which is now set to a file called **errors**.

We know that the **time** command is used to find out the time taken by a process to execute. The output of the **time** command always comes to the standard error device, which is the screen. If we want the output of **time** to go to some file, saying the following will not suffice.

$ time ls > myfile

This is because though the standard output (output of **ls**) was sent to **myfile**, standard error is still the screen, and that's where the time will be show. To send the time of execution also to **myfile**, we need to say

$ time ls > myfile 2>&1

This merges the standard output and standard error. As a result whatever is to go to the standard error would now be redirected to wherever the standard output has been redirected, i.e. to **myfile**.

Process Execution Metacharacters

These help with different ways of execution of commands.

When we want to run more than one command at the $ prompt in one stroke, we separate them with a semicolon. For example,

$ ls; who; banner Hi

This would result in the execution of **ls** first, then **who**, and lastly the **banner** command displays a big Hi.

If we wish certain commands to be executed in a sub-shell, we enclose them in parentheses.

$ (cd mydir ; pwd)
/usr/aal/mydir
$ pwd
/usr/aal

The parentheses causes a sub-shell to be invoked, in which a change of directory is executed. After executing a **pwd** in that sub-shell, the sub-shell ceases to exist. Back in the current shell, we are still in **/usr/aal**.

The metacharacter which delegates a given process execution to the background is **&**. If we want a long file to be sorted, and we know that it is going to take quite some time to sort this file, then we can mark it for background execution while we continue to work on something else.

```
$ sort abcd > abcd2 &
```

The trailing **&** entrusts the job to the background, leaving you free to do some other jobs in the foreground.

Conditional Execution Using **&&** and **||**

These metacharacters can be used to optionally execute a command depending on the success or failure of the previous command.

If we want the second command to be executed only if the first succeeds, we say

```
command 1 && command 2
```

Conversely, if we want the second command to be carried out only if the first fails, shell provides the metacharacter **||**.

```
$ command 1 || command 2
```

Let us illustrate this with an example.

Suppose you use **grep** to search a file for a word. On execution **grep** reports back to the shell whether the search was successful or not. Like other Unix commands, it reports the success or failure in terms of an exit status. If successful it returns an exit status 0. If something goes wrong, it returns a non-zero exit status. The **grep** command, for example, returns an exit status 1 if it fails to find the pattern, and an exit status 2 in case of syntax error or inaccessible files. We can check this status as shown below.

```
grep supplement paper > newpaper
if [ $? -eq 0 ]
then
      cat paper
fi
```

Instead of this code we can use a more compact code using the **&&** metacharacter. This is shown below:

```
grep supplement paper > newpaper  &&  cat paper
```

The command following the **&&** is performed only if the exit status of **grep** is 0, that is, only if the pattern 'supplement' is found in the file **paper**.

Similarly, in a command like

```
grep supplement paper > newpaper  ||  echo pattern not present
```

the command following the || is performed only if the initial command (**grep**) fails, that is, has a nonzero exit status.

Let us take a more complicated example of usage of **&&** and ||.

```
grep sachin addresses  ||  grep sachin adrfile  &&  cat afile
```

Here the pattern 'sachin' is searched first in the file **addresses**. If the search fails then the pattern is searched in the file **adrfile**. If this search is successful then the file **afile** is displayed on the screen.

What if the first **grep** is successful? The second **grep** is skipped and the **cat** is executed.

And what if both the **grep**s fail? Then **cat** is not executed. People familiar with programming (especially C) may be wondering which out of **&&** and **||** enjoys a higher priority.

The metacharacter which comes first enjoys a higher priority. The following figure summarises all the possibilities for the command:

command 1 || command 2 && command 3

Command1	Command2	Command 3 Executed?
Fails	Fails	No
Fails	Successful	Yes
Successful	Not executed	Yes

Figure 12.2

Can you prepare a similar table for the following command sequence:

command 1 && command 2 || command 3

Quoting Metacharacters

The following characters come under this category.

\   " "   ' '   ` `

\ takes away the special significance attached to any metacharacter. Consider the following statement:

$ echo This is a *

Looks like a simple statement. But the shell interprets the * at the end of the line as all files in the current directory. Hence, instead of echoing the * it echoes all files in the current directory.

To remove the shell dilemma, what we do in such cases is place a \ before the metacharacter.

```
$ echo This is a \*
This is a *
```

When preceded by a \, the * is echoed as it is. Note that the \ itself is not echoed in the output.

The single quotes ' ' tell the shell to take every enclosed character literally - absolutely no favourites. For example,

```
$ echo '$, \, ?, *, all just what they look!'
$, \, ?, *, all just what they look!
```

The back quotes replace the command they enclose with its output.

```
$ echo Today is `date`
Today is Sat Apr 27 17:05:56 IST 1996
```

By enclosing **date** in the back quotes, or the accent graves, as they are called, the shell understands that the output of **date**, is to be substituted here. Hence the output shown above.

The double quotes " " do pamper some metacharacters, namely, $, \ and ' '. When enclosed within " " these metacharacters are allowed to hold their special status. For example,

```
$ name=Unuck
$ echo "Your name is $name"
Your name is Unuck
```

Having set up a variable **name**, we **echo** the same using the metacharacter **$**. **$** indicates to the shell to take the value of the variable that follows it. The double quotes have not affected the special status **$** enjoys.

Positional Parameters and Special Parameters

The shell reserves some variable names for its use. **$1** through **$9** are ten shell variables, called positional parameters, which automatically collect the arguments passed at the command line. These were discussed in detail in Chapter 9.

Some special parameters are designated by the shell for yielding information about the environment in general and the process being executed. Here is a list of such parameters alongwith the meaning of each:

$$ PID of current shell
$?   Exit status of the last executed command
$!   PID of last background process
$-   Current shell settings
$#   Total number of positional parameters
$0   Name of the command being executed
$*   List of all shell arguments. Can't yield each argument separately.
$@**   Similar to **$*, but yields each argument separately when enclosed in double quotes.

Out of these we are already familiar with the parameters **$$, $?, $0, $#** and **$***. Let us examine the rest.

Oh, I Forgot...

Suppose you want to sort a long file and store the output in a new file. You would naturally get the process executed in the background such that you are free to carry out some other work in the foreground.

```
$ sort logfile > logrep &
23415
$
```

We have seen that whenever we run a process in the background the PID assigned to the process is displayed before displaying the $ prompt. Suppose now we get busy with some other work in the foreground. And in the middle of this foreground job you wish to find out whether the sorting is still going on, or is it over. To find this out you can do a **ps** and find out from the PID column the status of our sorting process. But what if we have forgotten the PID that was displayed when we fired the background process. No problem. We can still find out the PID by executing the simple command,

```
$ echo $!
23415
```

where $! stands for the PID of the last background process.

Naturally, if two processes are executed in the background then $! represents the PID of the second process. If we want to preserve the PID of the first process we may save the same in a variable as shown below:

```
$ sort logfile > logrep &
23415
$ first=$!
```

Debugging a Script

However small program you write it's not going to work correctly the first time around! This is because human beings are prone to mistakes. Moreover, a comma here and a semicolon there makes a lot of difference. If the grammar of your program goes wrong the shell informs you so the moment the erroneous statement gets executed. However, if the grammar is correct but there is a mistake in the logic the program would work, but would work incorrectly. At such times we would like to debug the program by tracing the flow of control, examining values of variables, checking whether the variable, filename and command substitution is being done properly or not etc.. To achieve this we have to simply add the following statement at the beginning of the script:

```
set -vx
```

Here, **v** ensures that each line in the shell script is displayed before it gets executed, and **x** ensures that the command along with the argument values that it may have is also displayed before execution. Let us illustrate this with an example.

```
# SS54
# Usage: SS54

echo Enter your name
read name
echo $name
set yankee doodle do
echo $1 $2 $3
```

Shown below is the normal execution of this script.

```
$ SS54
Enter your name
duckling
duckling
$
```

Let us now execute the same script after adding the line **set -vx** at the beginning of the script.

```
$ SS54
echo Enter your name
+ echo Enter your name
```

```
Enter your name
read name
+ read name
Dominique Domini
echo $name
+ echo Dominique Domini
Dominique Domini
set yankee doodle do
+ set yankee doodle do
echo $1 $2 $3
+ echo yankee doodle do
yankee doodle do
$
```

Note that by setting the **-v** option the line from the script which is about to get executed is displayed, whereas the lines which are preceded by the + sign have come courtesy the **-x** option. Also note that in the lines preceded by the + sign the variables have been substituted by their actual values. This way we come to know on what values is a particular command going to operate upon.

To know which options have been set we can use the parameter **$-** as shown below.

```
$ echo $-
vx
```

We can unset the debugging options that may have been set by saying,

```
$ set +vx
```

$* And $@

Let us look at the subtle difference between $* and $@ exemplified by the following script.

```
# SS55
# Usage: SS55 file1 file2 file3 ...

cat "$*"
cat "$@"
```

If we execute this shell script by saying,

```
$ SS55 f1 f2 f3
```

the two **cat** commands would become

```
cat "f1 f2 f3"
cat "f1" "f2" "f3"
```

On execution, the first of these commands would give an error since there does not exist a file with the name "f1 f2 f3". As against this, the second **cat** command would display the contents of the files **f1**, **f2** and **f3**. When not enclosed within "" **$*** and **$@** behave exactly similarly.

Exercise

[A]   What will be the output of the following program segments:

(a)   echo ?
       echo \?
       echo "?"
       echo '\?'
       echo "\?"

(b)   n="ask me"
       echo $n
       echo "$n"
       echo '$n'

(c)   a=b
        b=c d=c
        echo $$b
        echo $$$d

(d)   set ready the way as along with
        echo $# $$#

(e)   set -vx
        echo $-

(f)   a=
        [-z "$a"] && a=mafia
        echo $a

(g)   a=
        [-z "$a"] || a=mafia
        echo $a

(h)   (a="out of context")
        echo $a

(i)   a=stargazer
        (a=moongazer)
        echo $a

(j)   (date ; echo hello) > message

(k)   date ; echo hello > message

(l)   sort longfile > file &
        grep lion longfile > afile &
        echo $!

(m)   set mafia wars of Bombay
        echo $*

echo $@

(n) set shadow of Ignorance
echo "$*"
echo "$@"

(o) echo *
echo *
echo "*"
echo '*'

[B] State whether the following statements are True or False:

(a) Within ' ' there should always occur a Unix command and not a shell script.

(b) Within ' ' piping and redirection metacharacters cannot be used.

(c) If filenames are supplied as arguments to a script then **rm "$@"** would remove all files supplied as arguments.

(d) **$?** gives the PID of last background process, whereas **$!** gives the exit status of the last command executed.

(e) **SS40 2> myfile** would redirect the standard output and standard error to the file **myfile**.

[C] Suppose following files are present in the current directory:

ashish	arctan	dac.doc	dim.dwg	document
fag	fibonaccifinder	fog	folder	sam
si.c	tarun	zenith	zombie	

Which files would be listed by the following commands:

(a)   ls ?*?

(b)   ls fi*

(c)   ls [!fd]

(d)   ls [!fd]*

(e)   ls [!0-9][!asd]*

13

Tricks of The Trade

Controlling Terminal Input
Tackling Multiple Command Line Options
*trap*ing Signals
Functions
Executing Multiple Scripts
Exercise

With the knowledge of various control instructions and the shell metacharacters we would be able to tackle most programming situations. However, to add gloss to our programs and to improve our programming efficiency we need to look beyond what we have learnt so far. Things which will help us to change command names, control terminal input, tackle variety of options that may be supplied at the command prompt and the like. So here we go...

Controlling Terminal Input

We have been able to control the nature of output as it is echoed to the screen. **tput** helped us in positioning the output on the screen, whereas **echo** permitted us to display characters in bold, reverse video, blinking etc.

So far to read values from the keyboard during program execution we have used the **read** statement. However, **read** statement is limited in its reach. Anytime **read** statement is encountered we supply the values and faithfully hit the enter key and the values get stored in the variable(s) following the **read** statement. There are no variations available to this routine. Too drab, you would agree. What if we want to write a program which asks the user to supply a password from the keyboard? When this password is read using the **read** statement the password typed would naturally appear on the screen and the whole idea would be lost. In such a situation the **stty** command comes in handy. The following program shows how **stty** can be used in such a programming situation.

```
# SS55
# USage: SS55

old=`stty -g`
stty -echo iuclc
echo "Enter passwd: \c"
read pw
stty $old

if [ "$pw" = icit ]
then
        echo you supplied the correct password
else
        echo wrong password
fi
```

stty stands for 'set the options for a terminal'. It sets certain terminal I/O options for the device that is the current standard input and output. When used without arguments, it reports the settings of certain options. With the **-a** option, it reports all the option settings.

The **-g** option causes **stty** to output the current settings of the terminal as a list of fourteen hexadecimal numbers separated by colons. In our program we have used this option to store the current stty settings in the variable **old**. Next we have invoked **stty** with options **-echo** and **iuclc**. The **-echo** option ensures that what is typed doesn't get displayed on the screen and the **iuclc** ensures that even if we supply the password in uppercase it would be mapped to corresponding lowercase characters.

Once the password has been received we restore the original **stty** settings stored in the variable **old** and then check the supplied password against the legal password. Depending on whether it matches with our legal password we flash an appropriate message.

There are several options available with **stty**. You are referred to the manual for the details of each. Given below is only a list of commonly used options.

ignbrk	Ignores break on input.
-ignbrk	Does not ignore break on input.
igncr	Ignores carriage return on input.
-igncr	Does not ignore carriage return on input.
iuclc	Maps uppercase alphabets to lowercase on input.
-iuclc	Does not map uppercase alphabets to lowercase on input.
olcuc	Maps lowercase alphabets to uppercase on output.
-olcuc	Does not map lowercase alphabets to uppercase on output.
icanon	Enables canonical input (ERASE and KILL processing).
-icanon	Disables canonical input (ERASE and KILL processing).
echo	Echoes back every character typed.
-echo	Does not echo back every character typed.
min i, time i	(0 < i < 127) When **-icanon** is set, and one character has been received, read requests are not satisfied until at least min characters have been received or the timeout value time has expired and one character has been received.
sane	Resets all modes to some reasonable values. This option is useful when a terminal's settings have been hopelessly scrambled.

We would try to incorporate this password logic in a more practical situation later in this chapter.

Let us now look at another example which makes use of the **stty** command.

Example 13.1: Write a shell script to identify all zero byte files in the current directory and delete them. Before proceeding with deletion the shell script should get a confirmation from the user. Note that for deletion **rm -i** should not be used since it needs an Enter key to be hit after supplying **y** or **n**.

Identifying zero byte files in the current directory is fairly straight-forward. All that we have to do is use a file test. When we prompt the user for his response to 'delete y/n', his response would be collected using the usual **read** statement. However, there is a small hitch here. The **read** statement terminates only on hitting the enter key, whereas the problem specifies that the user should be required to supply only 'y' or 'n' in response to our prompt. To ensure this we should once again use the **stty** command as shown in the program given below.

```
# SS56
# Usage: SS56
# Remove 0 byte files in the current directory

        for file in *
        do
            if [ -f $file -a ! -s  $file ]
            then
                    echo "Delete $file y/n \c"
                    ans=""

                    stty -icanon min 0, time 0

                    while [ -z "$ans" ]
                    do
                        read  ans
                    done

                    if [ $ans = y  -o  $ans = Y ]
                    then
                            rm  -f  $file
                            echo " $file deleted..."
                    fi
```

```
          fi
      done

  stty sane
```

When **-icanon** is set and one character has been received, the **read** statement would continue to get executed till either:

(a)   At least **min** characters have been received

> or

(b)   The timeout value has expired and one character has been received.

If only **read choice** is used without the **while** loop then since **min** has been set to 0 control would just skip past the **read** statement since **min 0** means that **read** should read 0 characters. The **while** loop ensures that so long as at least one character is not received **read** continues to get executed.

time 0 ensures that read is terminated the moment one character is hit. This is because **time n** means wait till **n** seconds after a character has been hit.

Note that instead of preserving the original **stty** settings in a variable and restoring them at the end, here firstly we have changed the settings and then restored them using the **sane** option mentioned earlier.

Tackling Multiple Command Line Options

Many programs need multiple command line arguments to be specified at the time of execution. In such cases, firstly the program should check whether any arguments have been provided, then check that the arguments provided, if any, are valid, and finally perform appropriate action depending upon the arguments supplied.

We can carry out these checks using multiple **if** statements. However, the job becomes especially difficult when the multiple arguments are specified in any order that the user wishes. Let's justify this with an example.

Example 13.2: A friend of yours has promised to log in at a particular time. However, he has not kept the promise. You want to contact him as soon as he logs in. Write a shell script which checks after every one minute whether your friend has logged in or not. The logname should be supplied to the shell script at command prompt.

At the command prompt the user may optionally supply a **-m** option and a **-t interval** option. The **-m** option means whenever the user logs in we should be so informed not through **echo** but through **mail**. The **-t interval** option means check whether the user has logged in every **num** seconds. Write a shell script to achieve this.

Here is the shell script...

```
# SS57
# Usage SS57 [-m] [-t interval] logname

mailopt=false
interval=60

if [ $1 = m ]
then
      mailopt=yes
fi

if [ $2 = -t ]
then
      interval=$3
fi
```

```
    while true
do
        who I grep $4 > /dev/null
        if [ $? -eq 0 ]
        then
                if [ $mailopt = yes ]
                then
                        echo $4 has logged in I mail 'logname'
                else
                        echo $4 has logged in
                fi
                break
        else
                sleep $interval
        fi
done
```

We have tackled this program in an Chapter 11. However, that time we had not encountered the possibility of being informed by mail as well as checking whether the user has logged in at an interval supplied by the user. Note that the above program has not been sandpapered with error checks and is bound to fire in several situations:

(a)   If logname is not supplied at the command prompt
(b)   If positions of the **-m** and **-t** options are interchanged.
(c)   If interval is not supplied after the **-t** option.
(d)   If **-m** and **-t** options are not supplied and only logname is supplied.

Not that all these possibilities cannot be tackled using multiple nested **if** and **case** statements. But it would sure result into chaos. Instead things would become much smoother to program and understand if we use the **getopts** command. Let us see how. To begin with let us tackle **getopts** in its simplest garb. We would soon come back to the present example.

```
# SS58
# Usage: SS58 [-a/b]

getopts ab choice
case $choice in
    a) echo you entered a
       ;;
    b) echo you entered b
       ;;
    ?) echo wrong choice
esac
```

While executing this program the user is supposed to supply an option 'a' or 'b' at the command line. Look at the **getopts** command used in the program.

getopts ab choice

Here **ab** are the valid options and **choice** is the variable in which **getopts** will store the option supplied at the command prompt.

Thus **getopts** knows what are the valid command line options. On execution of the script **getopts** reads the options given by the user and decides whether they are valid or not and then leaves the rest to a **case** statement. **getopts** accepts single character options from the command line provided the option is preceded by a minus (-) sign. Thus, we should execute the above program by saying

$ SS58 -a

or

$ SS58 -b

In either case **getopts** scans the command line, picks up the option, compares it with the legal options and if a match is found stores the option in the variable **choice**. If we supply an illegal option by saying,

```
$ SS58 -z
```

getopts stores a '?' in the variable **choice** since the option supplied didn't match with any of the legal options.

Depending upon what is present in the variable **choice** the **case** statement then executes the appropriate instruction.

If we supply an illegal option, in addition to executing an appropriate statement from the **case**, **getopts** also flashes an error message as shown below.

```
$ SS58 -z
SS58: illegal option -- z
wrong choice
```

Observe that **getopts** does not assign the invalid choice ('z' in our case) to the variable **choice** because in that case, none of the **case** conditions will be true and no **case** statement will be executed, as it would be very difficult to devise a **case** statement that will take care of any option that the user may type in.

Note that when the option is supplied at the command line it must always be preceded by a minus sign. **getopts** actually scans the entire command line for the minus sign; if a minus sign is found, the single character immediately following the minus sign is taken as the option that the user has specified.

In SS58 we supplied only one option. What if the script is to tackle multiple options? We will have to call **getopts** repeatedly in a loop as shown in the following program.

```
# SS59
# Usage: SS59 [-a/b] [-c/d]
```

```
        while getopts abcd choice
        do
            case $choice in
                a) echo you entered a
                   ;;
                b) echo you entered b
                   ;;
                c) echo you entered c
                   ;;
                d) echo you entered d
                   ;;
                ?) echo wrong choice
            esac
        done
```

Let us see what happens when we execute this script.

```
    $ SS58 -a -c -z
    you entered a
    you entered c
    SS59: illegal option -- z
    wrong choice
```

Since we have supplied three options **getopts** will scan the command line thrice each time picking up one option. Having picked up the option it again checks for its legality. If found legal it assigns the option to the variable **choice**, otherwise assigns a '?' to **choice**. The **case** statement then appropriately processes whatever value is assigned to **choice**.

As with other Unix commands **getopts** too returns an exit status on execution. As long as there are options at the command line that **getopts** hasn't looked at yet, it would return a zero and the commands in the **while** loop would get executed. If the option retrieved from the command line is valid, the specified action for this option would be taken; if the option is not valid, the action common to all invalid options (the ? case) would be taken.

When there are no more options to be retrieved from the command line, **getopts** would return a non-zero exit status and the **while** loop would be terminated.

Let us now go one step further and see how can we tackle arguments that may be supplied with an option. For example, if we execute SS57 at command prompt by saying

> $ SS57 -m -t 120 aa12

120 becomes an argument for the option **-t**.

The following program shows how **getopts** takes care of arguments for an option.

```
# SS60
# Usage: SS60 [-a account] [-c creditlimit] [-d]

while getopts a:c:d choice
do
     case $choice in
          a) echo you entered a with argument $OPTARG
          ;;
          c) echo you entered c with argument $OPTARG
          ;;
          d) echo you entered d
     esac
done
```

Note how we have specified the valid options after **getopts**:

> getopts a:c:d choice

The ':' tells **getopts** that the options **-a** and **-c** would be followed by arguments, whereas the option **-d** would not be. Suppose we execute this script as follows:

```
$ SS60 -a a101 -c 5000 -d
you entered a with argument a101
you entered c with argument 5000
you entered d
```

When the command line is scanned by **getopts** it first encounters the option **-a**. **getopts** now checks whether it is a valid option or not. Since it is a valid option and there is a ':' after 'a' in the list of valid options ('a:c:d') **getopts** picks up the next argument from the command line and assigns to an internal variable OPTARG. **getopts** now returns an exit status 0. Hence the control-command in the **while** loop is satisfied and the control proceeds to the **case** statement. Here case 'a' gets satisfied and a message along with the value of OPTARG is echoed to the screen. Same thing happens when **getopts** encounters the **-c** option. This time 5000 is assigned to OPTARG and promptly printed out. Third time around **getopts** encounters the **-d** option. This time no value is assigned to OPTARG since there is no ':' after 'd' in the list of valid options. When the entire command line has been scanned **getopts** returns a non-zero exit status hence the **while** loop is terminated.

What if we do not supply an argument to, let us say, the **-c** option?

```
$ SS60 -a a101 -c
you entered a with argument a101
SS60: option requires an argument -- c
```

Now when **getopts** encounters the **-c** option it objects immediately since in the list of valid options 'c' is followed by a ':' but the argument is missing at the command line. That I suppose demonstrates the intelligence of **getopts**.

Note that if an argument is expected along with an option (remember that the colon in the script tells **getopts** that an argument is expected), the word immediately following the option on the command line is read as the argument to that option. Also, while an option cannot be specified without the minus sign, there is no rule saying that the argument to the option cannot begin with a minus sign.

Let us now see one final facility available with **getopts**. It provides a means by which we can find out exactly how many of the arguments provided at the command line were read by **getopts**.

getopts keeps count of the number of parameters read from the command line in an internal variable called OPTIND. By default the value of this variable is 1. It is incremented by 1 every time **getopts** comes across a valid option or argument to an option while scanning the command line. Look at the following program to verify this.

```
# SS61
# Usage: SS61 [-a account] [-c creditlimit] [-d]

while getopts a:c:d choice
do
        case $choice in
            a) echo you entered a with argument $OPTARG
            ;;
            c) echo you entered c with argument $OPTARG
            ;;
            d) echo you entered d
        esac
        echo $OPTIND
done
```

Figure 13.1 shows the values of OPTIND and $# for different arguments supplied at the command prompt while executing the above shell script.

Command line	OPTIND	$#	Remark
SS61 -a a101 -c 5000	5	4	
SS61 -a a101	3	2	
SS61 -a a101 -d	4	3	
SS61 -c 1200	3	2	
SS61 -d	2	1	
SS61 -d -a a101 -c 1300	6	5	
SS61 -a a101 -d -c 1300	6	5	
SS61	1	0	
SS61 -d 100	2	2	Error
SS61 -a	2	1	Error
SS61 -d -c	3	2	Error

Figure 13.1

Compare the values of OPTIND and $# in Figure 13.1. You can observe that if the options and arguments are supplied correctly the final value of OPTIND is always either greater than or equal to the value of $#. Any time the value of $# exceeds that of OPTIND it is a signal that something is wrong with the arguments supplied at command prompt. We will be utilising this result in out next program.

Note the last case in Figure 13.1. Even though the value of OPTIND is greater than $# there is an error. This error however would be trapped and reported by **getopts** itself since it doesn't find an argument after the option **-c**.

What if we execute SS61 in this fashion:

$ SS61 -a -c

This time the value of OPTIND would be 3 and that of $# would be 2. Moreover, no error would be reported since **getopts** believes that the word (**-c** in this case) following the option **-a** is an argument for this option. Though **getopts** cannot trap such errors (since there is no rule saying an argument cannot begin with a -) usually these errors get trapped when the value of this argument is used in further processing within the program.

Let us now get back to what we had begun with. We will rewrite the program for Example 13.2 using **getopts**. To prevent shuttling between pages the problem is reproduced below.

Example 13.2: A friend of yours has promised to log in at a particular time. However, he has not kept the promise. You want to contact him as soon as he logs in. Write a shell script which checks after every one minute whether your friend has logged in or not. The logname should be supplied to the shell script at command prompt.

At the command prompt the user may optionally supply a **-m** option and a **-t interval** option. The **-m** option means whenever the user logs in we should be so informed not through **echo** but through **mail**. The **-t interval** option means check whether the user has logged in every **interval** seconds. Write a shell script to achieve this.

Here is the program...

```
# SS62
# Usage: SS62 [-m] [-t interval] logname

mailopt=false
interval=60

while getopts  mt: choice
do
    case  $choice in
        m) mailopt=true
           ;;
        t) interval=$OPTARG
           ;;
```

```
                \?) echo Improper usage
                    exit
                    ;;
        esac
    done

    if [ $OPT.ND -ne $# ]
    then
        echo Improper usage
        exit
    fi

    count='expr $# - 1'
    shift $count
    logname=$1

    while true
    do
        who I grep $logname > /dev/null

        if [ $? -eq 0 ]
        then
            if [ $mailopt = true ]
            then
                set 'who am i'
                echo $logname has logged in I mail $1
            else
                echo $logname has logged in
            fi
            exit
        else
            sleep $interval
        fi
    done
```

With all that has been said about **getopts** and its facilities I hope you would be able to understand the program. The following points should prove helpful in understanding it.

(a) An option is always a single character preceded by a minus sign, whereas the argument may be of one or more characters and may or may not be preceded by a minus sign.

(b) On encountering an option **getopts** stores it in the variable at the end of the **getopts** command (the variable **choice** in the above program).

(c) On encountering an illegal option **getopts** stores a '?' in the variable at the end of the **getopts** command.

(d) On encountering an argument to an option **getopts** stores it in the variable OPTARG.

(e) By default the value of OPTIND variable is 1.

(f) The value of the variable OPTIND is incremented every time **getopts** encounters an option or an argument to an option.

(g) If the options and arguments have been supplied correctly the final value of OPTIND is either greater than or equal to that of $#.

*trap*ing Signals

It frequently so happens that while programming either by design or by accident the control falls in an infinite loop. There has to be a way of getting out of such indefinite loops. This facility is provided by the programming environment. For example, in DOS we have the usual Ctrl C to keep us from going round in circles. Unix too provides means to tackle such situations. These are:

(a)   Use a Ctrl d to log out of the shell.
(b)   Use the Del key.
(c)   Kill the process which has gone in an infinite loop from another terminal.
(d)   Kill the shell itself in which the infinite loop process is working.

While using any of these methods we are sending certain signals to Unix. But sometimes the requirement is such (as we would shortly see) that we want some process to ignore these signals. Or better still, we want some processes to carry out some other job on receiving these signals. Unix provides a command called **trap** to achieve this. Using this command we can see to it that the program terminating signals that we mentioned above can be persuaded to ignore the task that they were initially instructed to do. They can also be asked to do something totally unconnected with their original duties. Let us see how the **trap** command works.

Figure 13.2 shows the signal numbers associated with the ways by which we can terminate a process. The practice of giving numbers to the break signals is employed to make it easier to handle the large number of such signals that are available in Unix. These numbers are also used for identifying the signals to be trapped.

Signal	Signal Number
Exit	0
Ctrl d	1
Del	2
Ctrl \	3
Sure kill	9
Kill	15

Figure 13.2

Out of all the methods the Del key is most frequently used to terminate an ongoing process. To ensure that the Del key does not carry out the program termination job we should trap signal number 2 as shown below.

```
trap "" 2
```

If this command is given at the beginning of a program then when this program is executed the Del key cannot terminate the program in the middle of its work. The command tells Unix that we want to change the course of action to be employed by the system when it receives the signal number 2 from the user in the midst of program execution.

The new job to be performed on receiving the signal is to be given in double quotes. Here the double quotes do not enclose anything and so no alternate action will be performed by Unix on receiving signal number 2. This signal will thus be just ignored from now on.

We could also have told Unix that we want a listing of files in the current directory whenever we press Del when the program is executing. The **trap** command for this would look like

```
trap "ls" 2
```

Now if we hit a Del key in the middle of the program execution the files in the current directory would be listed immediately . If we press the Del key after the program execution is over it would of course have no effect and the file listing would not be generated.

Instead of **ls** we may have any other Unix command or even a shell script. Shown below are a few examples of the **trap** command.

Command	Action
trap "" 2	Does nothing on generation of signal number 2.

trap "ls -l" 2	Displays a long listing on generation of signal number 2.
trap "who" 2	Displays a list of users on generation of signal number 2.
trap "ls;who" 2	Displays file listing and current user listing on generation of signal number 2.
trap "ls;exit" 2	Displays file listing and terminates the process on generation of signal number 2.
trap "SS40" 2	Executes the shell script SS40 on generation of signal number 2.
trap "" 1 2 3	Does nothing on generation of signal numbers 1, 2 or 3.
trap "ls" 1 2 3	Displays file listing on generation of signal numbers 1, 2 or 3.

From the above examples it is evident that Del is not the only signal that can be trapped. A majority of the signals mentioned in Figure 13.1 can be trapped. There are some signals like signal number 9 that cannot be trapped. Hence no matter what **trap** statement we write, this signal will always stop program execution.

Let us now see a more practical use of the **trap** command. Consider the following example:

Example 13.3: Write a shell script which would display a message 'Terminal Locked' on the screen and wait for the user to hit a key. On receiving a key, it should accept a password and then unlock the terminal if the password matches.

At many Unix installations the users outnumber the terminals available. It may so happen that you leave your terminal and move on to your friend's terminal to get some help, only to find that when you return somebody has pressed a Ctrl-d at your terminal. As a result you were logged out. Then this person logged in and started working. To avoid such a situation you may like to lock your terminal before leaving your terminal. When somebody comes in and tries a Ctrl-d your script should ask for a password and since he may not be knowing your password his malicious intentions would be defeated. When you return and supply the correct password the script should terminate and you should be returned to the dollar prompt. The following program shows how this can be achieved.

```
# SS63
# Usage: SS63

trap "" 1 2 3
banner terminal
banner locked


read key
while true
do
        echo "Enter your password: \c"
        stty -echo
        read pw
        stty sane

        if [ "$pw" = icit ]
        then
                break
        else
                echo Wrong password. You are a illegal user.
        fi
done
```

To begin with we have trapped signals 1, 2 and 3. Next we have displayed the message 'Terminal Locked' on the screen. The first **read** statement receives a keypress and then the control goes in an infinite **while** loop. The password logic is fairly simple. What is the purpose of the infinite **while** loop? It ensures that the execution of the script doesn't come to an end even if an incorrect password is supplied. In fact this loop cannot be terminated by pressing Del or Ctrl d since these signals have been trapped and been instructed to do nothing.

Functions

Don't you think instead of 'ls' the good old 'dir' would have been a better name. Likewise, 'ren' and 'copy' would have been more suitable than a 'mv' and a 'cp'. No problem. We can still have DOS like commands for their Unix equivalents. Here is how.

```
# SS64
# Usage: SS64

dir( )
{
      ls
}

copy( )
{
      cp $1 $2
}

ren( )
{
      mv $1 $2
}
```

Here **dir()**, **copy()** and **ren()** are function names. When you execute this script it will put these functions in memory (like the variables). There onwards anytime you want to see the file listing all that you are required to say at the dollar prompt is

```
$ dir
dir: not found
```

What went wrong? Well, didn't we say that functions are like variables in one sense. If we initialise variables in shell script, execute the script and then attempt to echo the variables' value at the dollar prompt would the variables be available. Of course not. This so happens as the shell script gets executed in a subshell, and the subshell dies the moment the execution of the script is over. Likewise our functions also died the moment the execution of SS64 was over. Then what do we do to ensure that the functions don't die? Simple. Make the shell script to execute in the current shell. This is how it can be done.

```
$ . SS64
```

Note the '.' preceding SS64. It ensures that SS64 gets executed in the current shell. The space between the '.' and SS64 is necessary. If it is absent the shell considers '.SS64' as a hidden file. Let us now see whether the 'dir' command works.

```
$ dir
abc
adobe
bekar
binary
ss64
ss70
zombi
```

So here onwards we can see the directory listing using the 'dir' command. ls would of course continue to work. Likewise to rename files we can now say,

```
$ ren oldfile newfile
```

Like the variables present in the current shell, the functions available in the current shell can also be seen using the **set** command. Let us execute the **set** command after executing SS64 in the current shell.

```
$ . SS64
$ set
HOME=/usr/veena
HUSHLOGIN=FALSE
HZ=100
IFS=

LANG=english_us.ascii
LOGNAME=veena
MAIL=/usr/spool/mail/veena
MAILCHECK=600
OPTIND=1
PATH=/bin:/usr/bin:/usr/veena:/bin:.
PS1=$
PS2=>
SHELL=/bin/sh
TERM=ansi
TZ=IST-5:30
copy( ){
cp $1 $2
}
dir( ){
ls
}
ren( ){
mv $1 $2
}
```

Note that like the variables the functions also have been listed in the alphabetical order.

Now a few tips about the functions.

(a) Functions exist only in the shell in which they are defined. That is, they cannot be passed to subshells (whereas the variables can be).

(b) If the functions are executed in the current shell, then the changes made by these functions in values of variables remain effective even after the execution of the functions is over. For example, if we execute the following function, the system prompt remains as DB.

```
db( )
{
    PS1=DB:
}

$ db
DB:
```

(c) A function definition can stretch over as many lines as are necessary.

(d) You can put definitions of commonly used functions in the **.profile** file so that they are available whenever you login. Or you can store these functions in a file and execute that file when required in the current shell.

(e) Execution of a function is faster than a corresponding shell script since while executing a function the shell doesn't have to search the disk for the program, open the file and read the contents of the file into memory.

(f) Like variables, to remove the definition of a function from the shell we can use the **unset** command. For example,

```
$ unset dir
```

Let us now try to execute the **dir** function.

```
$ dir
dir: not found
```

(g) It is possible to have functions within a shell script which has
     other legal Unix commands and control instructions. For ex-
     ample, in the following program we have a function **usage( )**
     which can be called from several places in the shell script.

```
# SS65
usage( )
{
        echo Improper usage
        echo The correct usage is SS64 [-m] [-a logname] [-t]  [-r]
        exit
}

if [ $# -gt 5 ]
then
        usage
fi

# some more instructions

if some test
then
        usage
fi

# some more instructions
```

(h) If in addition to functions some other Unix commands or
     control instructions are present in the shell script then it is
     necessary that the functions appear physically before the com-
     mands and control instructions.

(i) If you execute the **exit** command inside a function it not only
     terminates execution of the function but also the execution of

the shell script that called the function. If you want to terminate just the execution of the function you may use the **return** statement.

(j)   Between a function and shell script of the same name priority goes to the function during execution.

Executing Multiple Scripts

We can easily call one script from another. All that we have to do is mention the name of the script to be called when we want to invoke it. For example, in the following program having executed the first two **echo** statements the shell script SS67 is executed. Once its execution is over the control comes back to SS66 which executes the **pwd** command and terminates.

```
# SS66
# Usage: SS66

echo Hello!
echo Today is 'date'
SS67   # calls the script SS67
pwd


# SS67
echo Now the control is in SS67
echo Returning back to the calling script...
```

Let us verify the output.

```
$ SS66
Hello!
Today is Sat May 4 19:05:55 IST 1996
Now the control is in SS67
echo Returning back to the calling script...
```

/usr/aa10

When SS67 is called the shell executes all instructions present in it and automatically returns the control back to SS66 (the calling script). Instead of returning back after executing all the instructions in SS67 sometimes we may want to return the control back to SS66 on satisfaction of some condition. This can be achieved by using an **exit** statement at the point from where the control is to be returned.

We can call any number of shell scripts any number of times from within a script. Also, we may call one shell script, which in turn would call another shell script, and so on. Such nesting of calls is allowed.

Exercise

[A]   State which of the following statements are True or False:

(a)   Functions once loaded in memory, can be removed only by logging out.

(b)   When you log in, the functions that you have declared automatically get loaded into memory.

(c)   Functions defined in the current shell are available to all the subshells invoked from the current shell.

(d)   Functions, like variables, can be made readonly.

(e)   A maximum of 256 functions can be defined in a file.

(f)   Functions get executed faster than the corresponding shell scripts.

(g)   The shell script containing functions should be executed in the current shell.

(h)   All shell scripts automatically get executed in the current shell.

(i)   The default value of OPTIND is 0.

(j)   OPTIND and OPTARG are Unix defined variables.

(k)   If the options and arguments of options supplied to the shell script are correct then the value of OPTIND would be greater than or equal to that of $#.

(l)   If a shell script is called from another then the called shell script should necessarily have a **return** statement.

(m)   The **trap** command can trap any signal.

(n)   If the statement **stty -echo** is followed by an **echo** statement, then the output of this statement would not be displayed on the screen.

(o)   An argument to a option cannot be preceded by a minus sign.

(p)   All Unix commands always have a single character options.

(q)   Settings made using **stty** in a shell script are effective only during the execution of the script. The original settings are restored the moment execution of the script is over.

(r)   We can trap a signal such that on occurrence of that signal a particular shell script gets executed.

[B]   Attempt the following:

(a)   A shell script can receive one or more out of the following four options:

Option	Meaning	Option	Meaning
-c	CGA mode	-v	VGA mode
-s	Single player	-t	Two players

Write a shell script using **getopts** which would receive one or more of these options from the command prompt, check their validity and display appropriate messages depending on the option selected.

(b) Write a shell script using **getopts** which can receive two options **-a** and **-p**. The option **-a** is either followed by an argument CGA or VGA, whereas the **-p** option is followed by an argument SINGLE or TWO. Your script should report which options have been used by the user as well as their validity.

(c) Write a shell script which works similar to the **wc** command. This script can receive the options **-l**, **-w** and **-c** to indicate whether number of lines, number of words or number of characters from the input stream are to be counted. The user may use any or all of these options. Your script should be intelligent to identify invalid options and reject them.

(d) Write a shell script containing a function **mycd()** using which you would be able to shuttle between directories. The function should work in the following manner:

```
$ mycd dir    # should cd into dir
$ mycd -      # should cd into previous directory
```

(e) Write a function **go()** which would change the $ prompt to the current directory name in which you are working. Thus, if you are working in the directory **/usr/aa10** the prompt should look like

/usr/aa10

If you execute the **go()** function as shown below

/usr/aa10> go abc

the prompt should look like

/usr/aa10/abc>

(f)   Write a function **mkcd()** which would create all the directories present in the path supplied to it as argument and change over to the last directory in this path. Thus,

$ mkcd d1/d2/d3/d4/d5

should create the five nested directories and change the present working directory to **d5**.

14 *Shell Miscellany*

W e know that when a user logs into the system, Unix starts up a shell called the login shell for that user. The login shell prompts the user for commands and executes them if they are valid. In addition to this it performs several other functions as we would shortly see. The login shell that you acquire, depends upon who you login as. For example, the login shell for the root, grants the user (who is called superuser) powerful and unlimited privileges as compared to the shell of an ordinary user, though both have invoked the same executable file, **/bin/sh**.

Functions of A Shell

The various functions that the shell carries out for us are discussed below.

(a)   It can act as a command. For example,

```
$ sh
$
```

This invokes a child shell (better known as a sub-shell). You can confirm this by listing the currently running processes using the **ps** command. Having gone into the sub-shell, to quit out of it we must either type **exit** or Ctrl-d. There is a better reason for invoking a sub-shell. We know that every shell script that we execute (unless otherwise mentioned) gets executed in a sub-shell. Also, before executing a script we have to use

chmod to grant ourselves an execute permission to it. We can avoid using **chmod** by executing the script as follows:

$ sh SS40

Here **sh** is acting as a command and SS40 as an argument for this command. Now the shell reads each command present in SS40 and executes it in the sub-shell. Does this mean that we can execute any user's shell script using the **sh** command? Yes and no. Yes, if you have a read permission to that script. And no if you do not have a read permission. Not only this, you cannot execute even your shell script using **sh** if you do not have a read permission to it.

In the last chapter we had seen how to trace the flow of control in a shell script using the **set -vx** command. Likewise we can say,

$ sh -vx SS40

and obtain the same effect.

(b)   It acts as a command interpreter.

When we are executing any command at the dollar prompt the shell first interprets our command and then transfers the control to the appropriate command file present on the disk.

(c)   It can act as a programming language.

We very well know this feature of the shell. It provides variables, control instructions, functions etc. which help in writing scripts to perform many complicated tasks.

(d)   It permits customization of user's environment.

Whenever we log in a file called **.profile** automatically gets executed. This file is similar to the AUTOEXEC.BAT file in DOS. This file can contain commands, variables, control instructions etc. Using these features we can customise our working environment as per our requirements. For example, we can change our prompt, decide what messages/information should be displayed when we log in, start execution of some processes in the background, schedule tasks for future execution, set up values of variables like MAILCHECK, PATH etc.

(e) It provides redirection and piping facilities.

We are well familiar with these facilities. So far we have seen these facilities being used with standard Unix commands and filters. However we can use them even with control instructions as shown below.

```
cat myfile |
while read line
do
      grep  camel $line
done
```

Here the output of **cat myfile** is being piped into the **while** loop. The **while** loop reads each line into the variable **line** and then **grep** searches and echoes those lines which contain the word 'camel' in them.

Likewise we can redirect the output of a **for** loop to some file as shown below:

```
for var in merry had a little lamp
do
      echo $var
done > newfile
```

Note that whenever piping or redirection is used in conjunction with a control instruction as shown above this instruction gets executed in a sub-shell. Thus, if some variables are set up in the loop, they won't be available in the parent shell when the execution of the loop gets over and the control returns to the parent shell.

(f)   It performs variable, filename and command substitution.

Consider the following command:

```
option="-l"
a='ls $option f*'
```

Here, we are using all the three substitutions mentioned above. Firstly, the variable substitution is done, whereby **$option** is replaced by the value of the variable **option**. Next the filename substitution is done during which a long listing of all files beginning with the character 'f' is obtained. Lastly, the command substitution is done in which the command present within the accent graves is replaced by the output of the command, in this case the long listing of files beginning with the character 'f'.

Variables Revisited

We have been using variables since our first shell script. Still some small but important details have been left out. Let us try to cover them here. Let us begin with exporting variables.

Exporting Variables

By default, any variable is available only in the shell in which it is defined. The following sequence of commands illustrates this.

```
$ a=20
```

```
$ sh
$ echo $a

$ exit
$ echo $a
20
```

After defining **a**, we invoked a sub-shell. This is achieved by saying **sh** at the prompt. We shall stay in this sub-shell until we leave it either by saying **exit** or **ctrl d**.

Since **a** was defined in the parent shell, it no longer holds any identity in the sub-shell. Having left the sub-shell, we can ensure that **a** is very much alive here by echoing it's value.

If we want variables to be available to all sub-shells we must **export** them from the current shell.

```
$ export a
```

Having done this, now when we invoke a sub-shell we obtain the same value for **a** as in the parent shell.

Try invoking sub-shells, and their sub-shells and you will always find yourself in the same environment - the dollar prompt is same, so is the secondary prompt. You'll find that values of the variables HOME and PATH too are always identical. Guess how is this achieved? These variables are exported, hence are made available to all sub-shells.

To obtain a list of all exported variables, we simply say **export** at the shell prompt.

```
$ export
```

All variables which have been exported are displayed along with their values. Note that this list contains variables that have been explicitly exported by the current shell and doesn't contain those that may have been inherited from the parent shell.

Note the following points:

(a)   A variable once exported from the parent shell becomes available to the sub-shell or any other shells launched from this sub-shell. This so happens because whenever a sub-shell is executed, the list of exported variables get copied to the sub-shell, while the local (unexported) variables in parent shell do not.

(b)   Once a variable is exported it remains exported to all sub-shells that are subsequently executed.

(c)   We can first create the variable and then export it or first export it and then create it. Thus the effect of

```
export a b c
a=100 b=200 c=300
```

is same as

```
a=100 b=200 c=300
export a b c
```

(d)   A variable once exported remains exported. If we are to unexport it we have to first unset it and then recreate it.

(e)   A variable can be exported from the parent shell to its subshell, but never the other way round. Thus if we create a variable **a** in a sub-shell and then export it, it would not become available to the parent shell.

(f)   If the sub-shell changes the value of an exported variables the value of this variable in the parent shell remains unchanged since the sub-shell always works only on the copy of the variable in the parent shell.

(g)   If an exported variable is modified in a sub-shell then to make this modified value available to a sub-sub-shell we must once again export the variable in the sub-shell.

Controlling Variable Assignments

The shell provides several ways for assigning values to variables under varying conditions. The action taken depends upon whether the variable is set or not, or whether the variable is null or not. The assignment is done using operators. These operators are more convenient than testing for the condition using an **if** statement.

Let's look at the first form of assignment. It looks like this:

        ${var-val}

If the variable **var** exists, then this expression has the value of the variable. If the variable doesn't exist (or is a null string), then the expression has the value **val**.

For example, look at the following sample code:

```
$ mydir=/usr/aa10
$ echo ${mydir-/usr/aa12}
/usr/aa10
```

First, we have defined the **mydir** variable to have a value '/usr/aa10'. Then, when we echoed the expression **${mydir-/usr/aa12}** we got '/usr/aa10' the value of **mydir**. Had **mydir** not been defined, '/usr/aa12' would have been echoed.

Let's now look at another example. Suppose there is no variable called **workingdir**.

```
$ echo ${workingdir-/usr/temp/aa3}
/usr/temp/aa3
$ echo $workingdir

$
```

Here, since **workingdir** was not existing the expression echoed '/usr/temp/aa3'. Look at the next **echo** statement carefully. It confirms that the value '/usr/temp/aa13' didn't get assigned to the variable **workingdir**. This variable still remains undefined.

What would be the practical use of this facility? We can use it when we want to use some default value for a variable and we want that if the variable is defined then this default value should be ignored and the new value be used. This is exemplified by the following script.

```
# SS68
option=${1--la}
ls  $option
```

If this script is executed without any argument then the variable **$1** would stand undefined hence the variable **option** would take the value **-la** and these options would be used by the following **ls** command. However, if an argument is supplied while executing this script, **$1** would stand defined hence the value of **$1** would be assigned to the variable **option** and this value would be used by the **ls** command.

There are three more conditional expressions which use braces; instead of -, they use =, +, and ?.

The **${var=val}** form works like the last expression except that if the variable is undefined, 'val' is assigned to the variable **var**. For example,

```
$ echo ${workingdir=/usr/temp/aa13}
/usr/temp/aa13
```

```
$ echo $workingdir
/usr/temp/aa13
```

If the variable is already defined, it is of course left unchanged. Note that with this form we are not allowed to use positional parameters. Thus the following statement would be invalid.

```
${1=-la}
```

A third variation is the expression **${var+val}**. It has the value 'val' if the variable is defined, otherwise it has no value.

```
$ tempfile=sundries
$ echo ${tempfile+trash}
trash
$ echo ${newfile+trash}

$
```

The fourth variation is **${var?message}**. If the variable **var** is defined, it works like the + form; but if the variable is not defined, then the message is printed, and the shell is exited.

For example, consider the following script.

```
# SS69
# Usage: SS69 [filename]

file=$1
cat ${file? File does not exist}
echo Through with the file!
```

Let's run this first without supplying the filename

```
$ SS69
File does not exist
$
```

Since no argument was supplied the variable **file** was undefined, hence the message was printed, and the script was terminated. This can be confirmed by the fact that the **echo** statement after the **cat** didn't get executed.

Let us now execute the script by supplying the filename:

```
$ SS69 newfile
Rapping on the window...
Flying through the night...
Through with the file!
```

Now that **file** was defined, the contents of **newfile** were displayed along with the message 'Through with the file'. This form of conditional expression is useful when you put error checking into a script. It lets you halt execution of a script if things start going wrong, as when we ran SS69 with **file** undefined.

Note that if you omit the message after the question mark, the system will print a default message and terminate the script.

At times braces are used simply to enclose the variable name, as in **${var}**. Ordinarily, **${var}** is the same as **$var**. However, the enclosed form can be used effectively to combine the value of a variable with other characters. This is of help if wish to construct strings which contain one or more variable values. The following example would clarify this statement.

```
$ opt=noecho
$ echo $optwas

$
```

This echoes a blank line since the shell believes that **optwas** is an undefined variable. However, the result would be different if we enclose the variable within a pair of braces.

```
echo ${var}was
noechowas
$
```

The moment we use braces the shell now recognizes the embedded variable Thus with braces we are able to construct a new word using the variable's value.

Note that we don't have to use the braces for a construction like

```
$ echo $file.c
noname.c
$
```

The reason is that the period is not a legal character for variable names, so the shell knows that the variable name must end before the period.

The following figure summarises all the operators that we have used above.

Expression	Meaning
${parameter-word}	Has parameter value if any. If not has the value word.
${parameter=word}	Has parameter value if any. Otherwise has the value word and sets parameter to word.
${parameter+word}	If parameter is set it is substituted by word, otherwise substitutes nothing.
${parameter?message}	Has parameter's value if any, otherwise substitutes message and exits from shell.

Figure 14.1

The eval Command

What do you think would be the output of the following code segment:

```
# SS70
# Usage: SS70
y=x
z=y
echo $$z
```

Let us try to execute it.

```
$ SS70
1342z
```

The output of the **echo** statement is surprising. It seems it should have printed 'x', since $z should have yielded 'y' and $y should have yielded 'x'. But that doesn't happen since the sequence $$ gives the PID of current shell. This PID gets printed followed by the character 'z'.

If we really wish to get the output as 'x' then we can do so using the **eval** command as shown below.

```
# SS71
# Usage: SS71
y=x
z=y
eval echo \$$z
```

Let us now execute it.

```
$ SS71
x
```

The **eval** command evaluates the command line to complete any shell substitutions necessary and then executes the command. This is needed when a single pass of shell substitution does not complete all the needed expansions. In our program when the statement

    eval echo \$$z

is scanned for the first time **$z** is replaced by **y** and then the command

    echo $y

is executed. This results in 'x' being echoed to the screen. Note that the '\' in this statement is necessary. When the statement is scanned the '\' ensures that the first **$** is preserved on the command line such that it can later be used to extract the value the variable **y**.

Thus the **eval** command tells shell to performs all its substitutions on **eval**'s arguments and then to execute the result as if it were a standard shell command line.

For the following statements can you find out how to echo the value 'w' using the variable **z**?

    x=w
    y=x
    z=y

The **eval** command is useful in shell scans that build up command line inside variables. If the variable contains any characters that must be seen by the shell directly on the command line i.e. not as a result of substitution then **eval** can be useful. ; | & < > and quotes must directly appear on the command line to have any special meaning to the shell.

Here are a few more examples of usage of **eval**.

(a)   Consider the following program.

```
# SS72
# Usage: SS72

output="myfile > yourfile"
cat $output
```

If we execute this script it reports that the file > does not exist. This is because I/O redirection is done before variable substitution. So once the variable has been substituted the shell cannot do redirection and thus attempts to **cat** three files on the screen: **myfile, >** and **yourfile**. Naturally, the shell doesn't find the file > in the current directory and hence reports an error. This problem can be overcome using the **eval** statement as shown below:

```
eval cat $output
```

(b)   Suppose we execute the following commands:

```
$ pipe='|'
$ ls $pipe wc -l
| not found
wc not found
-l not found
```

The errors result since input/output redirection and piping is done before variable substitution. Thus, when the shell scans the command line and doesn't' find any input/output redirection or piping symbols it goes ahead with the variable substitution. Therefore, |, **wc** and **-l** are passed to **ls** as arguments hence the error. A solution to this situation is usage of **eval** as shown below:

```
$ pipe='|'
$ eval ls $pipe wc -l
```

The first time the shell scans the command line it substitutes 'l' as value of the variable **pipe**. By the time substitutions on **eval**'s arguments are over and it's time to execute the command, it has become,

ls | wc -l

When this command is executed by the shell the output of **ls** is properly piped to **wc** which then reports the number of lines.

(c)   Consider the following command:

cat < ch*17

As we know, I/O redirection is done before filename substitution. Hence, before the shell can replace **ch*17** with files matching this skeleton, it would attempt to redirect standard input to **ch*17**. And since such a file does not exist in the current directory an error results. Again using **eval** would solve the problem.

eval cat \< ch*17

eval causes this command to be evaluated by the shell twice; once when **eval** is executed and once when the result of **eval** is executed.

The first evaluation replaces **ch*17** with **chapter17** and removes the \, then the shell executes the resulting command **cat chapter17**.

(d)   The following script shows how to get to the last argument supplied to the script using **eval**.

```
# SS73
# Usage: SS73 [ arg1 arg2 arg3 ... ... ]
eval echo \$$#
```

Let us see what this script outputs in two different executions.

```
$ SS73 fast faster fastest
fastest
$ SS73 fast faster fastest fassstessttt
fassstessttt
```

As you can see, the script is able to properly report the last argument provided at the command line. During execution, first time the first $ is ignored and the \ is removed by the shell from the statement. Also, this time **$#** gives total number of arguments. In the next scan it becomes **$3** during first execution and **$4** during the next. This value is then echoed to the screen.

(e)   **eval** is useful in assigning value to a variable using another variable as shown below.

```
# SS74
# Usage: SS74

x=100
ptr=x
eval $ptr=50
echo $x
```

Let us execute this script.

```
$ SS74
50
```

In the **eval** statement used in this script the value 50 is stored in the variable that **ptr** points to, i.e. in the variable **x**. Thus, the original value (100) of **x** is replaced by the new value (50). This is confirmed by the output of the **echo** statement.

Exercise

[A] State whether the following statements are True or False:

(a) An exported variable cannot be unset.

(b) A readonly variable cannot be exported.

(c) If value of the exported variable is changed in a sub-shell the changed value becomes available to the parent shell automatically.

(d) If value of the exported variable is changed in a sub-shell the changed value becomes available to the sub-sub-shell automatically.

(e) If output of a command is piped to a **while** loop the loop is executed in a sub-shell.

(f) If output of a **while** loop is redirected to a file then the loop gets executed in a sub-shell.

(g) While executing a script the shell acts as a compiler.

(h) The shell performs command substitution before filename substitution.

(i) On logging in the shell automatically executes the **.profile** file if it is present in your home directory.

[B] What would be the output of the following programs:

(a)
```
b=a
c=b
d=c
echo $$$c
eval echo $$$c
```

```
        eval echo \$$$c
        eval echo \$\$$c
        eval echo \$\$\$c
        eval eval echo \$\$\$c
        eval eval eval echo \$\$\$c
        eval eval eval echo \\\$$$c
```

(b)   echo Hello
       eval echo Hello
       eval eval echo Hello

(c)   i=0
       while [$i -le 10]
       do
            echo $i
            i='expr $i + 1'
       done > myfile
       echo $i

(d)   name=Sanjay
       surname=Khare
       echo ${name-Rahul}
       echo ${middlename-Rahul}
       echo ${surname+Arora}
       echo ${newname+Arora}

(e)   name=Sanjay
       surname=Khare
       echo ${name=Rahul}
       echo ${middlename+Rahul}
       echo ${surname-Arora}

(f)   m=thanks
       echo ${n?Not defined} is the value stored in n
       echo ${m?Not defined} is the value stored in n
```
```

15 System Administration

As we harped upon several times in earlier chapters, System Administrator is the ultimate authority in a Unix environment. But with this authority and power comes the responsibility to govern and care. To aid the genuine users in need of help and at the same time protect the system and the users from illegal users. So system administration is about setting standards and maintaining them. It's not as easy as it may sound. After all the system administrator has to live up to the expectations of all the users of the system. The various jobs that a system administrator has to carry out can be classified as shown below:

(a)   Add, change, and delete users, software and hardware.
(b)   Carry out routine maintenance activities like backup files and restore them on user's request.
(c)   Monitor system usage as related to disk and CPU.
(d)   Maintain services like mail and uucp.
(e)   Ensure system security.
(f)   Provide assistance to users when required.

The system administrator can carry out these jobs in three ways:

(a)   Using **sysadmsh**, the system administration shell.
(b)   Using the various system administration tools that come with the system.
(c)   Writing small shell scripts which in turn use the tools mentioned in (b).

Discussing the **sysadmsh** shell is beyond the scope of this book. Likewise, discussing each and every administration tool would require a separate text devoted only to system administration. Here we would discuss only those tools which can be used in writing some system administration shell scripts. Nevertheless let us find out where the administrator's tools reside. Figure 15.1 shows the directories that contain files and commands that affect system administration.

Directory	Description
/etc	Administrative and operational commands reside here, as well as passwd and group files
/usr/adm	Accounting directories
/usr/lib	Operational logs, cron tables, commands
/usr/lib/acct	Accounting commands
/usr/lib/uucp	uucp commands
/usr/news	Local news directory
/usr/pub	Public directories
/usr/tmp	Temporary directories

Figure 15.1

The major files and commands of concern to the system administrator are shown in Figure 15.2. Most of these files are ASCII data files which are used by system administration tools shown in Figure 15.3. As you can note most of the commands required for system administration reside in the **/etc** directory.

File	Description
/etc/brc	Executed at startup by **init**
/etc/checklist	Default file systems checked by **fsck**
/etc/group	Listing of group IDs and passwords
/etc/inittab	Event list for **init**
/etc/motd	Message of the day
/etc/mnttab	List of mounted file systems
/etc/passwd	Login and password file
/etc/profile	Custom shell script executed by **init**
/etc/rc	Startup shell script executed by **init**
/etc/termcap	Terminal capabilities database
/etc/wtmp	Log of login processes
/usr/adm/pacct	Accounting log
/usr/lib/cron/log	Log of **cron** processing
/usr/spool/cron/crontabs	Event list for **cron**

Figure 15.2

Directory	Description
/etc/config	Configures a Unix system
/etc/crash	Crashes the system
/etc/cron	Executes commands in/usr/lib/crontab
/bin/format	Formats a disk
/etc/fsck	Checks a file sytem
/etc/fsdb	Debugs file system errors
/etc/init	Initialises the system
/etc/killall	Kills all processes
/etc/labelit	Labels a disk or tape volume
/etc/mkfs	Makes a file system
/etc/mknod	Makes a special file node (e.g., named pipes)
/etc/mount	Mounts a file system
/etc/shutdown	Gracefully shuts the system down
/etc/umount	Unmounts a file system
/etc/volcopy	Volume-to-volume file system copy
/etc/wall	Sends a message to all users

Figure 15.3

Adding and Removing Users

Day-to-day work is where Shell truly shines as an aid for productive system administration. Almost everyday the administrator is required to add or delete a user or group from the system. Adding a user requires entries to be made in the **passwd** and **group** files. Also, directories and files need to be created and environment variables to be established. The following shell script shows how this can be achieved.

```
# SS75
# Usage: SS75
```

```
# shell script to open an account for a user

# get last user no
usernum='tail -1 /etc/passwd | cut -f3 -d":"'

# Increment user no
usernum='expr $usernum + 1'

# receive relevant information

echo "Which group will user belong to?"
read groupname
groupnum='grep $groupname /etc/group | cut -f3 -d":"'
echo "User's login name?"
read logname
echo "User's name and phone?"
read username

# add the information to the passwd file
echo "$logname:x:$usernum:$groupnum:$username:/usr/$log-
name:/bin/sh"  >> /etc/passwd

# create login and other directories
homedir=/usr/$logname
mkdir $homedir
mkdir $homedir/bin
mkdir $homedir/doc
mkdir $homedir/src

# add .profile file to user's account
cp /usr/lib/mkuser/sh/profile /$homedir/.profile

# give proper permissions to directories and files
chmod 755 $homedir $homedir/*
chmod 777 $homedir/src
chmod 700 $homedir/.profile
```

```
# make all files and directories owned by user and group
chown $logname $homedir $homedir/* $homedir/.profile
chgrp $groupname $homedir $homedir/* $homedir/.profile
```

The above shell script meets the basic needs for creating a new account. If the user requires more hooks into the additional subsystems of Unix like **lp**, **mail** etc. - the shell script will have to be enhanced to establish the environment variables required to make the user's entrance into the system as comfortable as possible.

The shell script to add a group to the **/etc/group** file would be similar to this script and can be written with a few modifications to this script. Likewise, we can write a shell script to delete the user. To do this all references to the user must be removed from the system. Try your hand at writing these two shell scripts.

Some More Daily Administration

In Chapter 7 we had seen how the **cron** daemon can carry out jobs assigned to it at predetermined regular intervals. It reads the **/usr/lib/crontab** file and executes the commands found there according to the time specifications. **cron** gives the system administrator a handy way of being everywhere, doing everything, without having to be on the system.

To remind you each entry in the **crontab** file has six fields. The first five fields tell **cron** when to execute the command: minute (0-59), hour (0-23), day (1-31), month (1-12), and day of the week (0-6, sunday = 0). To match a number of different times or days, a field may contain comma-separated numbers. To match any time or day, an asterisk (*) can be used in any of these fields. The sixth field contains the command to be executed.

The system administrator may use this facility to print the date and time on the console every 30 minutes and to **sync** the super block every 10 minutes as shown below:

```
0, 30                      * * * *   date > /dev/console
0, 10, 20, 30, 40, 50  * * * *   /bin/sync > /dev/null
```

The system administrator should use **cron** to handle as many routine tasks as possible. These include activities such as monitoring disk usage, cleaning up temporary files, keeping system logs to a reasonable size, printing accounting reports, administering subsystems such as **lp**, or any related administrative task.

Starting Up The System

Starting of the system is handled by a file **/etc/init**. It uses the file **/etc/inittab** during each of its startup states like mounting of disks or bringing the terminal devices (**/dev/tty**) on line. During startup a shell script called **/etc/rc** gets executed. It checks all the file systems for errors by calling a command called **fsck** (file system check), mounts the file system, and starts process accounting, **cron**, **lp**, and anything else that should be available when users enter the system.

Since **/etc/rc** is a shell script, it can be modified to ensure that the system comes up cleanly, ready for users. This shell script should evolve over a period of time to simplify system operation.

Shutting The System Down

Unlike DOS, it is of utmost important to shutdown the system systematically. Rash actions such as halting the machine from the console before all commands are killed, file system unmounted, accounting stopped, subsystems stopped, and so on, can generate all kinds of problems when you put on the system next time.

Unix provides a shell script called **shutdown** to close down the system systematically. **/etc/shutdown** can be modified by the system administrator to improve system reliability. Presented below is a sample script which contains the basic ingredients of the **shutdown** command.

```
# SS76
# Usage: SS76 [-y] [-g [hh]:mm] -f file
# shell script to shutdown the system systematically

# check whether you have an execute permission
if [ -x /usr/bin/id ]
then
      var='id'
      echo $var | grep uid=0 > /dev/null

      if [ $? -ne 0 ]
      then
            echo Only root can run this shell script
            exit
      fi
fi

# initialise default values for variables
grace=600
askconfirmation=no
hr=0
min=10
filesupplied=no

# process command line options, if any
while getopts yg:f: choice
do
      case $choice in
         -g) time=$OPTARG
            echo $time | grep ":" > /dev/null

            # if time supplied in hh:mm format
            if [ $? -eq 0 ]
            then
                  hr='echo $OPTARG | cut -d: -f1'
                  min='echo $OPTARG | cut -d: -f2'
            else
```

```
                        hr=0
                        min=$time
              fi

              # check validity of hours
              if [ $hr -lt 0 -o $hr -gt 72 ]
              then
                        echo grace period should be <= 72 hours
                        exit
              fi

              # check validity of minutes
              if [ $min -lt 0 -0 $min -gt 59 ]
              then
                        echo value of min should be between 0-59
                        exit
              fi
              ;;

     -f)    filesupplied=yes
            file=$OPTARG
            ;;

     -y)    askconfirmation=yes
            ;;

     ?)     echo Improper usage
            echo The correct usage is
            echo Usage: SS76 [-y] [-g [hh]:mm] -f file
            ;;
     esac
done

grace='expr $hr \* 3600 + $min \* 60'

# continue till grace period is greater than 60 seconds
while [ $grace -gt 60 ]
```

```
do
    left=`who | wc -l`

    # if more than one user has logged in right now
    if [ $left -gt 1 ]
    then
        # if a filename has been supplied then wall its contents
        if [ $filesupplied = yes ]
        then
            cat $file | /etc/wall
        else
            # otherwise wall the following message
            echo The system will be shut in $hr hours and $min minutes\n
                Please log off before that | /etc/wall
        fi

        # adjust the grace period such that the shutdown warning is
        # displayed every hour or every fifteen minutes if the grace
        # period is less than an hour.

        if [ $hr -gt 0 ]
        then
            hr=`expr $hr - 1`
            grace=`expr $grace - 3600`
            sleep 3600
        else
            if [ $min -ge 15 ]
            then
                min=`expr $min - 15`
                grace=`expr $grace - 900`

                # remain idle for next 15 minutes
                sleep 900
            else
                if [ $min -gt 0 ]
                then
                    min=`expr $min - 1`
```

```
                                grace='expr $grace - 60'

                                # remain idle for next 1 minute
                                sleep 60
                        fi
                    fi
                fi
            fi
done


# 1 minute left for shutdown

echo Shutdown has started...
date
echo
sync
cd /

trap "" 1 15
trap "exit" 2

# if confirmation has been requested
if [ $askconfirmation = yes ]
then
    echo "Do you really want to shutdown the system? y/n "
    read ans
else
    ans=y
if

if [ $ans = y -o $ans = Y ]
then
    echo The system will be shut down NOW!
    /etc/init  0
else
    echo False Alarm!! The system will not be brought down
    echo Shut Down aborted!!
```

```
            exit
   fi
```

The program is self-explanatory to a major extent. The command line options are processed using the **getopts** command. Then within a loop a shutdown message is sent to all logged in users every hour and every 15 minutes during the last hour. Once this time period expires the system is shut down using **/etc/init 0** after receiving a final confirmation.

One can think of improving the above program by including one more feature. Instead of straightaway shutting down the system on expiration of the grace period the system can be first placed in a single-user mode, then file systems can be checked, then it should ask whether disk or tape backups are to be made, execute the necessary commands for taking backups and then finally halt the system entirely.

We were unable to incorporate these features since so far we have not learnt how to backup the files, how to check the file systems etc. This in fact is going to be our next topic of discussion.

Disk Management

There are two types of backups that are frequently done in a typical Unix environment. The first type is done by the system administrator which involves backing up all system and user files. Such backups are taken on mass storage devices like magnetic tapes and fixed disks. Individual users can take backup of their work on cheaper storage mediums like floppies of different capacities. To take either kind of backups Unix provides a command called **tar**, a short-form for tape archive.

Before we can archive (backup) our files on the floppy we have to format it. Unix understands a wide variety of floppy disks though the 1.2 MB and 1.44 MB varieties are the ones which are more commonly used today. Remember that the floppy disk formats in Unix are not the same as in other operating systems such as MS-DOS. All disks used on a Unix machine, must be formatted under Unix only. Once formatted, it can be used in two ways in Unix:

(a) We can create a file system on the floppy disk and use it as if it is a directory on the hard disk. To do this we have to do two things. Firstly, we have to establish a file system on it using the **mkfs** command. Secondly, we have to mount this file system at a specific place (called mount point) on the file system of our hard disk.

(b) We access the floppy disk using the 'raw access' method which doesn't require creation of a file system on he floppy. This method is generally used during backing-up or archiving of data.

Irrespective of which method we decide to use we will have to first format the disk .Let us see how this can be done.

Formatting A Disk

To understand and interface with the different types of disks there are several files present in the **/dev** directory. These files are named as per the capacity and type of disks they intend to interact with. For example, for a 1.2 MB, double sided, 96 tracks per inch floppy disk there is a file called **rfd096ds15**. Here 'rfd' stands for raw floppy disk, 0 for floppy in drive A, 96 for tracks per inch, 'ds' for double sided and 15 for number of sectors per track. Given below are three more sample names:

(a) rfd196ds15 - same as above, except 1 indicating floppy in drive B.
(b) rfd048ds9 - 48 tracks per inch, 9 sectors per track raw floppy disk in drive A. i.e. a 360 KB disk.
(c) rfd0135ds18 - 135 tracks per inch, 18 sectors per track raw floppy disk in drive B. i.e. a 1.44 MB disk.

To format a floppy disk, we just have to say,

```
$ format  /dev/rfd096ds15
```

Naturally, if we are to format the 1.44 MB floppy disk present in drive B we would say

```
$ format  /dev/rfd1135ds18
```

Thus depending on the type of format desired and the capacity of the floppy disk the device name following the format command would change.

At times we can even skip the device name. In such an event the **format** command reads the device value specified in the **/etc/default/format** file. In our case this file contained the following values:

```
$ cat  /etc/default/format
# @ (#) format96 23.1 91/08/29
#
#
VERIFY=Y
DEVICE=/dev/rfd096ds15
$
```

This indicates that if we issue the format command without mentioning the device name it would format the disk in drive A as if it is a 1.2 MB (96 tpi) disk. This is shown below:

```
$ format
Insert floppy in drive; press <Return> when ready
formatting /dev/rfd096ds15 ...
track 79 head 1
done
verifying /dev/rfd096ds15 ...
track 79
```

```
done
$
```

As can be seen once the formatting was over, Unix went ahead and verified each formatted track since the VERIFY flag was set to Y in **/etc/default/format**. If during verification any errors in formatting are detected then they are appropriately reported. We can also use the verify option at command line as

```
$ format -v /dev/rfd096ds15
```

As mentioned earlier, once formatted we can use the floppy as a backup device, or create a file system on it, mount it in the original file system and use it as a directory. For the present let us follow the second path. Later on we would find out how to use it for taking backups.

Making A File System

A file system can be created on a formatted floppy using the **mkfs** command. Unlike **format** this command can only be used by the superuser of the system. So you'll have to approach him with your floppy disk and request him to create a file system on it and then mount it. This is what he is likely to do...

```
# /etc/mkfs /dev/rfd096ds15 2400:600
mkfs: default type (AFS) used
bytes per logical block = 1024
total logical blocks = 1200
total inodes = 608
gap (physical blocks) = 7
cylinder size (physical blocks) = 400
cluster size = 16
mkfs: Available blocks = 1157
#
```

Note that the command has been executes at the # prompt rather than the $ prompt since it is the # prompt at which the system administrator usually works. As can be seen **mkfs** takes a device name as its argument and creates a file system on that device. By default it creates a Acer File System on our disk. This is the default file system. We can use **mkfs** to create other types of file systems too. Note the second parameter supplied to **mkfs** 2400:600.

Here 2400 stands for the numbers of 512 KB blocks that may be present on the disk. For a 1.2 MB disk the number of blocks can be calculated as,

```
tracks/side * number of sides * sectors/track * bytes/sector / 512
= 80 * 2 * 15 * 512 / 512
= 2400
```

Mentioning fewer blocks than 2400 for a 1.2 MB disk would result into wasted disk space and mentioning more than 2400 would cause a fatal error since **mkfs** would not be able to find the specified number of blocks on the floppy disk.

The 600 following the colon indicates the number of inodes that we want to create in the file system. Usually this number is one fourth of the number of blocks.

We know that for each file that we create one inode gets consumed. Hence if we are expecting a lot of small sized files to be created on this file system we should give a larger inode count. If we don't then we may end up with a situation where there are free blocks available on the file system but all the inodes have been consumed.

Vice versa if we expect to create small number of large sized files on the file system then we should give a smaller inode count. This would avoid wasting of disk space to accommodate inode entries which may never get used.

If we want we can specify only the number of blocks and leave it for the system to decide the optimum inode count as shown below.

```
# /etc/mkfs /dev/rfd096ds15 2400
mkfs: default type (AFS) used
bytes per logical block = 1024
total logical blocks = 1200
total inodes = 304
gap (physical blocks) = 7
cylinder size (physical blocks) = 400
cluster size = 16
mkfs: Available blocks = 1176
#
```

Since we did not specify the number of inodes the system calculated 304 inodes for our file system of 2400 blocks.

While creating a file system if any data exists on the floppy disk, it will be promptly erased. Usually formatting and creating a file system is done only once. There onwards the file system is only mounted every time we decide to use the floppy disk. Let us now see how this mounting is done.

Mounting A File System

The file system built on the floppy disk can be linked into the existing file system on the hard disk using the **mount** command. Once mounted we can create files and directories in the new file system and treat it as a normal directory existing in a file system.

Like all file systems, each mounted file system too, has a root directory and all its directories fan out from the root. When we are mounting a file system, we are simply attaching its root directory to a particular point in the existing file system. This point of attachment is called the 'mount point' for that file system. The mount point of any new file system, must always be specified as a path from the root directory of the existing file system. Unix provides a default mount point called **/mnt**. Let us mount our file system at this mount point.

```
# /etc/mount /dev/fd096ds15 /mnt
```

Note that while mentioning the device we have mentioned only 'fd' in place of the normal 'rfd'. This is because once the file system has been created on the disk it no longer remains a 'raw' floppy disk.

The mount point **/mnt** is an empty directory in the root (/) directory, with root (superuser) as its owner. All users have the permission to access this directory.

Whether the floppy disk file system has been successfully mounted or not can be verified in two ways:

(a)   **cd** into the **/mnt** directory and create a few files and directories. If you are successful then these files and directories would be created on the floppy disk.

(b)   Run the **mount** command without any argument and it would list out all currently mounted file systems.

```
# mount
/ on /dev/root read/write on Wed May 01 12:04:42 1996
/mnt on /dev/fd096ds15 read/write on Wed May 01 17:54:22 1996
#
```

The output shows the root file system and the one that we mounted at the **/mnt** mount point.

If we want we can mount a file system at a mount point, other than the default mount point as shown below:

```
# /etc/mount /dev/fd096ds15 /usr/fdd
```

This command will mount the file system on the floppy at the **/usr/fdd** mount point assuming that the System Administrator has already created the directory **/usr/fdd**. This can again be confirmed by calling **mount** without any arguments.

```
# /etc/mount
/ on /dev/root read/write on Wed May 01 12:04:42 1996
/usr/fdd  on  /dev/fd096ds15 read/write on Wed May 01 17:54:22 1996
#
```

As long as the file system is mounted, Unix follows all normal procedures to keep the floppy up-to-date with the changes that you make. To confirm the status of the new file system, we can use the **dfspace** command.

```
# /etc/dfspace
/   :    Disk space: 35.72 MB of 253.85 MB available (14.07%).
/mnt:    Disk space:  1.14 MB of  1.17 MB available (98.00%).

Total Disk space: 36.86 MB of 255.02  MB available (14.46%).
```

When a file system is mounted, an entry is made in the 'mount table' of the system, maintained in a file. This mount table is read by the commands **df** which is called by **dfspace**. If we want we can write our own shell program which works similar to the **dfspace** script.

Here is how...

```
# SS77
# Usage: SS77
# reports the disk usage of each mounted file system

df -t > /tmp/dfoutput
t=`tty`

cumfree=0
cumtot=0
```

```
# change standard input
exec < /tmp/dfoutput

while read line
do
      # extract name of the file system
      fsys=`echo $line | cut -d":" -f1`

      # keep rest of the fields together
      rest=`echo $line | cut -d":" -f2`

      set -- $rest
      fblk=$1
      finode=$3

      # read the line which contains the total
      read line
      set -- $line
      tblk=$2
      tinode=$4

      # calculate the space in megabytes
      availmb=`echo "scale=2 \n $fblk * 512 / 1048576 - 0.0005" | bc`
      totmb=`echo "scale=2 \n $tblk * 512 / 1048576 - 0.0005" | bc`
      availper=`echo "scale=2 \n $availmb / $totmb * 100" | bc`

      echo "$fsys $availmb of $totmb MB available ($availper)"

      cumfree=`echo "scale=2 \n $cumfree + $availmb" | bc`
      cumtot=`echo "scale=2 \n $cumtot + $totmb" | bc`
done

cumper=`echo "scale=2 \n $cumfree * 100 / $cumtot" | bc`
echo "Total disk space :  $cumfree of $cumtot MB ($cumper)"

# reset standard input to terminal
```

```
exec  <  $t
```

```
# get rid of the temporary file
rm  -f  /tmp/dfoutput
```

And here is the output...

```
$ SS77
/ (/dev/root ) 35.7195 of 253.8495 MB available (14.00)
/mnt (/dev/fd096ds15 ) 1.1395 of 1.1695 MB available (97.00)
Total disk space :  36.8590 of 255.0190 MB (14.45)
```

Except for the places after the decimal point this output matches with that of the standard **dfspace** command. The shell script just reads the output of **df -t** which is earlier redirected into the file **/tmp/dfoutput**. The **df** commands gives the free disk space in terms of blocks. Our script just converts this into megabytes, calculates the percentage usage per file system and then prints out this statistics.

Remember that once the file system on the floppy disk has been mounted we should never remove the floppy from the drive unless the file system has been unmounted. This can be done using the **umount** command. Once again it is only the system administrator who can unmount a file system.

Unmounting A File System

The **umount** command can be used to unmount any existing file system. On execution **unmount** delinks the new file system from the root directory of the existing file system. On unmounting a file system the files on that file system remain undisturbed. Only thing that happens is they become inaccessible. To access the files once again the file system has to be remounted using the **mount** command. While unmounting the file system's mount point has to be mentioned as an argument.

```
# /etc/umount  /mnt
```

If the unmounted file system was existing on a floppy, now we can safely remove the floppy. Note that the **umount** command fails when a user has a file open in the file system or has used the **cd** command and is currently working in the file system.

```
# /etc/umount  /mnt
umount:  /mnt busy
```

This, ensures that the superuser does not unmount the default file system on the hard disk while users are working on it.

Usually when the system is shut down using the **/etc/shutdown** command, a command **unmountall** is called which unmounts all the file systems before the system is shut down. During startup, a **rc** script is executed which calls the command **mountall** which remounts the file systems.

Using A Raw Disk

We mentioned earlier that we can format a disk and then use it to take backups without being required to create a file system on it. This way the floppy disk can be used by individual users to backup their own files. The **tar** command is used to save and restore files to and from an archive medium like a tape or a floppy disk.

All users are permitted to use the **tar** command; it's usage is not restricted only to the superuser. Let us assume that a 1.2 MB formatted floppy is sitting in drive A and we want to backup files present in **/usr/aa1/cprogs** directory to this floppy. We can achieve this by saying

```
$ tar  -cv2  /usr/aa1/cprogs/*
Volume ends at 1100K, blocking factor = 5K
seek = 0Ka /usr/aa1/cproggs/ch1pr1.c 2K
```

```
seek = 3Ka  /usr/aa1/cproggs/ch1pr2.c  1K
seek = 4Ka  /usr/aa1/cproggs/first.c  1K
seek = 5Ka  /usr/aa1/cproggs/second.c  1K
seek = 6Ka  /usr/aa1/cproggs/trial.c  1K
```

Here the option **c** indicates that the files should be created anew on the floppy while taking the backup. The option **v** stands for verbose which ensures that all the messages about the actions of **tar** are displayed on the screen. And finally 2 stands for 1.2 MB disk. How come 2 represents 1.2 MB disk? Because while archiving files to any medium **tar** needs information like device name, blocking factor, volume size, and type of device. These values would obviously be different for different devices. Hence, instead of we being required to supply these values they are stored systematically in a file called **/etc/default/tar** as shown below:

```
$ cat /etc/default/tar
# @(#) def96.src  23.2 91/08/29
#     device                      block      size      tape
archive0=/dev/rfd048ds9            18         360        n
archive1=/dev/rfd148ds9            18         360        n
archive2=/dev/rfd096ds15           10        1200        n
archive3=/dev/rfd196ds15           10        1200        n
archive4=/dev/rfd096ds9            18         720        n
archive5=/dev/rfd196ds9            18         720        n
archive6=/dev/rfd0135ds18          18        1440        n
archive7=/dev/rfd1135ds18          18        1440        n
archive8=/dev/rct0                 20           0        Y
archive9=/dev/rctmini              20           0        Y
# The default device in the absence of a numeric or "-f device"
argument archive=/dev/rfd096ds15 10           1200        n
```

You can note that in this list the 1.2 MB disk has been given a number 2 and that's the reason we used it while issuing the **tar** command.

The usage of **tar** command differs slightly from the rest of the Unix command set. In **tar** options have two parts: a function option (**c** in the command that we used) followed by the function modifiers. It is necessary that each **tar** command must contain at least one function option and one or more function modifiers. The function option decides what function the **tar** command must perform (backup or restore) and the function modifiers control the manner in which the specified function must be executed. It is necessary that the function letters precede the function modifiers.

To restore the files from the floppy disk back to their original place we can issue the command,

```
$ tar -xv2
```

Here the function option is **x** which indicates that we want to extract the files from the backup medium and put them in their original place. **v** once again is a function modifier standing for verbose and 2 indicates that we are extracting files from a 1.2 MB floppy disk. Nowhere are we required to mention the name of the directory in which the files should be restored. This is because a file once backed up from a particular directory gets restored to the same directory on extraction.

We can of course extract only specific files my mentioning their full path name during extraction.

```
$ tar -xv2 /usr/aa1/cprogs/first.c /usr/aa1/myprogs/sample.c
x /usr/aa1/cprogs/first.c 2231 bytes 3K
x /usr/aa1/myprogs/sampke.c 2236 bytes 3K
```

This extracts only the files **first.c** and **sample.c** and places them back to their original place on the hard disk.

By now you must have appreciated the usefulness of the **tar** command. However, the multitude of options that it offers makes life difficult for the user. To make the learning process easier presented below is a figure indicating the function options and the function modifiers that are commonly used with the **tar** command.

Option	Description
Function options	
c	Creates a new archive
r	Appends files to the rear of the archive
t	Lists filenames backed up on the disk
u	Updates archive by appending files(s) if not already present or if modified
x	Extracts files from the tar archive
Function Modifiers	
v	Verbose mode; prints out status information
k	Prompts for additional floppies when existing archive becomes full.
e	Ensures that no file is split across a disk or tape

Figure 15.4

Monitoring System Usage

There is no such thing as a foolproof system. There are bound to be problems as people start using a system. What is important is that the system administrator must be able to anticipate problems and fix them when they occur. To be able to anticipate problems the system administrator must monitor certain system functions.

One of the most important things to manage on most systems is disk usage. This can be done using the commands **df** (reports free disk space), **du** (reports directory-wise disk usage) and **dfspace** (reports free disk space in terms of MB) which were discussed at length in Chapter 3. Using these commands the system administrator would be able to pinpoint any unreasonably high or rapidly growing disk usage. It is often found that a small community of users tend to use a large amount of disk space. Having identified such users the system administrator can write a script to monitor their disk usage more closely. The system administrator can automate this process so that the system tracks changes in disk usage, comparing one day against the next, and notifies him of any untoward activity.

If the amount of free space under a file system drops below a certain level the system administrator can either request the users to eliminate unnecessary files and directories thereby freeing valuable disk space or consider expanding the file system by adding more storage devices.

At times it is possible that both these options are ruled out. At such times the superuser may be required to apply some brute force and eliminate the following:

(a)   Temporary files in **/usr/tmp** directory.
(b)   Temporary files in **/usr/preserve** directory.
(c)   The file **/usr/adm/messages** which contains all boot time screens.
(d)   The file **/usr/adm/sulog** which contains the superuser's login time screens.
(e)   The secondary mail box file called **mbox** for each individual user.
(f)   All zero byte files in user's directories.

The following shell script shows how these files can be eliminated.

```
# SS78
# Usage: SS78
# eliminates unnecessary files to free some disk space

cd  /usr/tmp
rm -f * 2> /dev/null

cd /usr/preserve
rm -f * 2> /dev/null
```

```
# overwrite with nothing, results into a zero byte file
> /usr/adm/messages
> /usr/adm/sulog

# remove secondary mailboxes interactively
rm -i /usr/*/mbox

# locate and remove zero byte files from user's directories
find /usr/* -size 0c -exec rm { } \;
```

In this script except for the last line everything else is pretty self-explanatory. The **find** command helps in locating files which meet the search criteria. The general form of **find** command is,

```
find pathname-list expression
```

Usually Unix file systems are exhaustive having several directories and files in it. Often the depth of the directory tree is very large. If we are to **cd** into each of these directories to search a particular file we would have to spend several hours before we can reach every directory in the file system. The **find** command automates this process for us. It recursively descends into the 'pathname-list' supplied to search the file(s) mentioned in the 'expression'. Thus the 'pathname-list' contains the directories to be searched, whereas the 'expression' specifies the list of the files to be searched along with the criteria to carry out this search.

Let us illustrate this with a practical example.

```
$ find /usr/icit -name trial -print
/usr/icit/trial
/usr/icit/mydir/trial
/usr/icit/mydir/dir1/trial
/usr/icit/temp/trial
```

Here **/usr/icit** was the path that was searched for a file whose name was **trial** and on encountering such a file it's name along with the complete path was printed. Note that unless we use the **-print** option the file gets located but doesn't get printed. Also, appreciate how the **find** command descends into the directory tree starting from **/usr/icit**.

As with any powerful Unix command **find** too comes with several options. Instead of listing these options it would be worthwhile listing examples which make use of these options. So here is the list. Go through it carefully.

(a)   Search the file **aaa** from current directory downwards and print it.

       find . -name aaa -print

(b)   Find all files which begin with 'a' or 'b' from current directory downwards and print them.

       find . -name [ab]* -print

(c)   Search directories called **backup** from **/usr** directory downwards and print them.

       find /usr -type d -name backup -print

(d)   Search normal files called **backup** from **/usr** directory downward and print them.

       find /usr -type f -name backup -print

(e)   Search character special files called **backup** from **/usr** directory downwards and print them.

       find /usr -type c -name backup -print

(f)   Search block special files called **backup** from **/usr** directory downwards and print them.

```
find /usr -type b -name backup -print
```

(g)   Search all directories from **/usr** downwards for files whose inode number is 1234 and print them.

```
find /usr -inum 1234 -print
```

(h)   Search in root directory downwards all files which have exactly 2 links.

```
find / -links 2 -print
```

(i)   Search in root directory downwards all files which have less than 2 links.

```
find / -links -2 -print
```

(j)   Search in root directory downwards all files which have more than 2 links.

```
find / -links +2 -print
```

(k)   Search in current directory downwards all files whose owner is **aa1** and group is **grp**.

```
find . \( -user aa1 -a -group grp \) -print
```

(l)   Search in current directory downwards all files whose owner is **aa1** or whose name is **myfile**.

```
find . \( -user aa1 -o -name myfile \) -print
```

(m)   Search in current directory downwards all files which have permissions 777.

```
find . -perm 777 -print
```

(n)   Search in current directory downwards all files whose size is 10 blocks.

find . -size 10 -print

(o)   Search in current directory downwards all files whose size is 10 bytes (characters).

find . -size 10c -print

(p)   Search in current directory downwards all files whose size is greater than 10 bytes.

find . -size +10c -print

(q)   Search in current directory downwards all files whose size is less than 10 bytes.

find . -size -10c -print

(r)   Search in current directory downwards all files which were accessed exactly 7 days back.

find . -atime 7 -print

(s)   Search in current directory downwards all files which have not been accessed since last 7 days (or in other words which were accessed more than 7 days ago).

find . -atime +7 -print

(t)   Search in current directory downwards all files which have not been modified since last 7 days (or in other words which have been modified more than 7 days ago).

find . -mtime +7 -print

(u)   Search in current directory downwards all files whose status has changed (on creation or modification) more than 7 days ago.

find . -ctime +7 -print

(v)   Search in current directory downwards all files whose name is **core** and instead of printing their names execute a command **rm** on the searched files.

find . -name core -exec rm { } \;

Here, the { } indicate that the searched files would become arguments for **rm**. The semicolon is necessary and it has to be preceded by a \ to take away its special meaning.

(w)   Same as above except that this time it should ask for confirmation before executing the **rm** command.

find . -name core -ok rm { } \;

So much about managing and monitoring the disk usage.

CPU and access times can be monitored via the accounting data. By tracking and plotting the trend, the system administrator will have sufficient advance warning to install hardware upgrades and tune the system to meet the demands. He may also be required to develop additional commands to monitor the other services on the system like **mail** and **lp**.

Ensuring System Security

System security is one of the most important jobs that the system administrator has to perform. He should ensure the following:

(a)   **Prevent illegal users from accessing the system .**

(b)   Maintain integrity of the system.

(c)   Make sure that files of a user is accessible only to the owner or his group-mates.

To prevent unauthorised access, the system administrator should encourage users to change their passwords frequently. He should also use password ageing thereby forcing the users to change passwords after certain period of time.

Using **chmod** we can change the ownership of a program. For example, if you ever happen to get around to the terminal where the superuser has logged in and has gone somewhere. At such times if you set the user id bit of the program **/bin/sysadmsh**, copy it into your directory and then reset the original permissions and quietly walk off then you can become the superuser. Just execute the **sysadmsh** program that you copied in your directory. Since you have set the user ID bit for this file, on execution of this program the ownership of this program comes to you and then you can gain total control over the system. Neat trick, you would agree!

Well, if the system administrator wants he can easily detect whether somebody has played such a trick by running the following command:

```
find / -user root -perm 4000 -exec ls -lg { } \ ;
```

That brings us to the third part of security, i.e. data privacy. The superuser can easily ensure this since mounting and unmounting of file systems lies in the control of the superuser. Controlling data security is augmented by the **umask** command, which determines the default file and directory permissions.

As a precautionary measure the system administrator can periodically check for directories that can be read and written by anyone in the world:

```
find / -perm 777 -type d -print
```

The system administrator can also encourage users to set their own default security using a proper **umask** value and encrypting the important files. All these measures would help in preventing loss of data or system files.

Occasionally, the system administrator may be required to allow a group of users to access the machine without giving them all of the power of Unix. In such cases, while creating their accounts the system administrator may assign such users a restricted shell (**/bin/rsh**) rather than the usual Bourne (**/bin/sh**) or C shell (**/bin/csh**).

When such users log in, they will not be able to execute the **cd** command nor would they be able to change the value of PATH. For such users I/O redirection is NO NO and so also is executing commands that begin with **/**. This ensures that such users can cause little damage, inadvertently or otherwise.

Thus restricted shell lets the external users perform some necessary work, but prohibits them from going crazy in the system. However, the system administrator should not go overboard with restricted shell facility and start handing it out to every new user, thereby sentencing him to virtually life imprisonment. He is supposed to use his discretion in this regard. After all the goal of system administration is to help users do whatever they need to do.

Providing Assistance to Users

The system administrator should communicate to the users any changes that he incorporates in the system from time to time. This he can do by using communication commands like **mail, news, wall** and **motd**. The system administrator would be inviting user's wrath if they get stuck up, need help and don't know from where to get it. To avoid this the system administrator can write a simple shell script which indicates where and how to reach him. If there is more than one administrator and each specializes in certain Unix subsystems, then that information can be included too.

We have seen that shell programming can aid the system administrator in all the phases of administration. The system administrator has as much to gain from shell usage as any common Unix user. I hope you would be able to extend the shell scripts presented in this book so far to satisfy your specific needs.

Exercise

[A]   State whether the following statements are True or False:

(a)   The file **/bin/sysadmsh** can be executed only by the system administrator.

(b)   To mount a 1.2 MB floppy disk the command **mount /dev/rfd096ds15 /mnt** is correct.

(c)   The command **/etc/init 1** puts the system in single-user mode.

(d)   The command **/etc/init 0** halts the system.

(e)   It is necessary to format the floppy before using a **tar** command to store files on it.

(f)   There is no need to make file system on a disk if we are going to use it only to backup files on it.

(g)   A file system can be installed at any mount point other than **/mnt**.

(h)   A file can be copied across two different file systems.

(i)   A file system can be mounted and unmounted by any user.

(j)   A floppy can be formatted only by the system administrator.

(k)   Creating a file system on a disk means creating boot block, super block, inode table and data blocks on the disk.

(l)   Using **tar** we can archive files only on a magnetic tape.

(m)   It is necessary to unmount a file system before removing a floppy.

(n)   A **tar** command always needs at least one function option.

(o)   The number of inodes that can be created on floppy disks have been fixed according to their capacities.

[B]   How would you perform the following operations:

(a) **sync** the disk after every five minutes.

(b) Take backup of files in **/usr/cprogs** directory at 5 PM every day.

(c) List all backed up files present on a floppy disk.

(d) Extract a file **mylog** from a 1.44 MB disk.

(e) Find all files which begin with 'a' or 'b' with a digit as the second character from current directory downwards and print them.

(f) Delete all 5 byte files from the current directory downwards.

(g) Find all links of the **vi** editor.

(h) Search in current directory downwards all files which have more than 5 links.

(i) Search in current directory downwards all files whose owner is **aa1**, group is **grp** and it has not been accessed since last two years.

(j) Search in **/usr** directory downwards all directories which have permissions 444.

(k) Search in **/dev** directory downwards all block special files.

[C] Answer the following:

(a) Outline the jobs of a system administrator.

(b) What does each character in rfd1135ds18 connote?

(c) Can we delete the line VERIFY=Y from **/etc/default/format** and still be able to format a disk.

(d) How is **tar** command a little different than other Unix commands?

(e) What is the noticeable difference between options used by **find** command as compared to other Unix commands?

(f) Write the **crontab** entry for printing the report file **/usr/aa1/finacc/bsheeet** on first monday of every month.

(g) Write a interactive shell script which will request the user to put the 1.2 MB floppy in drive A, format it, make a file system on it with 2000 blocks and 500 inodes, mount it at a mount point **/fdd**.

(h) Write a shell script to send mail to groups of users by extracting their IDs from **/etc/group** file.

16 *Shell Program-ming Project*

Payroll Processing System
    Data Organisation
    Menus
    Report Formats
    Calculations
Working of The System
Program
Where Do You Go from Here...
Improve This Program...

S o far we have written small but useful shell scripts. The idea was always to introduce some new concept or a subtlety of shell programming. Now that we are through with most of the features of shell programming let us put together an entire system using shell scripts. Development of this system would encompass all that we have learnt so far. This would help you in two ways:

(a)   It would serve as a revision of all the concepts.
(b)   It would help you visualise in which situation which concept has to be used while writing professional level scripts.

However, instead of handing you the entire software on a platter, I thought it worthwhile to give you the overall picture and getting you started and then leaving it for you to develop some components of the software. We would try to develop a payroll processing system. So here we go...

Payroll Processing System

Shivley & Brett is a pharmaceutical company engaged in manufacture of life saving drugs. The company was established in the year 1982 with an employee strength of 75, with 8 officers. Since its inception, it has grown steadily over the years and today boasts a turnover of Rs. 130 millions. Today it has a strength of 600 employees out of which 125 are of officer cadre. There are five departments in the company, viz., Manufacturing, Assembly, Stores, Accounts and Maintenance. It has been the policy of the company to develop a technologically advanced work environment. In tune with this policy, the accounts department of the company has decided to computerise its payroll preparation. Since the payroll processing package for the company must be made to suit their requirements, the company has approached you to prepare the package. To begin with, the company has decided to implement computerised payroll processing only for the workers, with plans to include the officer staff only after the satisfactory completion of workers payroll processing.

Data Organisation

The workers in the company are divided into 5 categories, namely, Super skilled (SSK), Highly Skilled (HSK), Skilled (SKI), Semi skilled (SMS) and Unskilled (USK). The data about each worker in the company can be categorised as shown below:

General Data	Allowances	Deductions	Leave Record
Employee code	DA	Provident fund	Maximum CL
Name	HRA	ESI	Maximum ML
Department	CA	GIP	Maximum PL
Grade	CCA	Income tax	Cumulative CL
Sex	Special Pay 1	Profession tax	Cumulative ML
Address	Special Pay 2	Rent deduction	Cumulative PL
GPF no.	Gross Pay	LT loan installment	Cumulative LWP
GI scheme no.		ST loan installment	Attended days
ESI scheme no.		Special deduction 1	Monthly CL
Basic		Special deduction 2	Monthly ML
		Total deduction	Monthly PL
			Monthly LWP

This data can be organised into 2 different files:

(a)   Employee master data file - This contains that information about the employees which is relatively permanent. (EMASTER.DBF) (b)　Employee transaction data file - This contains data which varies from month to month. (ETRAN.DBF)

For maintaining one to one correspondence between records in master data file and transaction data file, the Employee code and Department in which the employee works would be present in both the data files. The fields in each data file would be as under:

EMASTER.DBF		ETRAN.DBF	
Description	Field Name	Description	Field Name
Employee code	e_empcode	Employee code	t_empcode
Name	e_empname	Department	t_dept
Sex	e_sex	Casual leave	t_cl
Address	e_address	Medical leave	t_ml
Name of city	e_city	Provi. leave	t_ pl
Pin code	e_pin	LWP	t_lwp
Department	e_dept	DA	t_da
Grade	e_grade	HRA	t_hra
GPF. no.	e_gpf_no.	CA	t_ca
GI scheme no.	e_gis_no.	CCA	t_cca
ESI scheme no.	e_esis_no.	Special pay 1	t_sppay_1
CL allowed	e_max_cl	Special pay 2	t_sppay_2
PL allowed	e_max_pl	Gross salary	t_gs
ML allowed	e_max_ml	GPF	t_gpf
Basic salary	e_bs	GIS	t_gis
Cumulative cl	e_cum_cl	ESIS	t_esis
Cumulative pl	e_cum_pl	Income tax	t_inc_tax
Cumulative ml	e_cum_ml	Profession tax	t_prof_tax
Cumulative lwp	e_cum_lwp	Rent deduction	t_rent_ded
Cumu. att.days	e_cum_att	Long term loan	t_lt_loan
		Short term loan	t_st_loan
		Special ded. 1	t_spded_1
		Special ded. 2	t_spded_2
		Total deduction	t_tot_ded
		Net pay	t_net_pay

Menus

The different menus to be developed in this system are as follows:

PAYROLL SYSTEM MAIN MENU
Database operations
Reports
Exit
Your Choice?

PAYROLL SYSTEM DATA BASE OPERATIONS
Master File Data Entry
Transaction Data Entry
Return to main menu
Your Choice?

PAYROLL SYSTEM MASTER DATA ENTRY
Add record
Modify record
Delete record
Retrieve record
Return to main menu
Your choice?

PAYROLL SYSTEM TRAN. DATA ENTRY
Add record
Modify record
Delete record
Retrieve record
Return to main menu
Your choice?

PAYROLL SYSTEM REPORTS MENU
Mailing Labels
Leave Status Report
Paysheet Printing
Summary Payroll Sheet
Return to main menu
Your choice?

PAYROLL SYSTEM SYSTEM MAINT. MENU
Close month
Close year & reorganise
Return to main menu
Your choice?

Report Formats

The formats of the different reports to be printed are as follows:

Mailing List

This report displays the entire mailing list of employees.

Clarence Elmsworth
Blandings Castle
Kalyan
411002

Jason Bourne
Whispering Palms, Madh Island
Bombay
400064

John Galt
A-2, Manish Nagar, Andheri
Bombay
400054

Michael Havilland
22, Shangri-la, Bandra
Banglore
560050

Leave Status Report

This report shows the status of leaves taken by an employee during the current year in terms of allowed leaves, leaves availed so far (cumulative) and leaves in balance.

Name : John Galt		Empcode:A10	Grade:HSK	Month:Mar96
CL allowed	ML allowed	PL allowed		
12	15	5		
Cum. CL	Cum. ML	Cum.PL	CumLWP	Cum. Att. days
3	4	0	0	82
Balance CL	Balance ML	Balance PL		
9	11	5		

Name : Jason Bourne		Empcode:A01	Grade: SSK	Month:Mar96
CL allowed	ML allowed	PL allowed		
15	20	5		
Cum. CL	Cum. ML	Cum. PL	Cum. LWP	Cum Att.days
1	0	0	0	102
Balance CL	Balance ML	Balance PL		
14	20	5		

Payslip

This report generates payslips of employees working in the factory.
Note that such reports are usually printed on pre-printed stationary.
In this system it has been printed only on the screen.

SHIVLEY & BRETT PVT. LTD.

Emp.code:A10		Sex: Male			Grade: HSK			Month:Mar		
Name: John Galt						Department: Assembly				
GPF No. 6132/A		GIS No.P6329			ESIS No. P6452					
Normal Days		Casual Leave		Medical Leave		Prov. Leave		LWP	Attended days	
31		2		1		0		0	28	
BS	DA		HRA	CA	CCA	SP 1	SP 2	GS		
520.0	1040.00		130.0	52.00	52.00	45.00	0.00	1839.00		
GPF	ESIS	GIS	IT	PT	Rent	Loan1	Loan2	S.D.1	SD.2	Tot.
156.0	75.00	115.0	0.00	20.00	50.00	0.00	75.00	0.00	0.00	491.0
Net Pay										
Rs. 1348.00						Receiver's signature				

Summary Payroll Sheet

This report gives department wise payment made for a particular month for all employees in each department.

Summary Payroll Sheet				
March 1996				
Department	**Total Employees**	**Gross Earnings**	**Gross Deductions**	**Net Payment**
MFG	132	32,040	3,530	28,510
ASSLY	67	21,030	2,850	18,180
STORES	19	17,550	1,870	15,680
ACCTS	22	18,490	2,115	16,375
MAINT	30	24,555	3,335	21,220

Calculations

The following table shows percentages used for calculation of various allowances and deductions for different grades of employees.

Grade	DA % of BS	HRA % of BS	CA % of BS	CCA % of BS	GPF **	ESIS	GIS	PT
SSK	200 %	30 %	10 %	10 %	10 %	Rs. 100	Rs. 115	Rs. 50
HSK	200 %	25 %	10 %	10 %	10 %	Rs. 100	Rs. 115	Rs. 50
SKI	100 %	25 %	10 %	10 %	10 %	Rs. 100	Rs. 115	Rs. 50
SMS	100 %	20 %	10 %	10 %	10 %	Rs. 100	Rs. 115	Rs. 20
USK	175 %	18 %	Rs. 150	10 %	10 %	Rs. 100	Rs. 115	-----

**** % of BS + DA

Quite naturally, this big a system cannot be implemented using a single shell script. In fact there would be several of them each doing a specific job and interacting with one another to work like a system as a whole. This once again is in tune with the Unix philosophy - build small parts, make them do their job well and then combine them, link them to build a powerful, robust system.

Given below is a list of the various shell scripts that are developed in this system along with the purpose of each. This will help you to keep track of the system as you read the listings given in the subsequent pages.

Shell Script	Purpose
paymain.prg	Does some initial house-keeping, Displays Main Menu and branches control to appropriate sub-menu.
writecentre	Writes a given string in the center of a given row either in Bold, Normal or Reverse video.
writerc	Writes a given string at the given row, column either in Bold, Normal or Reverse video.
dboper.prg	Displays Database Operations Menu and branches control to either Master or Transaction Data Entry Menu.
reports.prg	Displays Reports Menu and branches control to generate the appropriate report.
sysmnt.prg	Displays System Maintenance Menu and branches control to carry out appropriate house-keeping job.
mde.prg	Displays Master Data Entry Menu and branches control to carry out appropriate operation on employee master.
tde.prg	Displays Transaction Data Entry Menu and branches control to carry out appropriate operation on employee transaction file.
madd.prg	Adds new records to master file.
mmodi.prg	Modifies an existing record in master file.

Shell Script	Purpose
mdel.prg	Deletes an existing record from master file.
mret.prg	Retrieves record from master file and displays it on the screen.
tadd.prg	Adds new records to employee transaction file.
maillbl.prg	Prints mailing labels.
payprint.prg	Prints monthly payslips for employees on screen.
spaysheet.prg	Prints department-wise summary payroll sheet.
lsr.prg	Generates leave status report.
clmonth.prg	Closes the monthly transaction file.
clyear.prg	Closes the yearly transactions, updates master and reorganizes files and variables.

The overall breakup of the system on a file by file basis and their hierarchy of calling is given in Figure 16.1. Files which are general and are called by several other scripts are shown separately.

With this much detailing I suppose you would be able to follow the shell script listings given below. They have been suitably commented to help you understand the underlying logic.

Working of The System

The user just has to add records to the master and the monthly transaction file. While adding records to master file the program avoids any duplication of records since there must be a unique record for each employee. Also while adding records to the monthly transaction file the program makes sure that a record doesn't get added to the transaction file unless there is a corresponding record in the master file. Here too, the program prevents any unintentional or otherwise duplication of records.

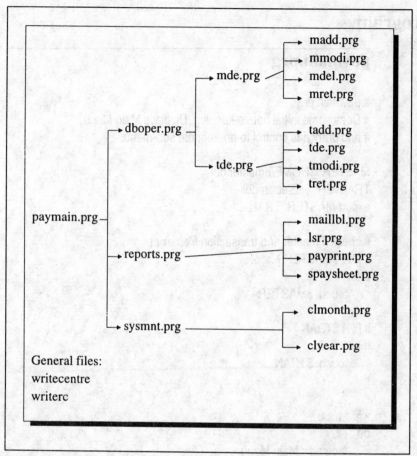

Figure 16.1

At the end of each month the user should generate all the reports through the reports menu. Before starting data entry for new transactions for a new month the user must specifically close that month's transactions through the 'Close month' option from the System Maintenance menu. At the end of the financial year the 'Close year' option from the System Maintenance menu should be exercised. It generates a transaction file which is a combination of all monthly transaction files in that financial year. It has been assumed that the financial year runs from April through March of next year.

Program

paymain.prg

```
# paymain.prg
# Does some initial house-keeping, Displays Main Menu
# and branches control to appropriate sub-menu.

MASTER=$HOME/emaster.dbf
TRAN=$HOME/etran.dbf
export MASTER  TRAN

# check if master and transaction files exist
if [ ! -f $MASTER ]
then
    touch  $MASTER
fi
if [ ! -f $TRAN ]
then
    touch  $TRAN
fi

while true
do
    # display Main Menu
    clear
    writecentre "Payroll Processing System" 7 "B"
    writecentre "Main Menu" 8 "N"
    writerc "\033[1mD\033[0matabase operations" 10 30 "N"
    writerc "\033[1mR\033[0meports" 11 30 "N"
    writerc "\033[1mS\033[0mystem maintenance" 12 30 "N"
    writerc "\033[1mE\033[0mxit" 13 30 "N"
    writerc "Your choice? " 15 30 "N"

    # receive user's choice
    choice=""
```

```
        stty -icanon min 0, time 0
        while [ -z "$choice" ]
        do
                read choice
        done
        stty sane

        # branch off to appropriate menu
        case "$choice" in
                [Dd]) dboper.prg ;;
                [Rr]) reports.prg ;;
                [Ss]) sysmnt.prg ;;
                [Ee]) clear
                        exit ;;
                *) echo \007 ;;
        esac
done
```

---

writecentre

```
# writecentre
# Writes a given string in the center of a given row
# either in Bold, Normal or Reverse video.

# check whether called properly
if [ $# -ne 3 ]
then
        echo improper arguments
        exit
fi

# position cursor
str=$1
row=$2
attr=$3
```

```
length='echo $str | wc -c'
col='expr \( 80 - $length \) / 2'
tput cup $row $col

# display string in Bold, Normal or Reverse video
case $attr in
     [bB])echo -n "\033[1m$str" ;;
     [nN])echo -n $str ;;
     [rR])echo -n "\033[7m$str" ;;
esac
echo -n "\033[0m"
```

writerc

```
# writerc
# Writes a given string at the given row, column
# either in Bold, Normal or Reverse video.

# check whether called properly
if [ $# -ne 4 ]
then
     echo improper arguments
     exit
fi

# position cursor
str="$1"
row=$2
col=$3
attr=$4
tput cup $row $col

# display string in Bold, Normal or Reverse video
case $attr in
     [bB])echo -n "\033[1m$str" ;;
     [nN])echo -n "$str" ;;
```

```
    [rR])echo -n "\033[7m$str" ;;
esac
echo -n "\033[0m"
```

dboper.prg

```
# dboper.prg
# Displays Database Operations Menu and branches control to
# either Master or Transaction Data Entry Menu.

while true
do
    # display Database Operations Menu
    clear
    writecentre "Payroll Processing System" 7 "B"
    writecentre "Data Base Operation" 8 "B"
    writerc "\033[1mM\033[0master File Data Entry"  10 30 "N"
    writerc "\033[1mT\033[0mransaction Data Entry" 11 30 "N"
    writerc "\033[1mR\033[0meturn to Main Menu" 12 30 "N"
    writerc "Your choice? " 15 30 "N"

    # receive user's choice
    choice=""
    stty -icanon min 0, time 0
    while [ -z "$choice" ]
    do
        read choice
    done
    stty sane

    # check user's choice and branch off to
    # appropriate Data Entry Menu
    case "$choice" in
        [Mm]) mde.prg ;;
        [Tt]) tde.prg ;;
        [Rr]) clear
```

```
            break ;;
        *) echo  \007 ;;
    esac
done
```

reports.prg

```
# reports.prg
# Displays Reports Menu and branches control to generate the
# appropriate report.

while true
do
    # display Reports Menu
    clear
    writerc "\033[36mPayroll Processing System\033[37m" 7 27 "B"
    writerc "\033[36mReports Menu\033[37m" 8 33 "N"
    writerc "\033[1mM\033[0mailing Labels" 10 30 "N"
    writerc "\033[1mL\033[0meave Status Report" 11 30 "N"
    writerc "\033[1mP\033[0maysheet Printing" 12 30 "N"
    writerc "\033[1mS\033[0mummary Payroll Sheet" 13 30 "N"
    writerc "\033[1mR\033[0meturn to main menu" 14 30 "N"
    writerc "Your choice? " 16 30 "N"

    # receive user's choice
    choice=""
    stty -icanon min 0, time 0
    while [ -z "$choice" ]
    do
        read choice
    done
    stty sane

    # check user's choice and branch off to
    # generate an appropriate report
    case "$choice" in
```

```
        [Mm]) maillbl.prg ;;
        [Ll]) lsr.prg ;;
        [Pp]) payprint.prg ;;
        [Ss]) spaysheet.prg ;;
        [Rr]) clear
                break ;;
        *) echo \007 ;;
    esac
done
```

---

sysmnt.prg

```
# sysmnt.prg
# Displays System Maintenance Menu and branches control to
# carry out appropriate house-keeping job.

while true
do
    # display System Maintenance Menu
    clear
    writerc "\033[36mPayroll Processing System\033[37m" 7 27 "B"
    writerc "\033[32mSystem Maintenance Menu\033[37m" 8 28 "B"
    writerc "c\033[1mL\033[0mose month" 10 30 "N"
    writerc "\033[1mC\033[0mlose year & reorganise" 11 30 "N"
    writerc "\033[1mR\033[0meturn to main menu" 12 30 "N"
    writerc "Your choice? " 14 30 "N"

    # receive user's choice
    choice=""
    stty -icanon min 0, time 0
    while [ -z "$choice" ]
    do
        read choice
    done
    stty sane
```

```
            # check user's choice and branch off to
            # carry out appropriate house-keeping job
            case "$choice" in
                [Ll]) clmonth.prg ;;
                [Cc]) clyear.prg ;;
                [Rr]) clear
                        break ;;
                *) echo  \007 ;;
            esac
done
```

---

mde.prg

```
# mde.prg
# Displays Master Data Entry Menu and branches control to
# carry out appropriate operation on employee master.

while true
do
        # display Master Data Entry Menu
        clear
        writecentre "Payroll Processing System" 7 "B"
        writecentre "Master File Data Entry" 8 "B"
        writerc "\033[1mA\033[0mdd records " 10 30 "N"
        writerc "\033[1mM\033[0modify records" 11 30 "N"
        writerc "\033[1mD\033[0melete record" 12 30 "N"
        writerc "\033[1mR\033[0metrieve record" 13 30 "N"
        writerc "r\033[1mE\033[0mturn" 14 30 "N"
        writerc "Your choice? " 16 30 "N"

        # receive user's choice
        choice=""
        stty -icanon min 0, time 0
        while [ -z "$choice" ]
        do
```

```
        read choice
done
stty sane

# check user's choice and branch off to perform
# appropriate operation on employee master
case "$choice" in
    [Aa]) madd.prg ;;
    [Mm]) mmodi.prg ;;
    [Dd]) mdel.prg ;;
    [Rr]) mret.prg ;;
    [Ee]) exit ;;
    *) echo  \007 ;;
esac
done
```

---

tde.prg

```
# tde.prg
# Displays Transaction Data Entry Menu and branches control to
# carry out appropriate operation on employee transaction file.

while true
do
    # display Transaction Data Entry Menu
    clear
    writecentre "Payroll Processing System" 7 "B"
    writecentre "Transaction Data Entry" 8 "B"
    writerc "\033[1mA\033[0mdd records " 10 30 "N"
    writerc "\033[1mM\033[0mmodify records" 11 30 "N"
    writerc "\033[1mD\033[0melete record" 12 30 "N"
    writerc "\033[1mR\033[0metrieve record" 13 30 "N"
    writerc "r\033[1mE\033[0mturn" 14 30 "N"
    writerc "Your choice? " 16 30 "N"

    # receive user's choice
```

```
            choice=""
            stty -icanon min 0, time 0
            while [ -z "$choice" ]
            do
                 read choice
            done
            stty sane

            # check user's choice and branch off to perform
            # appropriate operation on employee transaction file
            case "$choice" in
                 [Aa]) tadd.prg ;;
                 [Mm]) tmodi.prg ;;
                 [Dd]) tdel.prg ;;
                 [Rr]) tret.prg ;;
                 [Ee]) clear
                         exit ;;
                 *) echo \007 ;;
            esac
done
```

madd.prg

```
# madd.prg
# Adds new records to master file.

another=y
t='tty'

while [ "$another" = y -o "$another" = Y ]
do
    clear
    writecentre "Payroll Processing System" 1 "B"
    writecentre "Add Records - Master File" 2 "B"

    writerc "Employee Code: \c" 4 10 "B"
```

```
read e_empcode
if [ -z "$e_empcode" ]
then
    exit
fi

# check if such an employee code already exists
grep \^$e_empcode: $MASTER > /dev/null
if [ $? -eq 0 ]
then
    writerc "Code already exists. Press any key..." 20 10 "N"
    read key
    continue
fi

# read values of various fields
writerc "Name of Employee: \c" 5 10 "B"
read e_empname
writerc "Sex: \c" 6 10 "B"
read e_sex
writerc  "Address: \c" 7 10 "B"
read e_address
writerc "Name of city: \c" 8 10 "B"
read e_city
writerc "Pin code number: \c" 9 10 "B"
read e_pin
writerc "Department: \c" 10 10 "B"
read e_dept
writerc "Grade: \c" 11 10 "B"
read e_grade
writerc "GPF no. \c" 12 10 "B"
read e_gpf_no
writerc "GI scheme no.: \c" 13 10 "B"
read e_gis_no
writerc "ESI scheme no.: \c" 14 10 "B"
read e_esis_no
writerc "CL allowed: \c" 15 10 "B"
```

```
        read e_max_cl
        writerc "PL allowed: \c" 16 10 "B"
        read e_max_pl
        writerc "ML allowed: \c" 17 10 "B"
        read e_max_ml
        writerc "Basic Salary: \c" 18 10 "B"
        read e_bs

        e_cum_cl=0
        e_cum_pl=0
        e_cum_ml=0
        e_cum_lwp=0
        e_cum_att=0

        # write new record into employee master file
        echo $e_empcode:$e_empname:$e_sex:$e_address:$e_city:
        $e_pin:$e_dept:$e_grade:$e_gpf_no:$e_gis_no:$e_esis_no:
        $e_max_cl:$e_max_pl:$e_max_ml:$e_bs:$e_cum_cl:$e_cum_pl:
        $e_cum_ml:$e_cum_lwp:$e_cum_att | dd conv=ucase
            2> /dev/null >> $MASTER

        writerc "Add another y/n \c" 20 10 "N"
        read another
done
```

mmodi.prg

```
# mmodi.prg
# Modifies an existing record in master file.

another=y

while [ "$another" = y -o "$another" = Y ]
do
    clear
    writecentre "Payroll Processing System" 1  "B"
```

```
writecentre "Modify Records - Master File" 2 "B"

writerc "Employee Code: " 4 10 "B"
read e_empcode
if [ -z "$e_empcode" ]
then
     exit
fi

grep \^\$e_empcode: $MASTER > /dev/null
if [ $? -ne 0 ]
then
     writerc "Employee code does not exist. Press any key..." 10 10 "B"
     read key
     continue
fi

# transfer all other records to a temporary file
grep -v \^\$e_empcode: $MASTER > /tmp/emaster.mmm

mline='grep \^\$e_empcode: $MASTER'
oldIFS="$IFS"
IFS=':'
set -- $mline

writerc "Name: $2" 5 10 "N"
read e_empname

# if no change is made in employee name
if [ -z "$e_empname" ]
then
     e_empname=$2
fi

writerc "sex: $3" 6 10 "N"
read e_sex
```

```
# if no change is made in employee sex
if [ -z "$e_sex" ]
then
    e_sex=$3
fi

writerc "Address: $4" 7 10 "N"
read e_address
if [ -z "$e_address" ]
then
    e_address=$4
fi

writerc "City: $5" 8 10 "N"
read e_city
if [ -z "$e_city" ]
then
    e_city=$5
fi

writerc "Pin code No: $6" 9 10 "N"
read e_pin
if [ -z "$e_pin" ]
then
    e_pin=$6
fi

writerc "Department: $7" 10 10 "N"
read e_dept
if [ -z "$e_dept" ]
then
    e_dept=$7
fi

writerc "Grade: $8" 11 10 "N"
read e_grade
if [ -z "$e_grade" ]
```

```
then
    e_grade=$8
fi

writerc "GPF no: $9" 12 10 "N"
read e_gpf_no
if [ -z "$e_gpf_no" ]
then
    e_gpf_no=$9
fi

shift 9

writerc  "GI scheme no: $1" 13 10 "N"
read e_gis_no
if [ -z "$e_gis_no" ]
then
    e_gis_no=$1
fi

writerc "ESI sscheme no: $2" 14 10 "N"
read e_esis_no
if [ -z "$e_esis_no" ]
then
    e_esis_no=$2
fi

writerc "CL allowed: $3" 15 10 "N"
read e_max_cl
if [ -z "$e_max_cl" ]
then
    e_max_cl=$3
fi

writerc "PL allowed: $4" 16 10 "N"
read e_max_pl
if [ -z "$e_max_pl" ]
```

```
then
    e_max_pl=$4
fi

writerc "ML allowed: $5" 17 10 "N"
read e_max_ml
if [ -z "$e_max_ml" ]
then
    e_max_ml=$5
fi

writerc "Basic salary: $6" 18 10 "N"
read e_bs
if [ -z "$e_bs" ]
then
    e_bs=$6
fi

e_cum_cl=$7
e_cum_pl=$8
e_cum_ml=$9

shift 9
e_cum_lwp=$1
e_cum_att=$2

IFS="$oldIFS"

# append modified record to employee master file
echo $e_empcode:$e_empname:$e_sex:$e_address:$e_city:
$e_pin:$e_dept:$e_grade:$e_gpf_no:$e_gis_no:$e_esis_no:
$e_max_cl:$e_max_pl:$e_max_ml:$e_bs:$e_cum_cl:$e_cum_pl:
$e_cum_ml:$e_cum_lwp:$e_cum_att | dd conv=ucase
    2> /dev/null >> /tmp/emaster.mmm

# move new master over top of original
mv /tmp/emaster.mmm $MASTER
```

```
        writerc "Modify Another y/n " 20 20 "N"
        read another
done
```

---

mdel.prg

```
# mdel.prg
# Deletes an existing record from master file.

another=y
while [ "$another" = y ]
do
    clear
    writecentre "Payroll Processing System" 1  "B"
    writecentre "Delete Records - Master File" 3 "B"

    writerc "Employee Code to Delete: \c" 6 10 "B"
    read e_empcode
    if [ -z "$e_empcode" ]
    then
        exit
    fi

    # check whether employee code exists
    grep -y \^$e_empcode: $MASTER > /dev/null
    if [ $? -ne 0 ]
    then
        writerc "Employee code does not exist... Press any key" 10 10 "B"
        read key
        continue
    fi

    # rewrite all other records into a new file
    grep -vy \^$e_empcode: $MASTER > /tmp/emaster.ddd
    mv /tmp/emaster.ddd $MASTER
```

```
      # check whether there is a corresponding employee in transaction file
      grep -y \^$e_empcode: $TRAN > /dev/null
      if [ $? -eq 0 ]
      then
            # eliminate the corresponding record from transaction file too
            grep -vy \^$e_empcode: $TRAN > /tmp/etran.ddd
            mv /tmp/emaster.ddd  $TRAN
      fi

      writerc "Delete another y/n " 16 15 "B"
      read another
done
```

---

mret.prg

```
# mret.prg
# Retrieves record from master file and display it on the screen.

another=y

while [ "$another" = y -o "$another" = Y ]
do
      clear
      writecentre "Payroll maintenance System" 1  "B"
      writecentre " Retrieve Records - Master File" 2 "B"

      writerc "Employee Code: " 4 10 "B"
      read e_empcode

      if [ -z "$e_empcode" ]
      then
            exit
      fi

      # search employee code in master file
```

```
        grep \^\$e_empcode: $MASTER > /dev/null

        # if employee code doesn't exist
        if [ $? -ne 0 ]
        then
            writerc "Employee code does not exist. Press any key..." 10 10 "B"
            read key
            continue
        fi

        # separate out field values
        mline=`grep \^\$e_empcode: $MASTER`
        oldIFS="$IFS"
        IFS=':'
        set -- $mline

        # display field values on screen
        writerc "Name: $2" 5 10 "N"
        writerc "sex: $3" 6 10 "N"
        writerc "Address: $4" 7 10 "N"
        writerc "City: $5" 8 10 "N"
        writerc "Pin code No: $6" 9 10 "N"
        writerc "Department: $7" 10 10 "N"
        writerc "Grade: $8" 11 10 "N"
        writerc "GPF no: $9" 12 10 "N"
        shift 9
        writerc "GI scheme no: $1" 13 10 "N"
        writerc "ESI sscheme no: $2" 14 10 "N"
        writerc "CL allowed: $3" 15 10 "N"
        writerc "PL allowed: $4" 16 10 "N"
        writerc "ML allowed: $5" 17 10 "N"
        writerc "Basic salary: $6" 18 10 "N"

        IFS="$oldIFS"
        writerc "Retrieve another y/n " 20 20 "N"
        read another
done
```

tadd.prg

```
# tadd.prg
# Adds new records to employee transaction file.

clear
another=y
t='tty'
IFScolon=":"
IFSspace="$IFS"

# percentages used for calculation, according to employee grade
SSK="200 30 10 10 10 75 115 20"
HSK="200 25 10 10 10 75 115 20"
SKI="100 25 10 10 10 75 115 15"
SMS="100 22 10 10 10 75 115 15"
USK="17 20 10 10 10 75 115 0"

while [ "$another" = y -o "$another" = Y ]
do
    clear
    writecentre "Payroll Processing System" 1 "B"
    writecentre "Add Records - Tran. File" 2 "B"

    writerc "Employee Code: " 4 10 "B"
    read t_empcode
    if [ -z "$t_empcode" ]
    then
        exit
    fi

    mline='grep \^$t_empcode: $MASTER'
    mfound=$?

    # if employee code is not found in master
    if [ $mfound -ne 0 ]
```

```
then
     writecentre "Corresponding Master record absent" 7 "N"
     writecentre "Press any key..." 88888888 "N"
     read key
     continue
fi

grep \^$t_empcode: $TRAN > /dev/null
tfound=$?

# if employee code already exists in transaction file
if [ $tfound -eq 0 ]
then
     writecentre "Already exists, Cannot duplicate" 7 "N"
     writecentre "Press any key..." 8 "N"
     read key
     continue
fi

# read values of various fields
writerc "Department: " 5 10 "B"
read t_dept
writerc "Casual leave: " 6 10 "B"
read t_cl
writerc "Medical leave: " 7 10 "B"
read t_ml
writerc "Provisional leave: " 8 10 "B"
read t_pl
writerc "LWP: " 9 10 "B"
read t_lwp
writerc "Special pay 1: " 10 10 "B"
read t_sppay_1
writerc "Special pay 2: " 11 10 "B"
read t_sppay_2
writerc "Income tax: " 12 10 "B"
read t_inc_tax
writerc "Rent deduction: " 13 10 "B"
```

```
read t_rent_ded
writerc "Long term loan: " 14 10 "B"
read t_lt_loan
writerc "Short term loan: " 15 10 "B"
read t_st_loan
writerc "Special ded. 1: " 16 10 "B"
read t_spded_1
writerc "Special ded. 2: " 17 10 "B"
read t_spded_2

# extract grade and basic salary from master
grade=`echo $mline | cut -d":" -f8`
bs=`echo $mline | cut -d":" -f15`

# calculate various allowances and gross salary
set -- `eval echo \\$$grade`
t_da=`echo "scale=2\n$1 / 100.0 * $bs" | bc`
t_hra=`echo "scale=2\n$2 / 100.0 * $bs" | bc`
t_ca=`echo "scale=2\n$3 / 100.0 * $bs" | bc`
t_cca=`echo "scale=2\n$4 / 100.0 * $bs" | bc`
t_gs=`echo "scale=2\n$bs + $t_da + $t_hra + $t_ca + $t_cca +
          $t_sppay_1 + $t_sppay_2" | bc`

# calculate various deductions
t_gpf=`echo "scale=2\n$5 / 100.0 * ( $bs + $t_da )" | bc`
t_esis=$6
t_gis=$7
t_prof_tax=$8
t_tot_ded=`echo "scale=2\n$t_gpf + $t_esis + $t_gis + $t_prof_tax +
              $t_inc_tax + $t_lt_loan + $t_st_loan + $t_rent_ded +
              $t_spded_1 + $t_spded_2" | bc`

# calculate net salary
t_net_pay=`echo "scale=2\n$t_gs - $t_tot_ded" | bc`

# write new record to transaction file
echo $t_empcode:$t_dept:$t_cl:$t_ml:$t_pl:$t_lwp:$t_da:$t_hra:
```

```
$t_ca:$t_cca:$t_sppay_1:$t_sppay_2:$t_gs:$t_gpf:$t_gis:$t_esis:
$t_inc_tax:$t_prof_tax:$t_rent_ded:$t_lt_loan:$t_st_loan:
$t_spded_1:$t_spded_2:$t_tot_ded:$t_net_pay | dd conv=ucase
    2> /dev/null >> $TRAN


# find number of days in current month
days="31 28 31 30 31 30 31 31 30 31 30 31"
months=`date '+%m'`
totdays=`echo $days | cut -d" " -f $months`


IFS="$IFScolon"
exec < $MASTER


# read each record from master file
while read e_empcode e_empname e_sex e_address e_city e_pin
    e_dept e_grade e_gpf_no e_gis_no e_esis_no e_max_cl
    e_max_pl e_max_ml e_bs e_cum_cl e_cum_pl e_cum_ml
    e_cum_lwp e_cum_att
do
    IFS="$IFSspace"

    if [ $e_empcode = $t_empcode ]
    then
        # update cumulative leaves fields
        e_cum_cl=`expr $e_cum_cl + $t_cl`
        e_cum_ml=`expr $e_cum_ml + $t_ml`
        e_cum_pl=`expr $e_cum_pl + $t_pl`
        e_cum_lwp=`expr $e_cum_lwp + $t_lwp`
        net_days=`expr $totdays - $t_cl - $t_ml - $t_pl - $t_lwp`
        e_cum_att=`expr $e_cum_att + $net_days`
    fi


    # write record to master file
    echo $e_empcode:$e_empname:$e_sex:$e_address:$e_city:
$e_pin:$e_dept:$e_grade:$e_gpf_no:$e_gis_no:$e_esis_no:
$e_max_cl:$e_max_pl:$e_max_ml:$e_bs:$e_cum_cl:$e_cum_pl:
$e_cum_ml:$e_cum_lwp:$e_cum_att | dd conv=ucase
```

```
                    2> /dev/null >> /tmp/master.aaa
                    IFS="$IFScolon"
        done

        mv /tmp/master.aaa  $MASTER
        exec < $t
        IFS="$IFSspace"
        writerc "Add another y/n " 23 10 "N"
        read another
done
```

---

maillbl.prg

```
# maillbl.prg
# Prints mailing labels.

clear
t='tty'

writerc "Screen/Printer " 10 20 "B"
read ans
writerc "Please wait..." 12 22 "B"

exec < $MASTER

while true
do
        read line1

        # if record read successfully
        if [ $? -eq 0 ]
        then

                # separate out relevant fields
                name1='echo $line1 | cut -d":" -f 2'
                add1='echo $line1 | cut -d":" -f 4'
```

```
city1='echo $line1 | cut -d":" -f 5'
pin1='echo $line1 | cut -d":" -f 6'

# calculate lengths of various fields
ln1='echo $name1 | wc -c'
la1='echo $add1 | wc -c'
lc1='echo $city1 | wc -c'
lp1='echo $pin1 | wc -c'

# calculate blanks to be padded
bn1='expr 40 - $ln1'
ba1='expr 40 - $la1'
bc1='expr 40 - $lc1'
bp1='expr 40 - $lp1'

# pad blanks after name
count=1
while [ $count -le $bn1 ]
do
     name1="$name1 "
     count='expr $count + 1'
done

# pad blanks after address
count=1
while [ $count -le $ba1 ]
do
     add1="$add1 "
     count='expr $count + 1'
done

# pad blanks after city
count=1
while [ $count -le $bc1 ]
do
     city1="$city1 "
     count='expr $count + 1'
```

```
        done

        # pad blanks after pin
        count=1
        while [ $count -le $bp1 ]
        do
             pin1="$pin1 "
             count=`expr $count + 1`
        done
    else
        break
    fi

    # read another record from file
    line2=""
    read line2

    # separate cut relevant fields
    name2=`echo $line2 | cut -d":" -f 2`
    add2=`echo $line2 | cut -d":" -f 4`
    city2=`echo $line2 | cut -d":" -f 5`
    pin2=`echo $line2 | cut -d":" -f 6`

    # write fields from 2 records side by side
    echo "$name1 $name2" >> mail.lbl
    echo "$add1 $add2" >> mail.lbl
    echo "$city1 $city2" >> mail.lbl
    echo "$pin1 $pin2" >> mail.lbl
    echo >> mail.lbl

done

exec < $t

if [ "$ans" = S -o "$ans" = s ]
then
    echo
```

```
        pg  mail.lbl      # display mailing labels
else
        lpr  mail.lbl  # print mailing labels
fi

rm mail.lbl
```

payprint.prg

```
# payprint.prg
# Prints monthly payslips for employees on SCREEN.
# In practice the payslips are printed on
# pre-printed computer stationery. Hence printing on
# printer would have to be planned according to the
# page layout of the pre-printed form.

clear

writerc "Screen/Printer " 10 20 "B"
read ans

# calculate number of days in current month
month='date '+%B"
days="31 29 31 30 31 30 31 31 30 31 30 31"
tmp='date '+%m"
mdays='echo $days | cut -d" " -f $tmp'

another=y
t='tty'
IFSspace="$IFS"

while [ "$another" = y ]
do
    clear

    writerc "Employee Code: " 4 10 "B"
```

```
read empcode

if [ -z "$empcode" ]
then
    exit
fi

# search the employee code
grep \^\$empcode: $MASTER > /dev/null

# if the search fails
if [ $? -ne 0 ]
then
    writerc "Employee code does not exist. Press any key..." 10 10 "B"
    read key
    clear
    continue
fi

# build a horizontal dashed line
dln="-"
count=0
while [ $count -lt 78 ]
do
    dln="$dln-"
    count=`expr $count + 1`
done

clear
writerc "$dln" 0 1 "B"
writecentre "Shivley & Brett Pvt. Ltd." 1 "B"
writerc "$dln" 2 1 "B"

# set standard input to master file
exec < $MASTER

IFS=":"
```

```
# read till desired record is encountered
while read e_empcode e_empname e_sex e_address e_city e_pin
    e_dept e_grade e_gpf_no e_gis_no e_esis_no e_max_cl
    e_max_pl e_max_ml e_bs e_cum_cl e_cum_pl e_cum_ml
    e_cum_lwp e_cum_att
do
    if [ "$empcode" = "$e_empcode" ]
    then
        break
    fi
done

# set standard input to transaction file
exec < $TRAN

# read till desired record is encountered
while read t_empcode t_dept t_cl t_ml t_pl t_lwp t_da t_hra t_ca
    t_cca t_sppay_1 t_sppay_2 t_gs t_gpf t_gis t_esis t_inc_tax
    t_prof_tax t_rent_ded t_lt_loan t_st_loan t_spded_1 t_spded_2
    t_tot_ded t_net_pay
do
    if [ "$empcode" = "$t_empcode" ]
    then
        break
    fi
done

# reset standard input to terminal
exec < $t

IFS="$IFSspace"

# display various field values at appropriate places
writerc "Employee code:"  3 1 "B"
writerc "$e_empcode" 3 15 "N"
writerc "\033[1mSex:\033[0m$e_sex" 3 24 "N"
```

```
writerc "\033[1mGrade:\033[0m$e_grade" 3 40 "N"
writerc "\033[1mMonth:\033[0m$month" 3 66 "N"
writerc "\033[1mName:\033[0m$e_empname" 5 1 "N"
writerc "\033[1mDepartment:\033[0m$e_dept" 5 50 "N"
writerc "\033[1mGPF NO.:\033[0m$e_gpf_no" 7 1 "N"
writerc "\033[1mGIS NO.:\033[0m$e_gis_no" 7 25 "N"
writerc "\033[1mESIS NO.:\033[0m$e_esis_no" 7 48 "N"
writerc "Normal Days" 9 1  "B"
writerc "Casu.Leav" 9 21 "B"
writerc "Medical Leave" 9 32 "B"
writerc "Prov. Leave" 9 48 "B"
writerc "LWP" 9 61 "B"
writerc "Attended Days" 9 66 "B"
writerc "$mdays" 10 1 "N"
writerc "$t_cl" 10 21 "N"
writerc "$t_ml" 10 32 "N"
writerc "$t_pl" 10 48 "N"
writerc "$t_lwp" 10 61 "N"
writerc "$e_cum_att" 10 66 "N"
writerc "BS" 12 1 "B"
writerc "DA" 12 10 "B"
writerc "HRA" 12 25 "B"
writerc "CA" 12 32 "B"
writerc "CCA" 12 39 "B"
writerc "S.P.1" 12 48 "B"
writerc "S.P.2" 12 54 "B"
writerc "GS" 12 61 "B"
writerc "$e_bs" 13 1 "N"
writerc "$t_da" 13 10 "N"
writerc "$t_hra" 13 25 "N"
writerc "$t_ca" 13 32 "N"
writerc "$t_cca" 13 39 "N"
writerc "$t_sppay_1" 13 48 "N"
writerc "$t_sppay_2" 13 54 "N"
writerc "$t_gs" 13 61 "N"
writerc "GPF" 15 1 "B"
writerc "ESIS" 15 10 "B"
```

```
            writerc "GIS" 15 18 "B"
            writerc "IT" 15 25 "B"
            writerc "PT" 15 32 "B"
            writerc "RENT" 15 39 "B"
            writerc "Loan1" 15 48 "B"
            writerc "Loan2" 15 54 "B"
            writerc "S.D.1" 15 61 "B"
            writerc "S.D.2" 15 68 "B"
            writerc "Total" 15 74 "B"
            writerc "$t_gpf" 16 1 "N"
            writerc "$t_esis" 16 10 "N"
            writerc "$t_gis" 16 18 "N"
            writerc "$t_inc_tax" 16 25 "N"
            writerc "$t_prof_tax" 16 32 "N"
            writerc "$t_rent_ded" 16 39 "N"
            writerc "$t_lt_loan" 16 48 "N"
            writerc "$t_st_loan" 16 54 "N"
            writerc "$t_spded_1" 16 61 "N"
            writerc "$t_spded_2" 16 68 "N"
            writerc "$t_tot_ded" 16 73 "N"
            writerc "Net Pay" 18 1 "B"
            writerc "Rs. $t_net_pay" 19 1 "N"
            writerc "Receiver's Signature" 19 59 "B"
            writerc "$dln" 20 1 "B"

            writerc "Want to display another payslip y/n " 22 10 "N"
            read another
    done
```

---

spaysheet.prg

```
# spaysheet.prg
# Prints department-wise summary payroll sheet.

clear
```

```
# possible departments in the company
dept="MFG:ASSLY:STORES:MAINT:ACCTS"

t='tty'
IFSspace="$IFS"
IFScolon=":"

month='date '+%B''
year='date '+%Y''

# display report titles
writecentre "Payroll Processing System" 1 "B"
writecentre "Summary Payroll Sheet" 2 "B"
writecentre  "$month $year" 3 "B"

# display column headings
writerc "Total" 5 20 "B"
writerc "Gross" 5 35 "B"
writerc "Gross" 5 50 "B"
writerc "Net" 5 70 "B"
writerc "Department" 6 5 "B"
writerc "Employees" 6 20 "B"
writerc "Earning" 6 35 "B"
writerc "Deduction" 6 50 "B"
writerc "Payments" 6 70 "B"

count=1
row=8

# run the loop for 5 different departments in the company
while [ $count -le 5 ]
do
    # pick up one department
    var='echo $dept | cut -d":" -f $count'

    # initialise variables
    tot_emp=0
```

```
gross_earn=0
gross_ded=0
net_pay=0
IFS="$IFScolon"

# set standard input to transaction file
exec < $TRAN

# read records from transaction file
while read t_empcode t_dept t_cl t_ml t_pl t_lwp t_da t_hra t_ca
     t_cca t_sppay_1 t_sppay_2 t_gs t_gpf t_gis t_esis t_inc_tax
     t_prof_tax t_rent_ded t_lt_loan t_st_loan t_spded_1 t_spded_2
     t_tot_ded t_net_pay
do
     IFS="$IFSspace"

     # if department matches
     if [ "$t_dept" = "$var" ]
     then
          tot_emp=`expr $tot_emp + 1`
          gross_earn=`echo "scale = 2\n $gross_earn + $t_gs" | bc`
          gross_ded=`echo "scale = 2 \n $gross_ded + $t_tot_ded" | bc`
          net_pay=`echo "scale = 2 \n $net_pay + $t_net_pay" | bc`
     fi

     IFS="$IFScolon"
done

# reset standard input to terminal
exec < $t

# output summary values of one department
writerc "$var" $row 5 "N"
writerc "$tot_emp" $row 20 "N"
writerc "$gross_earn" $row 35 "N"
writerc "$gross_ded" $row 50 "N"
writerc "$net_pay" $row 70 "N"
```

```
                IFS="$IFSspace"
                row='expr $row + 1'
                count='expr $count + 1'
        done

        IFS="$IFSspace"

        writerc "Press any key..." 24 10 "N"
        read key
```

lsr.prg

```
# lsr.prg
# Generates leave status report.

clear

# initialise variables
another=y
t='tty'
month='date '+%B''
IFSspace="$IFS"

while [ "$another" = y  -o  "$another" = Y ]
do
        clear
        writecentre "Payroll Processing System" 1 "B"
        writecentre "Leave Status Report" 2 "B"

        writerc "Employee Code: " 4 10 "B"
        read empcode

        if [ -z "$empcode" ]
        then
                exit
```

```
fi

grep \^$empcode: $MASTER > /dev/null
if [ $? -ne 0 ]
then
    writerc "Employee code does not exist. Press any key..." 10 10 "B"
    read key
    continue
fi

IFS=":"

# set standard input to master file
exec < $MASTER

# search for the desired employee code
while read e_empcode e_empname e_sex e_address e_city e_pin
    e_dept e_grade e_gpf_no e_gis_no e_esis_no e_max_cl e_max_pl
    e_max_ml e_bs e_cum_cl e_cum_pl e_cum_ml e_cum_lwp
    e_cum_att
do
    if [ "$empcode" = "$e_empcode" ]
    then
        break
    fi
done

# reset standard input to terminal
exec < $t

IFS="$IFSspace"

# calculate balance leaves
bal_cl=`expr $e_max_cl - $e_cum_cl`
bal_ml=`expr $e_max_ml - $e_cum_cl`
bal_pl=`expr $e_max_pl - $e_cum_pl`
```

```
# display leave status

writerc "                       " 4 1 "N"
writerc "\033[1mName:\033[0m$e_empname" 5 1 "N"
writerc "\033[1mEmpcode:\033[0m$e_empcode" 5 35 "N"
writerc "\033[1mGrade:\033[0m$e_grade" 5 55 "N"
writerc "\033[1mMonth:\033[0m$month" 5 66 "N"

writerc "CL Allowed" 7 1 "B"
writerc "ML Allowed" 7 15 "B"
writerc "PL Allowed" 7 35 "B"
writerc "$e_max_cl" 8 1 "N"
writerc "$e_max_ml" 8 15 "N"
writerc "$e_max_pl" 8 35 "N"

writerc "Cum.Cl" 10 1 "B"
writerc "Cum.ML" 10 15 "B"
writerc "Cum.PL" 10 35 "B"
writerc "Cum.LWP" 10 55 "B"
writerc "Cum.Att.Days" 10 66 "B"
writerc "$e_cum_cl" 11 1 "N"
writerc "$e_cum_ml" 11 15 "N"
writerc "$e_cum_pl" 11 35 "N"
writerc "$e_cum_lwp" 11 55 "N"
writerc "$e_cum_att" 11 66 "N"

writerc "Balance CL" 13 1 "B"
writerc "Balance ML" 13 15 "B"
writerc "Balance PL" 13 35 "B"
writerc "$bal_cl" 14 1 "N"
writerc "$bal_ml" 14 15 "N"
writerc "$bal_pl" 14 35 "N"

writerc "Another employee y/n " 21 10 "N"
read another
done
```

clmonth.prg

```
# clmonth.prg
# Closes the monthly transaction file.

clear
writecentre "Payroll Processing System" 2 "B"
writecentre "Close Current Month" 3 "B"

set 'date'
cur_mth=$2

if [ -f  "etran$cur_mth.dbf" ]
then
     writecentre "Month has already been closed. Press any key..." 15 "B"
 read key
 exit
fi

count='wc -l $MASTER'
set $count
mcount=$1
count='wc -l $TRAN'
set $count
tcount=$1

# if all records have not been entered in transaction file
if [ $mcount -gt $tcount ]
then
     writecentre "Transaction file incomplete. Cannot close month." 15 "B"
     writecentre "Press any key..." 16 "B"
     read key
     exit
fi

mv $TRAN  etran$cur_mth.dbf
```

```
touch $TRAN

# check for success
if [ $? -eq 0 ]
then
     writecentre "Month successfully closed... Press any key" 15 "B"
else
     writecentre "Unable to close month... Press any key" 15 "B"
fi
read key
```

clyear.prg

```
# clyear.prg
# Closes the yearly transactions, updates master and reorganizes.

clear
writecentre "Payroll Processing System" 2 "B"
writecentre "Close Year & Reorganize" 3 "B"

t='tty'
oldifs="$IFS"

writecentre "Please wait... trying to close year" 10 "B"

yr='date '+%y''
if [ -f "etran$yr.dbf" ]
then
    writecentre "Year has already been closed. Press any key..." 12 "B"
    read key
    exit
fi

# since financial year is from Apr to Mar
months="Apr:May:Jun:Jul:Aug:Sep:Oct:Nov:Dec:Jan:Feb:Mar"
IFS=:
```

```
set $months
count=1

flag=0
while [ $count -le 12 ]
do
        if [ -f "etran$1.dbf" ]
        then
                cat etran$1.dbf >> etran$yr.dbf
                rm  etran$1.dbf
                flag=1
        fi

        count='expr $count + 1'
        shift
done

if [ $flag = 0 ]
then
    writecentre "Month has not been closed. Press any key..." 12 "B"
    writecentre "Close month before closing year. Press any key..." 13
"B"
    read key
    exit
fi

# set standard input to master file
exec < $MASTER

# prepare master file for new financial year
while read e_empcode e_empname e_sex e_address e_city e_pin
      e_dept e_grade e_gpf_no e_gis_no e_esis_no e_max_cl e_max_pl
      e_max_ml e_bs e_cum_cl e_cum_pl e_cum_ml e_cum_lwp
      e_cum_att
do
      e_cum_cl=0
```

```
                    e_cum_pl=0
                    e_cum_ml=0
                    e_cum_lwp=0
                    e_cum_att=0
                    IFS="$oldifs"
                    echo $e_empcode:$e_empname:$e_sex:$e_address:$e_city:
                    $e_pin:$e_dept:$e_grade:$e_gpf_no:$e_gis_no:$e_esis_no:
                    $e_max_cl:$e_max_pl:$e_max_ml:$e_bs:$e_cum_cl:$e_cum_pl:
                    $e_cum_ml:$e_cum_lwp:$e_cum_att >> /tmp/master
                    IFS=":"
            done

            IFS="$oldifs"
            mv /tmp/master $MASTER

            # reset standard input to terminal
            exec < $t
            writecentre "Year has been closed successfully. Press any key..." 12
            "B"
            read key
```

Where Do You Go from Here...

Phew! That was one long program listing. I Hope you understood the
underlying logic. I can appreciate that such big programs cannot be
imbibed to the last detail at first shot. But if you take it apart file by
file the whole process of understanding would become a little easier.
Now you can think of developing on your own the following
programs which have been left as an exercise to the reader.

(a)   tmodi.prg - Modification of an existing record in the transac-
       tion file.
(b)   tdel.prg - Deletion of an existing record in the transaction file.
(c)   tret.prg - Retrieval of an existing record from the transaction
       file.

Improve This Program...

However good one does anything there is always a scope for improvement. So also is true with this program.

You can improve this program in several ways. Some of these are mentioned below:

(a)   The program is not sand-papered with error checks. (This was done to simply keep the programs compact and easy to understand.) For example, while performing data entry the program doesn't do data validation. That is, if the user supplies Basic salary as alphanumeric or Name as numeric the program blindly accepts this. The data validation can be done for each field. Though this is not entirely impossible using the shell techniques that we know, a better idea would possibly to call a C routine which can do the data validation more efficiently.

(b)   The program has been hard-coded to implement only five different types of departments present in the company. Also, the program assumes there are certain fixed grades of employees. You can improve upon this by making the program work for any number of departments and grades of employees. It would be a good idea to read the percentages used for calculation of various allowances and deductions from an initialisation file when the program is run every time rather than hard-coding these facts within a program.

(c)   No facility has been provided to take backup of current master and transaction files. This can be implemented through the System Maintenance menu.

(d)   One more menu called File Tools can be implemented which would permit the usual file operations like copying, deletion, catenation, renaming etc. such that the user doesn't have to quit from the software just to perform these common chores.

Index

READER'S EVALUATION

I t is our sincere endeavour to publish books which are specifically designed to meet your requirements. Your feedback on our titles would be of crucial help to us in this endeavour. Please spare some of your valuable time to fill the form given below and mail it to:

Publishing Manager,

BPB Publications,

20, Ansari Road, Daryaganj, New Delhi 110002

Looking forward to receiving your valuable comments and suggestions.

Title: **Unix Shell Programming**

Author: Y. P. Kanetkar

ISBN: 81-7029-753-2

Please tick the appropriate box below each question as per the following rating code:

1. COVERAGE (have all relevant topics been included in the book?)

Excellent	Good	Average	Bad

2. PRESENTATION (have the topics been clearly explained?)

Excellent	Good	Average	Bad

3. DEPTH (have the topics been explained in sufficient detail.?)

Excellent	Good	Average	Bad

4. EXAMPLES/SAMPLE PROGRAMS/EXERCISES (Are these clear and illustrative?)

Excellent	Good	Average	Bad

5. Is there any other topic which you would like to be included in the book?
   (i)
   (ii)
   (iii)

6. Is there any topic which you feel should be explained in a better manner?
   (i)
   (ii)
   (iii)

7. Is there any other book on this subject which you have been using? If yes, please state title, author and publisher.

8. How does this book compare with the other one?
   (i) Coverage in this book is better/much better/same/worse.
   (ii) Presentation in this book is better/much better/same/worse.
   (iii) Depth in this book is more/much more/same/lesser.
   (iv) Examples/sample programs in this book are better/much better/ same/worse.

9. Did you experience any difficulty in obtaining this book in your town? Yes/No

10. How did you come to know about this book?
    (i) From friends/fellow students
    (ii) From teacher/instructor
    (iii) Saw it in the bookshop
    (iv) Through an advertisement/book reviews in magazine(s).

Name: _____

Affiliation: _____

Qualification: _____

Address: _____

The best of C/C++ & BORLAND C/C++ . . . from BPB

UNIX/XENIX

Prata	Advanced UNIX: A Programmer's Guide
Felps	Illustrated UNIX System V
Morgan	Inside XENIX
Norton	Peter Norton Guide to UNIX
Reichard	Teach Yourself. . . UNIX - 3rd Edition
Cuthbertson	The ABC's of SCO UNIX
Reilly	UNIX Power Tools (W/CD-ROM)
Mukhi	Working with UNIX

C

Stevens, R	Advanced Fractal Programming in C
Stevens, AL	AL Stevens Teaches C (W/D)
Stevens, A	C - DATA BASE Development
Pugh, K	C Language for Programmers
Holzner, S	C with Assembly Language
Kanetkar, Y	C - Projects (W/2D)
Lal, V	Database Management Using C (W/D)
Shukla	Data Structure Using C Lab Workbook (W/D)
Kanetkar, Y	Working with C (for DOE - 'A' & 'B' Level)
Radcliffe, R	ENCYCLOPEDIA C
Kanetkar, Y	EXPLORING C
Stevens, R	GRAPHICS Programming in C
Ladymon, R	Graphics User Interface Programming with C
Beam, J	Illustrated C Programming
Zolman, L	Illustrated C
Phillips, D	Image Processing in C (W/D)
Abolrous, A	Learn C in Three Days
Kanetkar, Y	Let Us C - 2nd Revised Edition
Holmes	Programming with ANSI C
Bolon, C	Mastering C
Dharaskar	The Hidden Treasure of C
Siegel, C	Teach Yourself - C - 2nd Revised Edition
Mukhi, V	The 'C' Odyssey - Vol. I-DOS
Mukhi, V	The 'C' Odyssey - Vol. II-ADVANCED DOS
Mukhi, V	The 'C' Odyssey - Vol. III-UNIX
Mukhi, V	The 'C' Odyssey - Vol. IV-NETWORK & RDBMS
Mukhi, V	The 'C' Odyssey - Vol. V-C++ & GRAPHICS
Mukhi, V	The 'C' Odyssey - Vol. VI-WINDOWS
Mukhi, V	The 'C' Odyssey - Vol. VII-OS/2
Goodwin	User Interface in C
Kanetkar, Y	Understanding Pointers in C
Kanetkar, Y	Undocumented DOS Through C
Hunter, B	Understanding C
Kanetkar, Y	Writing TSR's through C

C++

Ladd, S	Applying C++ (W/D)
Stevens/Wattins	Advanced GRAPHICS Programming in C & C++
Aklecha, V	A Comprehensive Guide to C++
Eckel	Black Belt C++ : Master Collection for Programmers
Shukla	C/C++ Programming Lab Workbook
Pappas/Murray	C++ Programmer's Guide (W/D)
Ladd, S	C++ Components & Algorithms (W/D)
Stevens, AL	C++ Database Development (W/D)
Holmes, M	C++ Communications Utilities (W/D)
Oualline, S	C - Elements of Style for C & C++
Homes, BJ	Convent to C & C++
Gurewich	Mastering C++ (From C to C++ in Weeks) (W/D)
Parsons, D	Object Oriented Programming with C++
Riley	Programming On-Line Help Using C++
Stevens, Al	Teach Yourself C++ (W/D) - Revised Edition
Rao	C++ Neural Networks & Fuzzy Logic (W/D)
Smith, N	Write Your Own Programming Language Using C++
Neibauer, A	Your First C/C++ Program (W/D)

All these and many more authoritative titles are available at your bookshop. In case of any difficulty, please contact our distributors.